BEING AN EFFECTIVE TEACHER
Role of Psychological Dimensions

Being an Effective Teacher

Role of Psychological Dimensions

(Study of Secondary School Teachers in Punjab)

Kamalpreet Kaur Toor

SHIPRA

Rs. 1250

ISBN: 978-93-86262-09-7

First Published in India in 2017

Being an Effective Teacher: Role of Psychological Dimensions (Study of Secondary School Teachers in Punjab)

Published by:

SHIPRA PUBLICATIONS
LG 18-19, Pankaj Central Market,
I.P. Ext., Patparganj, Delhi 110092, India
Ph.: +91 1147322068/9650028065
Email: info@shiprapublication.com
Website: www.shiprapublication.com

Dedicated to the placid personality of

Late S. Bhajan Singh Toor

A source of inspiration to all and

Also enlightened my ways through his divine luminosity.

Acknowledgements

I bow my head before Waheguru, "the Almighty", for bestowing his benevolence upon me by virtue of which I could reach this stage of my academic career.

Words are insufficient to express my deep gratitude to Professor Meenakshi, Department of Education and Community Service, Punjabi University, Patiala for providing inspiring guidance and consistent advice in this endevour.

I am grateful to Professor Kulwinder Singh, Department of Education and Community Service, Punjabi University, Patiala, for the valuable suggestions, which helped me in grasping various dimensions of the theme undertaken.

No appropriate words could be traced in the present lexicon to convey my thanks to my parents S. Kuldeep Singh Toor and Sr. Surjit Kaur Toor. I pay sublime obeisance to them as their persistent inspiration, sacrifices, patience and moral support gave me strength to move forward accompanied by their unconditional love which led to the completion of this assigned investigation. Every bit of what I am today, I owe it all to them. I am always indebted to my Chacha ji (uncles) and my Chachi ji (aunties) for the way they groomed me and enabled me to achieve my academic dreams. It gives me immense pleasure to acknowledge the love, support, motivation and good wishes extended to me by my friends in all manners. I extend my hearty thanks to them for withstanding by me during this phase of my life.

Kamalpreet Kaur Toor

Contents

Acknowledgements vii
List of Tables xi
List of Figures xiii

1. Effectiveness of the Teacher: Psychological Dimensionality **1**

- Teacher Effectiveness 3
- General Intelligence 13
- Social Intelligence 18
- Emotional Intelligence 22
- Relationship between General Intelligence, Emotional Intelligence and Social Intelligence 29
- Creativity 32
- Interrelationship of Creativity and Intelligence 41
- General, Social, Emotional Intelligence and Creativity of Effective Teachers 44
- Teacher Effectiveness and its Psychological Correlates: Research Evidence 49
- Significance, Objectives, Hypotheses and Delimitations 54

2. Research Methodology **59**

- Research Tools 59
- The Standard Progressive Matrices (SPM) (1958) 60
- Universe and Sample 65
- Data Collection 65
- Scoring and Tabulation 67
- Statistical Treatment of Data 70

3. Analysis and Interpretation of Data **74**

A : Teacher Effectiveness and its Psychological Dimensionality: Descriptive Analysis **74**

- Descriptive Analysis of Teacher Effectiveness, General 74

Intelligence, Emotional Intelligence, Social Intelligence and Creativity of Secondary School Teachers

- Identification of More and Less Effective Secondary School Teachers 78
- Descriptive Analysis of General Intelligence, Emotional Intelligence, Social Intelligence and Creativity of More and Less Effective Secondary School Teachers 79

B : Teacher Effectiveness and its Psychological Dimensionality: Multivariate Analysis 81

- Comparison of General, Emotional, Social Intelligence and Creativity of Secondary School Teachers in relation to Gender, Type of School and Teacher Effectiveness 81
- Correlational Analysis 94
- Regression Analysis 98
- Path Analysis 100
- Discriminant Analysis 101
- Discussion of Results 105
- Testing of Hypotheses 118

4. The Way Forward: Recommendations and Suggestions 130

Glossary 136
Bibliography 143
Index 172

List of Tables

2.1: Area Wise Distribution of Items in Teacher Effectiveness Scale 70
2.2: Test-Retest Reliability and Inter-Correlation of the Progressive Matrices and Mill Hills Scales at Different Ages 71
2.3: Factors Wise Distribution of Emotional Intelligence Scale 71
2.4: Distribution of Dimensions in Social Intelligence Scale 71
2.5: Split-Half Reliability and Test-Retest Reliability Coefficients of Social Intelligence Scale 72
2.6: Divergent Production Abilities and their Test Names 72
2.7: Test-retest Reliabilities of Divergent Production Abilities 72
2.8: Product Moment Correlations between Divergent Production, Abilities and Baqer Mhedi's Test of Creative Thinking (verbal) 73
2.9: District wise Number of Schools and Teachers Covered in Sample 73
2.10: Weightages for Unusuality of Responses of Divergent Production Abilities 73

3.1: Descriptive Analysis of Teacher Effectiveness, General, Emotional, Social Intelligence and Creativity of Secondary School Teachers (N = 850) 122
3.2: Distribution of More and Less Effective Secondary School Teachers (Gender and Type of School) 122
3.3: Descriptive Analysis of General, Emotional, Social Intelligence and Creativity among More and Less Effective Secondary School Teachers 122
3.4: Distribution of Sample in Terms A×B×C Factorial Design 123
3.5: Means and SDs of General, Emotional, Social Intelligence and Creativity of Secondary School Teachers in Terms of Gender X Type of School X Teacher Effectiveness 123
3.6: Mean Performance of General, Emotional, Social Intelligence and Creativity among Secondary School Teachers in terms of Gender X Type of School X Teacher Effectiveness 124
3.7: Summary of Analysis of Variance (Gender X Type of School X Teacher Effectiveness) on General, Emotional, Social Intelligence and Creativity of Secondary School Teachers 125

3.8: The t-values of Testing Significance of Mean Difference on General Intelligence in Teacher Effectiveness × Gender (A×B) Interaction 126
3.9: The t-values of Testing Significance of Mean Difference on General Intelligence in Teacher Effectiveness × Type of School (A × C) Interaction 126
3.10: The t-value Testing Significance of Mean Difference on Creativity in Teacher Effectiveness × Gender (A×B) Interaction 127
3.11: Coefficients of Correlation of Teacher Effectiveness with General, Emotional, Social Intelligence and Creativity among Secondary School Teachers 127
3.12: Inter-correlation of General Intelligence, Social Intelligence, Emotional Intelligence and Creativity among Total Group of Secondary School Teachers 127
3.13: Contribution of General Intelligence, Emotional Intelligence, Social Intelligence and Creativity to Teacher Effectiveness among Secondary School Teachers 128
3.14: Direct, Indirect and B Values on Teacher Effectiveness among Secondary School Teachers 128
3.16: Standardized Canonical Discriminant Function Coefficients of Teacher Effectiveness 129
3.17: Structure Matrix Correlations with Teacher Effectiveness 129
3.18: Canonical Discriminant Function Coefficients of Teacher Effectiveness 129
3.19: Classification Results 129

List of Figures

1.1:	Mcber's (2000) Model of Teacher Effectiveness	7
1.2:	Clark and Walsh's (2002) Model of Effective Teacher	8
1.3:	Mayer and Salovey's (1997) Cognitive Model of Emotional Intelligence	24
1.4:	Bar-On (1997) Relational Model of Emotional Intelligence	25
1.5:	Spencer and Spencer (1993) Model of Emotional Intelligence	27
1.6:	Scope of Emotional Intelligence by Mayer, Roberts and Barsade, 2008	32
1.7:	Person, Process, Product, Press	33
1.8:	The Relationship between General Mental Ability and Emotional Intelligence (Campbell, 1990)	46
1.9:	Role of Emotional Intelligence in Teaching	47
2.1:	Distribution of Sample	66
3.1(a):	Teacher Effectiveness × Gender (A × B)	86
3.1(b):	Teacher Effectiveness × Gender (A × B)	86
3.2(a):	Teacher Effectiveness × Type of School (A × C)	88
3.2(b):	Teacher Effectiveness × Type of School (A × C)	88
3.3(a):	Teacher Effectiveness X Gender (A × B)	92
3.3(b):	Teacher Effectiveness X Gender (A × B)	93
3.4:	Path Model Showing Effects of General Intelligence, Social Intelligence, Emotional Intelligence, Creativity on Teacher Effectiveness	101

1

Effectiveness of the Teacher

Psychological Dimensionality

Education is the best media for the all-round development of human personality. It is the process of bringing up individual for living a congenial, homogeneous and comfortable social life. Joeti Bhai Desai once said that "a child can never be taught, he/she can be brought up". So education is the process of developing the hidden potentialities of a child. Therefore, in order to educate youngsters, a process which may encourage and motivate them to think, reason, analyze, comprehend and learn by activating and employing inner capabilities has to be devised. It is for this reason that education is imparted from the very beginning—informally, non-formally and finally in formals way. All the educational institutions of the state follow a formal system of education stipulated for national educational aims. The present form of formal education is the latest process of education which is carried out through teaching by the teacher. Teaching is a two way interactive process through which the teacher aims to ignite a thought process in the minds of the students. For the implementation of formal education, a sound educational infrastructure for the educational institutions is needed. As a primary condition, there should be a spacious building with well-equipped classroom. Every class room should have a chalk board, a store room for storing teaching aids, and good display bulletin boards. It should also have well equipped library, art room, workshop for crafts, a play ground, a canteen, office, rooms and staffroom etc. The key functionaries of any educational institution are the teachers. Without the teachers an educational institution cannot function at all. It can also be said that the teachers are the life force of any educational institution. They are instrumental in making the functioning of an education institution possible.

Since the origin of human race and subsequent evolution of human societies in the world, teacher has played a vital role as a constructive moulder and upbringer of the youth. A teacher educates the youth in all aspects of life and gives them orientation in important dimensions of human life like socialization, moralization, training and in helping them acquire skills for earning livelihood and inculcating good desirable life habits.

Teachers constitute a very vast academic community engaged in teaching profession throughout the world. It is necessary that educational institutions like schools, colleges, technical institutions and universities should have intelligent, qualified, diligent, sincere, proficient and dedicated teachers. In this respect it also becomes important to highlight the qualities of a good teacher. If the educational authorities are not conscious about the necessary qualities of a teacher, neither the implantation of curriculum of the school or other educational institutions nor the preconceived educational aims can be implemented or achieved.

Dr. S. Radha Krishnan, the great teacher and philosopher and former president of India, addressed the nation of 5th September 1964 (Teacher's Day) and spoke about the importance of teachers in society.

> "Teachers have a vital role to play in the progress and development of the country; for on them depends how the new generation is trained to face the increasing responsibilities of citizenship and administration. And yet if the teachers have to perform their duties well, the people and the government must ensure them reasonable conditions of the life and work".

Education of children depends upon schools, their infrastructure, curriculum and teachers. This has been clearly mentioned by Kothari Education Commission (1966) which categorically states that the destiny of India is being shaped in its classrooms. This commission has placed great emphasis on the relevance of school education and the importance of teacher. Highlighting the importance of teachers in education Whitehead wrote in 1929 "Everything depends on the teachers".

Moreover, Kothari Education Commission (1966) has also placed a tremendous emphasis on the role of teacher which is reflected in the statement—

> "of all the different factors which influence quality of education and its contribution to national development, the quality, competence and character of teachers are undoubtedly the most significant".

Teacher plays a pivotal role in educational administration. As such a teacher must be philosophically, sociologically and psychologically sound so that his wisdom and accomplishments are imbibed by the students. Jensen (1948) also describes the following crucial qualities of a teacher in his "teacher characteristics" study.

I. ***Personal Qualities:*** These include emotional stability as revealed by the interaction of teachers with pupils and associates, honesty, fairness and objectivity.
II. ***Professional Qualities:*** These include classroom practices of a teacher relating specially to, learning process, skill and knowledge.
III. ***Social Qualities:*** These include face to face relationships with students and associates.

Thus it can be said that the effectiveness of the teacher largely depends on the sum total of personal, professional and social qualities. Good knowledge of content matter, methodology of teaching and personal attributes such as intelligence, emotional and social intelligence, creativity, mental health, adjustment and values etc. are of great importance for a teacher's success in imparting educational.

However, this book focuses on the following attributes of a teacher.

- Teacher Effectiveness
- General Intelligence
- Social Intelligence
- Emotional Intelligence
- Creativity

Teacher Effectiveness

Dictionary meaning of effectiveness is the 'quality of being effective'. The term 'teacher effectiveness' and 'effective teacher' can be used interchangeably. The term teacher effectiveness implies the possession of a multitude of skills in different combinations according to the requirements of different contexts. There can be no single yardstick to measure the effectiveness of a proficient teacher. It is commonly seen that different terms like good, popular, successful are used to describe the effectiveness of a teacher. More precisely effectiveness refers to the quality of being adequate to accomplish a purpose by producing the intended or expected result. An effective teacher is generally successful in leaving a deep, vivid and lasting impression. Moreover, the qualities of a good teacher can be established and understood only in relative terms. This makes it necessary to enumerate the qualities of a successful or effective teacher as compared to those of ineffective ones. Mitzel, (1960) reported that effectiveness of the teacher can be assessed through three type of criteria: Process, Product and Presage. In this schema teacher effectiveness is concerned with process and product while effective teacher is concerned with presage. Based on Mitzel's schema for determining the effectiveness of a good teacher in more concrete terms the following yardsticks have been adopted in the present work.

(i) Composites of judgements or rating by peer and head, self rating, observation of classroom practices (Process).
(ii) Test of qualities commonly associated with teaching success.
(iii) Measures of pupil change or students learning outcomes (Product).
(iv) Personal attributes (Presage).

Effectiveness of a teacher stems from a combination of knowledge, skills and personal characteristics (Katz, 1993). The characteristics which are correlated with effectiveness are good knowledge of subject matter, ability to organize learning materials, ability to successfully communicate knowledge to the students and ability to deal with classroom situations (Gupta and Jain, 2007). Apart from this personal characteristics like enthusiasm for teaching, effective communication, adaptability to change, consistent acquisition of knowledge, competence, acceptance of difference, patience, willingness to take risks, flexibility, creativity, hard work and sense of humour are commonly associated with the idea of quality teaching (Taylor and Wash, 2003; Colker, 2008).

Kapoor and Gupta (1983) have defined teacher effectiveness as the efficacy exhibited by a teacher in instructional strategies, classroom management, personal disposition, evaluation, interpersonal relations, job involvement, initiative and enthusiasm, professional values, innovativeness in the every day teaching learning situation. While Good (1959) defined effectiveness of the teacher as the interplay and interaction between physical, intellectual and psychological interests of the students, content matter, and the evaluation procedures. Flanders and Simon (1969) on the other hand foreground the relationships between the characteristics of teachers, teaching acts and their effects on the educational outcomes of classrooms and defined the concept of effective teacher in terms of certain qualities like sense of huemour, ability to explain, to understand, to manage class and helping and being fair with the students. An effective teacher helps the students in the development of basic skills, understanding, proper work habits and desirable attitude, value judgement and adequate personal adjustment (Ryan, 1969).

Encyclopedia of Educational Rresearch defines the term 'Teacher effectiveness' in terms of the results a teacher achieves or the amount of progress the pupils make toward some specified goal of education. Teacher effectiveness is regarded not as a stable characteristic of the teacher as an individual but as a product of the interaction between teacher characteristics and other factors that vary according to the situation in which a teacher works. Teacher effectiveness can be understood as the effective linkage of teacher competence and teacher performance with the accomplishment of teacher goals. Several assumptions which are related to effectiveness of teacher are implicit in this definition (Anderson, 1991). An initial assumption is that an effective teacher tends to be aware of and actively pursues goals; the second assumption is that vast majority of teacher goals are or should be concerned either directly or indirectly with learning of the students. It can also be maintained that effective teachers are those who achieve the goals they set for themselves or the goals which have been set for them by others, such as school principles, education administrators, and parents. According to Ornstein (1991), effective teachers must have a body of knowledge essential for teaching, and should also know how to apply it. By integrating these two conceptions, effective teachers may be assumed as those who possess the relevant competence (including necessary professional knowledge, skills, and attitudes) and who use the competence appropriately to achieve their set goals. Teacher effectiveness factors typically include certain kind of leadership, a shared vision, an orderly atmosphere, maximized learning time, careful monitoring of students progress (Teddlie and Reynolds, 2000).

Daniel Muijs and David Reynolds (2001) in their book "Effective Teaching: Evidence and Practice" have discussed the importance of teacher effectiveness. According to these writers, effective teacher is one who possesses (a) Teaching skills of direct instruction, interactive teaching, classroom management, review and practice, behaviour management, effective use of problem solving and higher order thinking skills. (b) Specific teaching skills, like developing social skills of students, enhancing self-esteem among students, teaching students with special educational needs, and taking account of individual differences. (c) Skill of teaching specific subjects like literacy, mathematics, information and communication technology skills and professional development.

In one of the traditional approaches, teacher effectiveness defined by Medley (1982) proposed that the structure of teacher effectiveness should include nine important components: pre-existing teacher characteristics (i.e. the knowledge, abilities, and beliefs that a teacher possesses on entering into teacher training program); teacher competence (i.e. the set of knowledge, abilities and beliefs that is a part of teacher training program); teacher performance (i.e. the behaviour of a teacher at teaching that may change when the teaching environment undergoes a change); student learning experience (i.e., the experience from interactions between teacher and the students in the process of teaching and learning); student behaviour or learning outcomes (i.e., the progress students make towards a defined educational goal); teacher training (for building up teacher competence); external teaching context (including school organizational structure, management, culture, teaching facilities, resources, curriculum, school goal and mission, etc); internal teaching context (including class size and composition, pupil abilities, classroom climate, teacher-pupil relationship, etc); and individual student characteristics (i.e., individual student's previous learning experience, physical and intellectual ability, learning styles, and other personal characteristics).

In 1978, Wimberly *et al.* discussed some dimensions which are related with effectiveness of teachers. These are as under:

Student Development: Enhancing intellectual skills, better interpretative powers and new viewpoints combined with greater learning stimulation and understanding into student development dimension.

Teacher Task Responsiveness: This includes clear and fair grading procedures, informing students where they stand and expeditious return of examination and assignments.

Respect for Students: Consideration of rights and needs of students.

Teacher Capability: Teachers command of the subject, interest in subject and command of material.

Encouragement to Students: Professional integrity, stimulation, complimenting students, encouraging participation.

Mcber's (2000) Model of Teacher Effectiveness

In the "Effective Teaching" study conducted for Department of Education and Skills by Hay McBer (DFEE, 2000) which is based on the interviews of teachers, three main elements relating to effectiveness of the teacher have been identified.

Professional Characteristics: These includes teacher leadership qualities, their ability to relate to others, their analytic and conceptual thinking skills, their professionalism and expectation setting abilities.

Classroom Climate measured through interviews with pupils: It includes pupils' perceptions of the clarity of each lesson, an orderly climate, clear behaviour standards, a perception of teacher fairness, presence of opportunity for pupils to participate and feeling emotionally supported in class, the perception that classroom is a safe, comfortable, interesting and exciting place.

Teaching Skills: Teaching Skills such as time on task, high expectations, effective planning, varied teaching, classroom and behavioural management and effective use of assessment and homework (*see* Fig. 1.1).

The three main characteristics given in Mcber's model if found in a teacher can significantly influence overall performance. The three factors are different in nature. Professional characteristics and teaching skills are factors which are related to what a teacher brings to the job. Professional characteristics are ongoing patterns of behaviour that combine to influence the performance of a teacher. Teaching skills on the other hand are micro-behavioural aspects that an effective teacher constantly exhibits when teaching in a class. Classroom climate is an

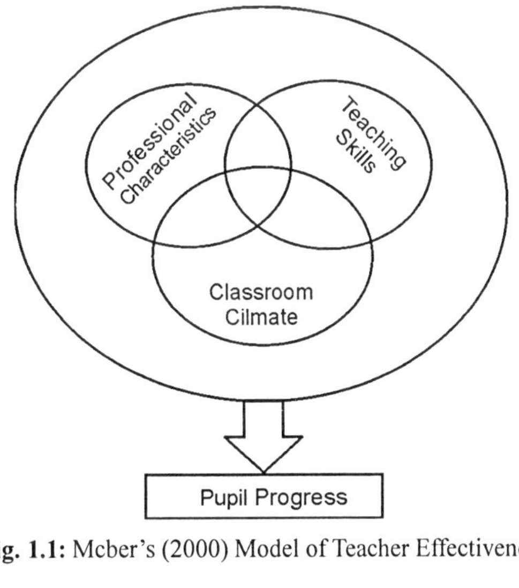

Fig. 1.1: Mcber's (2000) Model of Teacher Effectiveness

output measure. It allows teachers to understand how the pupils in the class feel about the learning climate created by them which in turn influences their motivation to learn.

Clark and Walsh's (2002) Model of an Effective Teacher

This model emphasizes not only the domains of effective teaching which receive greatest attention in teacher education and evaluation such as content knowledge, pedagogical knowledge and more recently, pedagogical content knowledge but also takes into account the teacher's personal knowledge and knowledge of context. It suggests that it is not just the knowledge that teachers have in these domains but the way this knowledge overlaps and interacts both, within the teacher and with the teacher's physical, social, intellectual and emotional environment that has to be taken into consideration (*see* Fig. 1.2).

Discipline Knowledge: Discipline knowledge encompasses an understanding of the salient concepts, relating concepts, ideas and skills of the subject. Content knowledge or discipline knowledge is the first prerequisite of ability to effectively teach a particular discipline.

Pedagogical Knowledge: The art and science of teaching is pedagogy. It includes the knowledge about classroom management, organization of classroom activities, methods for motivation of students, personal knowledge about particular students and social interactional skills.

Knowledge of Context: Context includes the knowledge of classroom, school, culture, community, educational system and students.

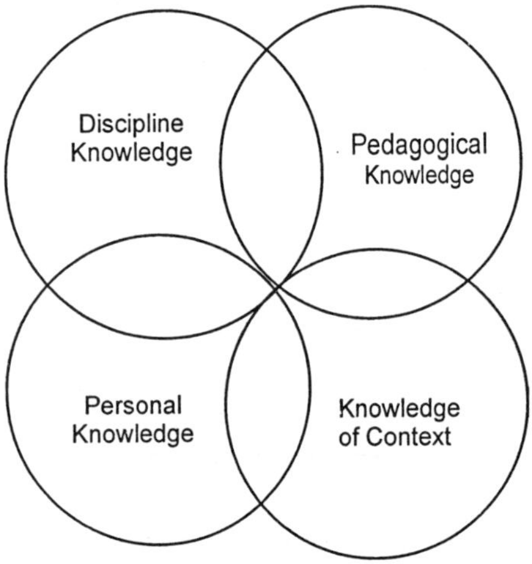

Fig. 1.2: Clark and Walsh's (2002) Model of Effective Teacher

Personal Knowledge: Components of personal knowledge are moral code of behaviour such as honesty, integrity, teacher's personal philosophy and self belief.

The sum total of different types of knowledge results in effective teaching. An effective teacher shows superior performance in terms of education outcomes. He constantly assesses and understands the moral as well as intellectual ends for which he teaches. When a teacher lacks all these attributes he loses his effectiveness and is regarded as an ineffective teacher.

In recent years the concept of total teacher effectiveness has emerged. This is markedly different from the traditional concepts of teacher effectiveness. The concept of teacher effectiveness in traditional sense is deficient in the sense that it focuses mainly on the individual level of teacher or student and ignores the complex inter-relatedness of the performance of teachers and students. In 1993, Cheng and Tsui developed a conceptual framework of total teacher effectiveness in terms of multiple domains (affective, behavioural and cognitive), multiple levels (individual, group, and school), multiple factors (teachers and students) and multiple layers (performance, competence, experience and outcomes) in order to discuss the complexity of teacher effectiveness. The new concept can be termed *Total Teacher Effectiveness* because it provides a holistic picture of the nature of teacher effectiveness by taking into consideration multiple domains of competence and performance of teachers and students at the multiple levels. This framework assumes that teacher effectiveness is related to teacher's teaching process and student's learning process. Therefore, the conception of teacher effectiveness involves two important categories of actors (teachers and students) at three different levels (individual, group, and school). The processes and effects of teaching and learning may get manifested in the behaviour, affective, and cognitive domains of different actors at different levels.

In 2004 Campbell *et al.* gave a model of differentiated teacher effectiveness. They conceptualized that the effectiveness of a teacher is a combination of teacher knowledge and teacher behaviour both of which are related to students' achievement. The model of differentiated teacher effectiveness proposes that a teacher might be differentially effective (subjects, differential pupil characteristics, different roles and different contexts). A teacher has to teach pupils with different levels of intelligence and pupils with special educational needs. A teacher has also to work in the direction of developing leadership for school improvement and developing teaching for problem solving.

Stronge (2007) in his book "Qualities of Effective Teacher" identified the common attributes of behaviour that characterizes effective teacher. According to his thesis, the positive and negative attributes of behaviour exhibited by teachers determine their effectiveness in the classroom and ultimately, the impact they have on student achievement. Teachers are effective because of the way in which various personal and professional factors combine and are executed in a classroom. Several specific characteristics of teacher responsibilities and teacher behaviours of effective teacher are listed for each of the following categories.

- Effective teacher as a person
- Classroom management and organization
- Planning and organizing for instruction
- Implementing instruction
- Monitoring student progress and potential

Effective Teacher as a Person

Rosenshine and Furst (1971) research on teacher performance criteria reviewers reported clarity to explain concepts, variability in employing a variety of instructional materials, enthusiasm, task orientation, student's opportunities to learn criterion materials are strongly related to behaviour of the effective teacher.

Kottler *et al.* (2005) have discussed human dimensions of effective teacher like creativity, honesty, emotional stability, patience, ability to challenge and motivate, novelty, good management, easy accessibility, warmth and quality of being emphatic. Woolfolk (2004) described personal and professional characteristics of effective teacher such as, knowledge of subject matter, clarity and organization, warmth and enthusiasm, explanation and direct Instruction. Chickering and Gamson (1991) consistently identified knowledge of subject matter, organizational skills, enthusiasm, clarity and interpersonal skills, as marks of effective teacher.

The personal and professional characteristics of effective teachers as perceived by students were quality of being caring, communicative and creative (being innovative, imaginative, non-traditional), disciplinarian, showing fairness (reasonable, impartial), flexible, humorous, knowledgeable (possessing knowledge of subject matter, change in education, knowledge of student needs), good listening skills, good classroom management, ability to use different modalities, ability to motivate, demonstrating passion for teaching, patience, ability to build relationships, showing respect to others, maturity to value opinions of others, ability to challenge students, well and having a good and pleasing personality (optimistic, positive, enthusiastic) apart from being understanding (Brown and McIntyre, 1993; Schulte *et al.* 2008).

On the other hand qualities as perceived by head of educational institutions are ability to maintain discipline, possessing teaching skills, intelligence, physical health, personality, resourcefulness, scholarship, preparation, fairness and co-operation (Menon, 1949). In a study of effective teaching by Johnson (1997) school board members, principals and teacher were asked to answer the question, "what is the makeup of an effective teacher?" Each group focused on what was important from their respective points of view. However, they concurred on three important points: knowledge and being caring are important effectiveness attributes; communication and classroom management are vital to the success of teaching; process and mastery are important products of teaching.

Hence, it can be concluded that attributes of an effective teacher as a person are listening, caring, understanding, knowledge of students as individuals, nurturing attitude, warmth and encouragement and overall love for children (Wentzel, 1997; Langar, 2000). Effective teaching includes positive attitudes about life and teaching and promoting a congenial, collaborative work environment (Mitchell, 1998; SECTQ, 2003).

Classroom Management and Organization

Effective teachers are more consistent and proactive in classroom management as compared to less effective teachers, who are permissive and inconsistent (Molnar *et al.* 1999) and have a heightened awareness of all actions and activities in the classroom (Wang *et al.* 1993). Effective teachers handle routine tasks promptly and efficiently (Bain and Jacobs, 1990; Cotton, 2000). Effective teachers manage and attend to the needs of all students within the class, communicate and reinforce behavioural expectations with clarity, manage the learning environment responsibly (Good and Brophy, 1997; Marzano, 2003) and create positive, warm, class room climate (Taylor *et al.* 2000; Walker-Dalhouse, 2005). An exceptionally effective teacher is one who demonstrates extraordinary abilities in the areas of teaching; communication of material, motivation of students, provision of an environment conductive to learning, maintenance of student interest, classroom management and appropriate relationship with students (Malikow, 2005-2006).

Planning and Organizing for Instruction

An effective teacher recognizes academic instruction as central to his or her role and focuses classroom time on teaching and learning and tries to link instruction to real-life situations of students (Brain and Jacobs, 1990). An effective teacher follows a consistent schedule and maintains procedures and routines, handles administrative tasks quickly and efficiently, prepares materials in advance, limits disruption and interruptions (Berendt and Koski, 1999; Zohorik *et al.* 2003; Brophy and Good, 1986; Cotton, 2000).

Implementing Instruction

Effective teachers lay stress on the importance of higher mental processes, such as problem solving techniques, analytical thinking, and creativity. An effective teacher uses different instructional strategies according to achievement levels and needs of students (Brain and Jacobs, 1990; Brookhart and Loadman, 1992) and lay greater emphasis on individualization in their teaching (Molnar *et al.* 1999; Walberg, 1984; Wenglisky, 2002). Effective teachers facilitate open discussion within the classroom and promote student self-regulation (Day, 2002) and are concerned with having students learn and demonstrate understanding of meaning than memorization and emphasize higher order thinking skills (Demmon-Berger, 1986; Marzano *et al.* 1993). Effective teachers are accepting, supportive and persistent in challenging and engaging students in all aspects of instruction.

Monitoring Student Progress and Potential

Monitoring and assessing student development and work is a complex task. For this, effective teachers employ the tools at their disposal to make a positive impart on students, including uses of homework and feedback. Effective teacher clearly explains homework, relates homework with students' capacity and gives grades and holds discussions in the class. Effective teachers plan and implement good monitoring strategies and encourage students to monitor their own learning and progress (Wharton-McDonald *et al.* 1998). Effective teachers give feedback in a manner that is supportive and encouraging to students (Peart and Campbell, 1999).

In the light of different perspectives it can be summarized that effective teachers have friendly, mature relationships with their students, and demonstrate caring, humour and commitment. It can be implied from the above discussion that classroom climate, teaching strategies, teachers' social and emotional behaviour and attitude towards students are major factors associated with effective teaching.

General Intelligence

The origin of the concept of general intelligence lies in antiquity. A perusal of the *Great Books of the Western World* (1987) indicates that some of the concepts of intelligence date back to the ancient Greeks (Sternberg, 1990). Beginning with Homer, a sixth century B.C., to John Locke, an empiricist philosopher of the nineteenth century, the dominant view about intelligence in the Western world has been that there are different kinds or aspects of intelligence and that people differ in these aspects. In general, intelligence was taken as an important natural human disposition. Different philosophers and thinkers have approached the idea of intelligence from different perspectives. Homer saw intelligence as "an entity", Plato as the "ability to learn", Aristotle as "quick wit", Augustine as "good qualities", Aquinas as "universal deeper understanding", Montaigne as "ability to seek out knowledge and truth", Pascal as "precise intellect and mathematical intellect", and Locke "distinguished between wit and judgement".

It was only Adam Smith, an important economist and philosopher of the nineteenth century, who traced an economic origin of the differences in talent. Immanuel Kant believed that intelligence comprised of understanding, judgment and reason. J.S. Mill was particularly interested in the faculty of originality which is one of the facets of intellect. William James remarked that humans and non-humans differ in their ability to associate ideas by similarity. The motives behind measurement of intelligence in the twentieth century were predominantly social motives. Intelligence was not explored from a scientific perspective. The first systematic attempt to develop a test of intelligence was made by Alfred Binet, a Frenchman. He started work at the request of French Ministry of Education, in 1904. Unlike Galton who reduced intelligence to sensory, perceptual, and motor processes, Binet argued that the core of intelligence consisted of more complex mental processes such as memory, imagery, comprehension, and judgment. Binet and Simon produced their first 'Metrical Scale of Intelligence' which was designed for children aged 3 to 12 years, arranged in order to difficulty. The concept of I.Q. was added afterwards when Binet's Stanford-Binet Test was revised.

In 1912 Stern proposed the use of the ratio of mental age, over chronological age, while in 1916 Terman published the revision of Binet-Simon Intelligence Test which was based on variety of items selected according to the abilities of children in terms of mental age, over chronological age and teachers' judgements. This test was revised in 1937 and again in 1960 to include a variety of items such as vocabulary, block counting, abstract words, finding reasons, word meaning and repeating digits. Then The Wechsler Adult Intelligence Scale (WAIS) was devised in 1939 by David Wechsler and revised in 1955.

Conceptual definitions of intelligence include opinions of experts or lay persons about what constitutes intelligence or intelligent thought and behaviour. In the implicit approach definitions or characteristics, attributes and conceptions of intelligence have been gathered from people asking them what they meant by intelligence and what people say intelligence is. In this intelligence is viewed as a stipulative concept, one that achieves its meaning as a result of the way in which people position it to mean a certain thing.

The most famous study of experts' conception of the scope of intelligent behaviour has been carried out by the editors of the 'Journal of Educational Psychology Intelligence and its Measurement' (1921). In this compilation, fourteen experts gave their views on the nature of intelligence with definitions such as the following:

1. The power of good responses from the point of view of truth or facts (E.L. Thorndike).
2. The ability to carry on abstract thinking (L.M. Terman).
3. Sensory capacity, capacity for perceptual recognition, quickness, range or flexibility of association, facility and imagination, span of attention, quickness or alertness in response (F.N. Freeman).
4. Having learned or ability to learn to adjust oneself to the environment (S.S. Colvin).
5. Ability to adapt oneself adequately to relatively new situations in life (R. Pintner).
6. The capacity for knowledge and knowledge possessed (B.A.C. Henmon).
7. A biological mechanism by which the effects of a complexity of stimuli are brought together and given a somewhat unified effect in behaviour (J. Peterson).
8. The capacity to inhibit an instinctive adjustment, the capacity to redefine the inhibited instinctive adjustment in the light of imaginarily experienced trial and error, and the capacity to realize the modified instinctive adjustment in overt behaviour to the advantage of the individual as a social animal (L.L. Thurstone).
9. The capacity of acquire capacity (H. Woodrow).
10. The capacity to learn or to profit by experience (W.F. Dearborn). Sensation, perception, association, memory, imagination, discrimination, judgment, and reasoning (N.E. Haggerty).

Cross-culturally the conception of intelligence has been found to be different in different cases. The differences between eastern and western conceptions of intelligence have transcended ancient times and persist even in the present day. In a general sense, Western culture emphasizes on speed of mental processing. On the other hand, other cultures may even be suspicious of quality of work that is done very quickly. Yang and Sternberg (1997) studied contemporary Taiwanese Chinese conception of intelligence and found five factors:

a. A general factor, much like the 'g' factor in conventional western test.
b. Interpersonal intelligence
c. Intrapersonal intelligence
d. Intellectual self-assertion
e. Intellectual self-effacement

In a related study with different results, Chen (1994) found that factors underlying Chinese conceptualization of intelligence are non-verbal reasoning ability, verbal reasoning ability, and rote memory. The difference may be owing to different sub-populations of Chinese, to differences in methodology, or to differences in periods during which the studies were conducted.

Chen and Chen (1988) found non verbal skills, verbal reasoning, social skills and numerical skills considered most relevant skills in measuring intelligence.

In Eastern Concept of Intelligence discernment and judgment, are also considered important factors and are given precedence over quickness in thinking. Traditional Indian views on intelligence (Das, 1994) or *Budhi* (in Sanskrit), involved concepts, such as wisdom, prudence, emotion, societal values and relations. The internal structure of wisdom comprises a unique blend of cognitive, interpersonal, social and personality attributes. This shows intelligence includes not only reasoning but also will and emotion. Srivastava and Mishra (2007) in their book 'Rethinking Intelligence' analyzed lay people's responses and yielded broad conceptual dimensions of intelligent behavior like cognitive competence, social competence, emotional competence and entrepreneurial competence. It can be argued that the differences between the East and West may be due to differences in the kinds of skills valued by the two kinds of cultures.

Further explicit approach of intelligence is based or at least tested, on data collected from people performing tasks presumed to measure intelligent functioning and serve as the basis for scientific hypotheses. The three basic units to the discussed under this approach are stimulus response bond (S-R), the factor, and the elementary information process (as component).

The S-R bonds proposed by Thorndike (1928) under which forms of intelligence were viewed in terms of ability to learn i.e. building simple SR bonds. Gagne (1970) was able to identify eight kind of learning involved in S-R bonds.

a. signal learning (Pavlovian conditioning)
b. S-R learning (Operant conditioning)
c. Chaining (Complex operant conditioning)
d. Concept learning
e. Verbal association
f. Discrimination
g. Rule learning
e Problem solving

In the factorial approach factor has been considered as the basic unit of analysis. The paradigm has been called 'differential, 'psychometric' or 'factorial' on the basis of trends worked out by finding inter correlations among mental tests.

Charles Spearman (1927) gave the earliest factor theory of intelligence which comprises two kinds of factors, general factors and specific factors. General ability, or 'g' as measured by general factor, is required for performance on mental tests of all kinds. Specific ability as measured by each specific factor is required for performance on just one mental test. Spearman suggested that the ability underlying the general factor could be understood as a kind of mental energy.

Godfrey Thomson (1939) accepted Spearman's hypothesis of a general factor running through the range of mental ability tests. Thomson disputed Spearman's claim that the general factor represented a single underlying source of individual differences. Instead he proposed that appearance of a general factor was due to the working of multitude of mental "bonds" including references, learned associations and performance of any particular task or activities.

Thurstone (1938) accepted Spearman's theory and identified primary mental abilities as verbal comprehension, word fluency, numbers, spatial visualization, perceptual speed, memory and reasoning.

Guilford (1967) in his structure of intellect model proposed that intelligence comprises of 120 elementary abilities, each of which involves the action of some operation upon some content to produce some product.

Vernon (1971) has proposed that intelligence can be described as comprising abilities at varying levels of generality. At the highest or most general level is a general factor, encompassing all tasks. This is followed by (1) major group factors, including a verbal educational factor and practical-mechanical factor (2) minor group factors; and (3) specific factors.

Cattell (1971) and Horn (1968) held that intelligence involves two dimensions, crystallized intelligence, measured by tests such as vocabulary and general information and fluid ability, measured by tests such as abstract analogies and abstract series completions.

Horn (1994) has greatly expanded hierarchical concept as proposed by Cattell. He has suggested that 'g' can be split into their more factors nested under fluid and crystallized abilities. These three other factors are visual thinking (gv), auditory thinking (ga) and speed (gs).

Under the third approach called the component approach scientists attempted to analyze directly the process involved in intellectual behaviour rather than trying to find behavioural correlates. These three approaches are not mutually exclusive. They are in fact complementary.

Triarchic Theory of Intelligence of Sternberg (1985) suggested the intelligent behaviour is the product of applying thinking strategies handling new problems creatively and quickly and adapting to contexts by selecting and reshaping our environment. The three aspects are described as:

(a) *Analytic:* (Componential Intelligence) ability to think abstractly, process information, verbal abilities.
(b) *Creative (Experimental Intelligence):* Ability to formulate new ideas and combine unrelated facts; creativity ability to deal with novel situations and make new solutions automatic.
(c) *Practical (Contextual Intelligence):* Ability to adapt to a changing environment to make the most of opportunities—problems solving in specific situations.

J.B. Carroll (1997) in his "The Three Stratum Theory of Cognitive Abilities" presented hierarchical model of intelligence which conceptualized a three level theory of intelligence. The Three Stratum Theory identified these three levels as general ability, a few broad abilities (such as fluid and crystallized abilities, learning, and memory, visual and auditory perception, processing speed) and at least 70 specific abilities such as language development, memory, simple reaction time. General ability may be related to the maturation and functioning of the frontal lobe of the brain, while specific abilities may be connected to the other parts of the brain. Characteristics of generally intelligent person mentioned by Mayor *et al.* (2001) are attributes such as adaptability in behaviour constituting problem solving, verbal facility and common sense in interactions with the real world. The general concept of intelligence refers to one's overall ability to adapt through effective cognition and information processing. This involves the use of higher order mental abilities to perceive patterns and logically reason to solve problems. Abstract reasoning may be the primary aspect of general intelligence but there are other factors also which affect the measurement of general intelligence. In a testing situation, the intelligence manifested by a person is dependent on the input a person is receiving and general knowledge base from which that person operates. General intelligence is often broken down into different intelligences based on what inputs are being processed. General intelligence is specifically test for verbal intelligence and spatial intelligence

Gardner (1983, 1993) has been foremost among theorists arguing that human cognitive abilities are best envisaged as several independent forms of intelligence.

(a) *Linguistic:* Sensitivity to sound, meaning of words and the function of language.
(b) *Logical/Mathematical:* Ability to discern logical patterns, numerical patterns, symbols and complex chains of reasoning.
(c) *Bodily/Kinesthetic:* Ability to control body movements and manipulate objects skillfully.
(d) *Spatial/Visual:* Ability to accurately perceive the visual-spatial world and make transformations based on those perceptions.
(e) *Musical:* Ability to produce and appreciate rhythm, pitch and *musical expression.*
(f) *Interpersonal:* Ability to sense and respond to the moods, temperaments, motivations and desire of others.
(g) *Intrapersonal:* Ability to understand personal feelings that guide behaviour, knowledge of personal strengths, weaknesses and desires.

Social Intelligence

"Social intelligence" is frequently defined as the "ability to deal with people". The term social intelligence, "social adaptability" and "sociability" are sometimes used inter changeably. Gilliland and Burke (1926) expand this simple definition as follows: The sociable individual may be defined as having the ability to get on agreeably. He is well adapted for society, friendly, fond of mixing with others. In short, he is the type of individual usually called a "good mixer". The search for a construction of social intelligence has had a long and unstable history. Walker and Foley (1973) in a comprehensive review of the literature on social intelligence go on to explain that social intelligence is a cyclical concept, seeming to come in and go out of favour in repeated cycles over time. Four major approaches to understanding the construct of social intelligence are explained here under:

Definitional approach of social intelligence refers to the conceptual proximity with the psychometric view of social intelligence as defined by E.L. Thorndike (1920) i.e. "the ability to understand and manage men and women, boys and girls—to act wisely in human relations". Thus it is contended that social intelligence is the ability to perceive one's own and other's internal states, motives and behaviours and to act toward them optimistically on the basis of the information perceived. According to this appoarch intelligence is grouped into three clusters. These are referred to as (i) abstract intelligence (the ability to understand and manipulate with verbal and mathematics symbols); (ii) concrete intelligence (the ability to understand and manipulate with objects); (iii) social intelligence (the ability to understand and relate to people).

Moss and Hunt (1927), define social intelligence as the ability to g*et* *al*ong with others. In a similar manner, Hunt (1928), defined social intelligence as the construction in terms of one's ability of the best ways to deal with people. Strang (1930) expanded upon Hunt's definition by emphasizing the role of prior knowledge (about people) in the exercise of social intelligence. Vernon (1933) combined aspects of past definitions with some new ideas when he defined social intelligence. According to Vernon social intelligence includes the ability to g*et al*ong with people in general, knowledge of social matters, a sense of ease in dealing with other people, susceptibility to stimuli from other members of a group, and insights into the states and traits of others. Wedeck (1947) expanded upon the last aspect of Vernon's definition by defining social intelligence as one's ability to judge correctly the feelings, moods, and motivations of others. Perhaps all of these various definitions are best and most succinctly summarized by Wechsler's (1958) definition of social intelligence as one's facility in dealing with human beings. Weinstein (1969) speaks of social intelligence as the ability to accomplish interpersonal goals. Marlowe (1986) indicates social intelligence to be the "ability to understand the feelings, thoughts, and behaviours of persons, including oneself, in interpersonal situations and to act appropriately upon that understanding".

In implicit theoretical approach, one seeks to discover what various groups of people mean by social intelligence by investigating their implicit and usually tacit theories of the construct. Studies carried out by Bruner *et al.* (1958) and by Cantor (1978) on people's conceptions of intelligence revealed many characteristics that were highly social in nature. This kind of approach was also formalized by Sternberg *et al.* (1981). The factors uncovered in both these studies are: practical problem solving, verbal ability and social competence. Briefly, these investigators factor-analyzed the rating of both the experts and laypersons in order to study how distinctively characteristic the behaviours of intelligent, academically intelligent, and everyday intelligent people are. In the entire factor analysis a single most important factor that merged was labeled "social competence". Ford and Miura (1983) used a related approach to studying social intelligence. Four main dimensions of what we are calling social intelligence emerged from their study: *prosocial skills*; *leadership skills*; *social ease; self-efficacy*.

The psychometric approach to understand social intelligence involves both the definitional and theoretical approaches adding standard kinds of psychological theorizing. The third psychometric approach describes social intelligence in terms of scores on various kinds of tests. In George Washington Social Intelligence Test (GWSIT, 1949) six aspects of social intelligence have been given:

- Judgement in social situations
- Memory for names and faces
- Observation of human behaviour
- Recognition of the mental states behind minds
- Recognization of mental states from facial expression
- Social information
- Sense of humour

Guilford's (1967) structure of intellect model postulates operations, contents and products. Guilford considers his system to be an expansion of the intelligence proposed by Thorndike. Thus, the symbolic and semantic content domains correspond to abstract intelligence, the figural domain to practical intelligence, and behavioural domain to social intelligence.

Kaukiainen *et al.* (1995) explained dimensions of Peer-Estimated Social intelligence (PESI).

- Perception of others
- Social flexibility

- Successful achievement of one's goals
- Behavioural outcomes

Wong *et al.* (1995) have, in their work, discussed dimensions of social intelligence, social perception, social insight and social knowledge.

Silvera *et al.* (2001) constructed 'The Tromso Social Intelligence Scale'; and defined social intelligence as "the ability to understand other people and how they will react to different social situations". In other words their study is in the realm of pure social cognition.

The social-experimental approach uses measures such as self-ratings, teacher ratings, and interviewer ratings of social competence, peer nominations, and measures of goal directedness, empathy, social maturity, moral-developmental level to assess social-intelligence skills (Ford, 1982) and reflecting a more goal-oriented approach. Ford and Tisak (1983) defined social intelligence as "one's ability to accomplish relevant objectives in specific social settings". Social intelligence represents the efforts of individuals to solve problems of daily life and work towards desired goals (Cantor and Harlow, 1994). Cantor and Kihlstorm (1987) defined social intelligence as a form of intelligence specifically geared to solving problems of social life, and in particular managing the life tasks, current concerns or personal projects which the person selects for him or herself or which other people impose on him or her from outside.

Greenspan (1979) proposed a hierarchical model of social intelligence, in which, social intelligence consists of three components:

- Social Sensitivity: reflected in role making and social inference
- Social Insight: including social comprehension, psychological insight, and moral judgement.
- Social Communication: referential communication and social problem solving (Cunnigham, 1997).

Goleman (2006) held that the ingredients of social intelligence can be organized into three broad categories:

- Social awareness: refers to a spectrum that runs from instantaneously knowing another's inner state, to understand his feelings and thoughts and to know complicated social situations. It includes primal empathy, attunement, empathic accuracy and social cognition.
- Social facility builds on social awareness to allow smooth and effective interactions. The spectrum of social facility includes synchrony, self presentation and concerns.

Social competence has been defined as the possession and use of the ability to integrate thinking, feeling and behaviour to achieve social tasks and outcomes valued in host context and culture (Topping *et al.* 2000).

Social intelligence is contrasted with other kinds of intelligence such as problem solving intelligence—an ability to solve logically complex problems, or emotional intelligence—an ability to monitor one's own and others emotions and to use the information to guide one's thinking and actions. Social intelligence has been discussed as an ability of an actor/agent to relate to other actor/agents in a society, understand them, and interact effectively with them (Fruchter *et al.* 2005).

Emotional Intelligence

Our mind works in three ways—cognition, affect and motivation. Cognition includes functions such as memory, reasoning, judgement and abstract thought. Affect includes emotions, moods, evaluations and other feeling states. Emotions appear to be involved in all aspects of human interaction. Our emotions are something that we are familiar with and use in our daily life, as well as something that we recognize readily in everyday situations as we read people's face or body language. Emotional intelligence does not only entail being aware of one's own emotions but also using these emotions in functional ways. First, emotions can be useful in terms of directing attention to pressing concerns and signaling what should be the focus of attention (Frigda, 1988; George and Brief, 1996). Second, emotions can be used in choosing among alternatives and taking decisions. The ability to anticipate how one would feel if certain events took place can help decision makers choose among multiple options (Damasio, 1994). Third, emotions can be used to facilitate certain kinds of cognitive processes. As mentioned earlier, positive moods can facilitate creativity, integrative thinking and negative moods can facilitate attention to, detection of errors and careful information processing (Isen *et al.* 1987; Sinclair and Mark, 1992; Salovey *et al.* 1993).

By 2007, there was wide diversity in the conceptions of emotional intelligence. Some researchers defined this form of intelligence as the ability to reason about emotion, whereas others equated the concept with different traits such as flexibility, happiness and self-regard (Locke, 2005). It is believed that emotional intelligence determines the potential to learn practical skills that are based on the five elements of self-awareness, motivation, self-regulation, empathy and adaptability in relationships. Ciarrochi *et al.* (2000) conceptualized emotional intelligence an individual's perception, expression, understanding and management of emotions. These are directly related to the major life events that they have experienced. These emotions are then interpreted and adapted according to those life events, leading to life outcomes, either positive or negative. Hence, the importance of being able to understand and mange an emotion as it is applied to life.

The concept of emotional intelligence derives partly from earlier ideas about social intelligence which was first determined by Thorndike in 1920's as one of the many different types of intelligence that individuals possess. Thorndike defines social intelligence as the ability to understand people. Emotional intelligence is included in Gardner's inter and intra-personal intelligence in his "Theory of Multiple Intelligence" which came out in 1983. The inter-personal intelligence consists of the ability to understand others. Intra-personal intelligence is the ability to develop an accurate model of the self and use it effectively throughout life. Moreover, in this conceptualization these skills are understood to be necessary for social interaction and the understanding of one's emotions and behaviour.

However, there is a lot of ambiguity that surrounds the concept of emotional intelligence. No doubt, it is a function of the brain. It is concerned with processing and utilization of emotional information. Besides, it is different from cognitive intelligence.

Many authors and theoreticians have dwelt on the concept of emotional intelligence. The most important definitions seem to fall under the following main branches:

Cognitive Model of Emotional Intelligence

This model primarily focuses on the assumption that emotions convey knowledge about a person's relationship with the world e.g., fear indicates the perception of threat that a person is facing, happiness is indicative of a harmonious relationship with others and anger generally reflects perception of injustice. As such certain general rules and laws can be employed in recognizing and reasoning with feelings. Salovey and Mayer (1990) have theorized that emotional intelligence involves the ability to perceive accurately, the appraisal and expression of emotions, the ability to assess and/or generate feelings when they facilitate thought, the ability to understand emotions and emotional knowledge and the ability to regulate emotions to promote emotional and intellectual growth (*see* Fig. 1.3).

According to Mayer and Salovey's (1997) Cognitive Model, emotional intelligence consists of four separate components or branches.

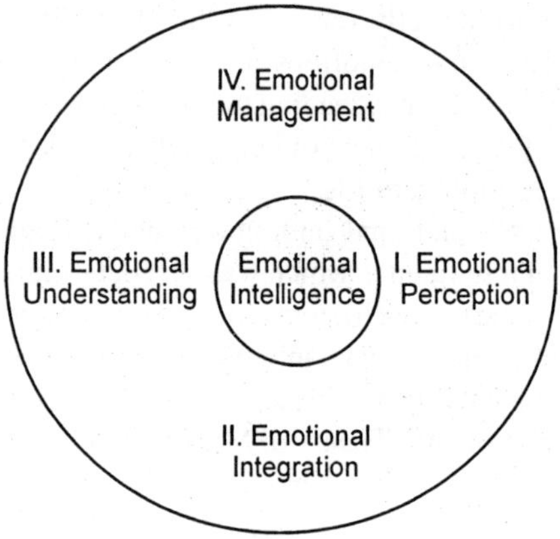

Fig. 1.3: Mayer and Salovey's (1997) Cognitive Model of Emotional Intelligence

(*a*) *Perceiving and identifying emotions:* The ability to perceive how you and those around you are feeling.

(*b*) *Facilitation of thought:* Ability to generate emotion and then reason with this emotion.

(*c*) *Understanding emotions:* Ability to understand complex emotions and emotional 'chains', how emotions transit from one stage to another.

(*d*) *Managing emotions:* The ability which allows you to manage emotions in yourself and in others.

Affective Regulation Model of Emotional Intelligence

Goleman (1995, 1998) viewed emotional intelligence as the ability to know and manage one's own emotions, recognize them in others and to handle relationships. Goleman (1995) calls emotional intelligence "a master aptitude, and capacity that profoundly affects all other abilities, either facilitating or interfering with them".

According to Goleman's model following are the main components of emotional intelligence:

(*a*) *Emotional Self-awareness:* It includes accurate self-assessment and self-confidence.

(*b*) *Emotional Self-management:* It includes self-control, trust worthiness, conscientiousness, adaptability, achievement, orientation and initiative.

(*c*) *Relationship Management:* It includes the development of leadership, influence, communication, change catalyst, conflict management, building bonds, team work and collaborations.

Relational Model of Emotional Intelligence

A more comprehensive definition given by Bar-on (1997) defines emotional intelligence "an array of non-cognitive capabilities, competencies and skills that influence one's ability to succeed in coping with environmental demands and pressures." The five main domains of this model are intra-personal skills, inter-personal skills, adaptability, stress management and general mood (*see* Fig. 1.4).

It includes:

(a) *Intra-personal E.Q:* The ability to be aware of, to understand, and to express oneself;

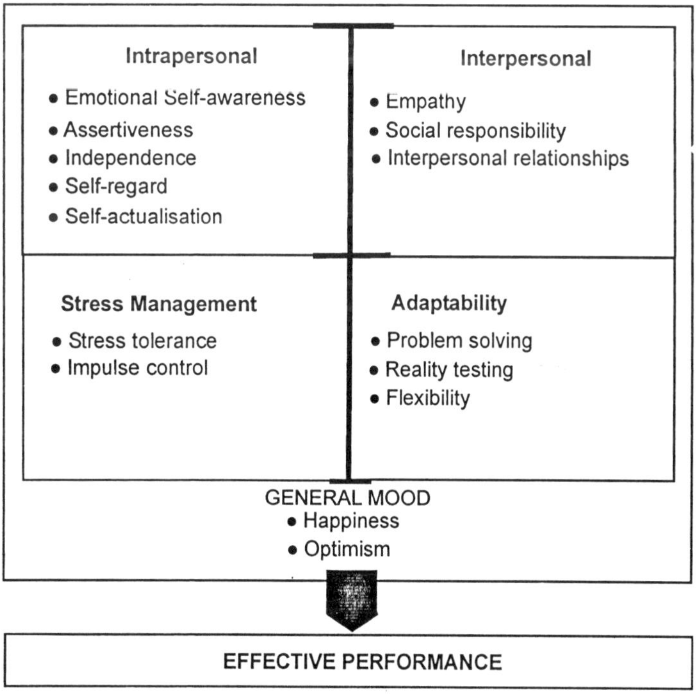

Fig. 1.4: Bar-On (1997) Relational Model of Emotional Intelligence

(b) *Interpersonal E.Q*: the ability to be aware of, to understand, and to relate to others;
(c) *Stress management E.Q*: the ability to deal with strong emotions and control one's impulses;
(d) *Adaptability E.Q*: the ability to adapt to change and to solve problems of a personal or a social nature; and
(e) *General mood E.Q*: the ability to look at the brighter side of life and to enjoy oneself and others.

A careful perusal of the above models reveals that all these models tend to place greater emphasis on harnessing emotions of one's own self and that of others for one's own benefit. In this sense, emotional intelligence has been visualized more as ability, or a mental skill to be distinguished from characteristic way of behaving (traits) and non-intellectual abilities (talents).

Cooper's Model of Emotional Intelligence

According to Cooper (1996/1997) emotional intelligence can be divided into five attributes which are as follows:

(a) *Current environment:* includes life pressures and life situations.
(b) *Emotional literacy:* includes emotional self-awareness, emotional expressions and emotional awareness of others.
(c) *E*.Q. competencies: includes intentionality, creativity, resilience, inter-personal connections and constructive discontent.
(d) *E.Q. values and attitudes:* includes outlook, compassion, intuition, trust, personal power and integrated self.
(e) *E.Q. outcomes:* includes general health, quality of life, relationship quotient and optimal performance.

Spencer and Spencer (1993) Model of Emotional Intelligence

On the basis of Goleman's work Spencer and Spencer (1993), proposed the following constituents of personal and social competencies which constituted emotional intelligence (*see* Fig. 1.5).

Four Dimensions of Emotional Iintelligence proposed by Davies *et al*., 1998

1. Appraisal and expression of emotion in one's self: relates to an individual's ability to understand his/her deep emotions and to be able to express emotions naturally.
2. Appraisal and recognition of emotions in others: relates to an individual's ability to perceive and understand the emotions of the people around him/her.

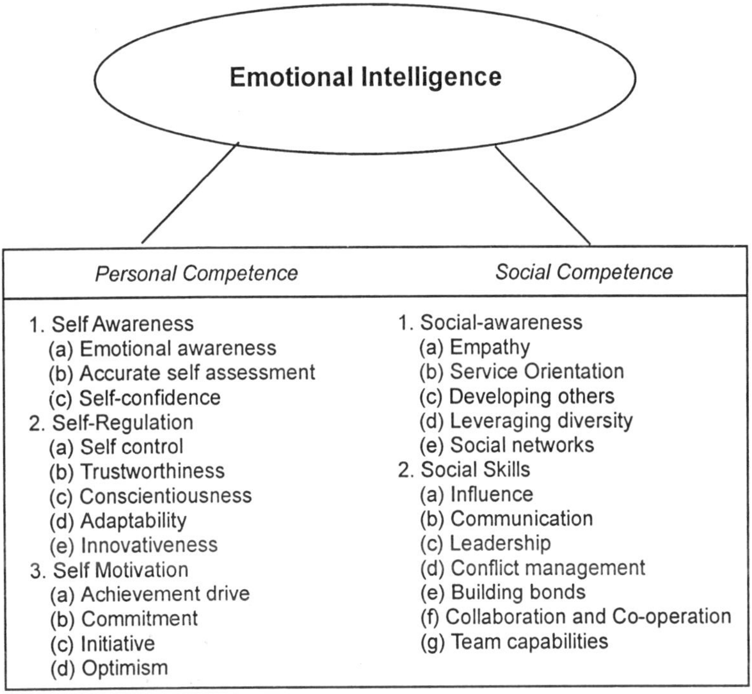

Fig. 1.5: Spencer and Spencer (1993) Model of Emotional Intelligence

3. Regulation of emotion in one's self: relates to the ability of a person to regulate his/her emotions, enabling recovery from psychological distress. A person with high ability in this area would be able to return quickly to normal psychological states after rejoicing or being upset.
4. Use of emotions to facilitate performance: relates to the ability of a person to make use of emotions by directing them towards constructive activities and personal performance.

Indian Viewpoint on Emotional Intelligence

The Indian view on emotional intelligence is rooted in the rich traditional, religious and philosophical context focusing on the role of family and society in shaping one's emotions. Social concerns such as well-being of others and fulfilling one's duty constitute a dominant part of achievement goals, with social skills respecting elders or helping others constituting the salient means of achieving these goals (Dalal, Singh and Mishra, 1988).

The Indian view of self is characterized largely as inter-dependent. Certain valued traits in the Indian culture like respecting elders, caring, kindness, benevolence, non-violence are typical emotional expressions. These are grounded in the cultural traditions and have been passed down for one generation to another. Peace of mind and freedom from worries have been emphasized as aspects of self and reflect Indian values. In Indian thought, the self is viewed as an experiencing subject or an unchanging centre of awareness. Yoga and ways of meditation are considered means of discovering the true self. The Indian self is constructed around 'we', 'our' and 'us' in contrast to western 'I' and 'my'. This implies that the Indian notion of self is always conceived in relation to the social context. People with such self-perception try to fit in with the significant others, fulfill obligations and duties and have intimate and lasting friendships. Emotional learning in the Indian context needs to be viewed as a life-long process of personal exploration (looking inward) towards the discovery of true self. This process is accompanied by concepts such as *Yoga, Karma* (deeds), *Jitendriya* (person who is able to manage and regulate one's emotions), *Dharma* (duty), *Vratas* (ordinances), caring and benevolence. Though not empirically tested, yet the existence of these ideas cannot be denied since they have found expressions in literature, folklore, popular songs, idioms and other Indian expressions.

Emotional intelligence in the Indian context cannot be viewed as a homogenous trait or as mental ability devoid of social concerns like respecting elders, concern for others and fulfilling one's duties. In fact, the Indian notions of emotional intelligence are related with ways in which an individual deals with different situations-emotional, social or otherwise. These culture specific ways of behaving, therefore, are basic to the notion of emotional intelligence. It is due to these reasons that individuals approach emotions differently—across cultures, sub-cultures, within society or families.

Studies of Lutz and White (1980) and Miller (1984) have shown emotions to be dependent on cognitive appraisals of experience as well as to be a culturally grounded process. For example, peace of mind and being free of worries have been emphasized as aspects of self in India. People in individualistic cultures often have greater skills in entering and leaving news social groups. They make "friends" easily, and by "friends" they mostly mean non-intimate acquaintances. In contrast, Misra (2001) and Triandis *et al.* (1988) found that people in collectivist cultures like India have fewer skills in making new "friends" but the term "friends" in their case implies a life-long intimate relationship, with several obligations.

The Indian tradition has also from time-to-time and through different religious and social customs, emphasized some independent but inter-related concepts in relation to stress and suffering such as—detachment, impulse control and transcendence (Palsane and Lam, 1996).

The definitions and statements by some Indians who have worked in understanding the concept of emotional intelligence provide an exposition into the understanding about emotional intelligence.

Singh (2003) defines emotional intelligence as the ability of an individual to appropriately and successfully respond to a vast variety of emotional stimuli being elicited from the inner self and immediate environment. Emotional intelligence constitutes three psychological dimensions: emotional sensitivity, emotional maturity and emotional competence, which motivate an individual to recognize truthfully, interpret honestly and handle tactfully the dynamics of human behaviour.

Mohan (2003) defines emotional intelligence is a positive combination of a deep insight into one's emotional and cognitive capacities and a charming flair of communication, empathy and motivation, leading to personal optimism, inter-personal confluence and organizational excellence.

Sanwal (2004) expresses the view that emotional Intelligence is the awareness of use of emotions and their utilization within the parameters of individual cognitive styles to cope with situations and problems.

Chadha (2005) offers the thesis that all forms of intelligence have an emotion base. Using your emotions as a source of energy to accomplish the self-defined goals is what emotional intelligence consists of.

Malekar (2005) in his work has explained that emotional intelligence is a set of factors which involve awareness of self and managing emotions, developing oneself through the power of empathy and motivation and building strong relationship with people.

Relationship between General Intelligence, Emotional Intelligence and Social Intelligence

Most of the early day psychologists focused exclusively on cognitive aspects, such as memory and problem solving while dealing with the concept of intelligence. In a major departure from the traditional approach, David Wechsler (1958) recognized non-intellective elements along with "intellective elements" and defined intelligence as "the aggregate or global capacity of the individual to act purposefully, to think rationally, and to deal affectively with his environment". In the late 1950's David Wechsler asserted that "social intelligence is just general intelligence, applied to social situations". According to this view abstract or general intelligence enters into and overlaps with social intelligence. Correlation between social intelligence test and general intelligence test shows that the individuals who have high general intelligence tend to have high social intelligence. The same ability, namely, the ability to adjust one's self to new situations, seems to be needed in both social and non social situations (Strang, 1930). The traditional concept of social intelligence as purely cognitive assumes that social intelligence may be different from general intelligence. The old view saw social intelligence as the application of general intelligence to social situations—a largely cognitive aptitude. However, when ordinary people were asked to list what in their opinion made a person intelligent, social competence emerged as a prominent natural category. Whereas most early psychologists placed emphasis on verbal and problem solving skills the new concept of social intelligence defines it mainly as interpersonal talent. Gardner (1983) describes interpersonal intelligence as empathy, or the awareness and appraisal of the subjective feeling evoked in one's self by others as well as the awareness and appraisal of non-verbal expressions of others with emotional content. Emotional intelligence could be viewed as collective effort of interpersonal and intrapersonal intelligence but social intelligence gives importance to interpersonal abilities. Social intelligence is the key element which makes people succeed in life. Social intelligence is the capacity of the individual to interact with his environment effectively. The interpersonal relation in various work environments is itself a reflection of social intelligence. Social intelligence is most similar to emotional intelligence in that adaptability and functionality of an individual's cognitions are stressed in the current social environment. In this construction little importance is given to the perception and integration of emotional information. In the 1990's, as the localization of emotions in the brain became better understood, Mayer noted, "Emotional intelligence could be groomed as the replacement number of the triumvirate where social intelligence failed".

Social Intelligence abilities related to Emotional Intelligence

Emotional Intelligence	*Social Intelligence*
Self awareness	Social awareness • Primal empathy • Empathic accuracy • Listening • Social cognition

(*Contd.*)

Emotional Intelligence	*Social Intelligence*
Self-management	Social facility or Relationship management • Synchrony • Self-presentation • Influence • Concern

It may be noted that self-awareness (intrapersonal intelligence), empathy and handling relationships (interpersonal intelligence) are essentially dimensions of emotional intelligence. Thus, emotional intelligence represents as alternative grouping of tasks to social intelligence. On one hand, emotional intelligence is broader than social intelligence, including not only reasoning about the emotions in social relationships, but also reasoning about internal emotions that are important for person (as opposed to social) growth. On the other hand, emotional intelligence is more focused than social intelligence in that it pertains primarily to the emotional (but not necessarily verbal) problems embedded in personal and social problems. Together with cognitive intelligence, emotional and social intelligence form important components of general intelligence. One of the major differences between the two is that former is related primarily to higher order mental processes like reasoning, while the latter focuses more on perceiving, immediate processing and applying emotional and social context, information and knowledge. It has also been suggested that another fundamental difference between the two may be that cognitive intelligence is strategic in nature, while emotional and social intelligence is more limbically tactical for immediate behaviour suited more for survival and adaptation (Golman, 1993; Bar-On, 1997; Stein and Book, 2009).

Emotional Intelligence is closely related to two other scientific concepts: intelligence and emotion. Intelligence and emotion have commensal connotations for most psychologists. Intelligences involve abilities to understand information; emotions are coordinated responses to the environment. Emotional Intelligence is the ability to reason about emotions as well as the capacity to use emotions and emotional information to assist reasoning (*see* Fig. 1.6).

There is no doubt that cognitive abilities and emotional intelligence act interactively to determine success in actual life situations, the research evidence explaining the relationship between intelligence and emotional

Emotional Intelligence

Emotional intelligence is an ability to understand and to problem solve that involves

- Managing emotional Reponses
- Understanding emotions and emotional meanings
- Appraising emotions from situations
- Using emotion for reasoning
- Identifying emotions in faces, voices, posters, and context

Emotion

Emotions are coordinated responses to changes in the environment that involves:

- Invoking specific subjective experiences
- Activating relevant cognitions, especially
- Related to taking action in relation to the self and environment
- Coordinating bodily states so as to prepare for certain reactions (e.g., fight or flight)
- Appraising the ongoing situation for changes

Intelligence

Intelligence are abilities to understand and problem solve about information that involve:

- Reasoning about abstract relationship (fluid intelligence)
- Storing material in an organized fashion in memory (crystallized intelligence)
- Learning targeted material
- Inputting material through sensory and perceptual channels
- Processing information quickly

Fig. 1.6: Scope of Emotional Intelligence by Mayer, Roberts and Barsade, 2008

intelligence is not clear. The correlation between IQ and EI has been reported to range from 0.00 to 0.36 depending on the measures used. Using his own EI measure, Mayer *et al.* (2000) reported a zero correlation with fluid intelligence and a 0.36 correlation with verbal IQ. There was no significant correlation between IQ and EQ (Bar-on *et al.* 2003). Total EQ score correlated +0.12 with full IQ score on the Wechsler Adult intelligence scale (WAIS) in a study of 40 adults (Pallazza and Bar-on, 1995). The total EQ-i total scored +0.01 with Raven Progressive Matrices in one study (Hee-Woo 1998) and +0.01 in another study (Fund, 2000). Ciarrochi, Chan and Chaputi (2000) reported a correlation of +0.05 for the Multi Factor Emotional Intelligence Scale (MEIS) and the Raven Progressive Matrices.

Creativity

The concept of creativity is complex in nature. It is difficult to understand it by adopting one single definition. Different viewpoints have been put forward to explain the concept, emphasizing different aspects of creativity. By and large, psychologists seem to agree that creativity involves the ability to produce original ideas and to perceive new relationships among unrelated or remotely related things. It does not involve just an ability to produce original ideas. Creativity is multifaceted. Creativity research, rather than having one universal definition, has used a variety of definitions, theories and assessment approaches.

Repucci (1960) reviewed fifty to sixty definitions and classified them into six major groups or classes. The first group, labeled *Gestalt or Perception types*, places emphasis on the recombination of ideas or restructuring. The second is *end product or innovation oriented*, the third class is *Aesthetic or Expressive*—with emphasis upon self-expression; the fourth group of definitions is characterized as *Psychoanalytic or Dynamic.* These define creativity in terms of certain interactional strength ratios of the id, ego and superego. A fifth class called *Solution thinking,* emphasizes the thinking process rather than the actual solution of the problem. The last class is labeled *Varia* simply because there is no easy way of characterizing these definitions.

Welsch (1980) proposed the thesis that creativity is the process of generating unique products by transformation of existing products. These products, tangible and intangible, must be unique only to the creator, and must meet the criteria of purpose and value established by the creator.

A widely known and accepted concept of creativity, called the 'FourP' model, is based on the assumption that creativity can be defined as a holistic multi-dimensional concept (*see* Fig. 1.7).

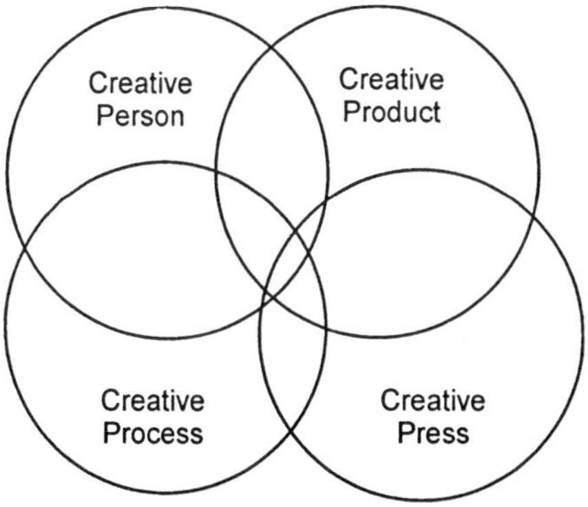

Fig. 1.7: Person, Process, Product, Press

Source: Firestien (1993).

Rhodes (1961) developed a framework for a unifying approach to creativity; forming four strands. These strands are the creative person (clustered around personality-related traits and the mental ability of the person to create something new), the *creativity process* (the function of the mind in creating ideas in the creative person like searching, combining and synthesizing), *creative product* (the outcome or product being original, unique, valuable and novel), and the *creative press* (or environment) which influence the ecological impression on the person and upon his mental processes and outcomes. Mooney (1963) and Rhodes (1967) have referred to these kinds of definitions as the "FourP" creativity.

Creativity as Person

Definitions in term of 'person' refer to the person who is creative in terms of physiological and temperamental attributes including attitudes, habits and values. According to Guilford (1963) creativity is combination of attitude factors and disposition that enables a person to use his distinctive potentialities in novel ways. Some personality-oriented psychologists conceive creativity in terms of the person. Considerations of the creative person typically fall into three general categories: (A) cognitive characteristics (B) personality and motivational qualities and (C) special events or, experiences during one's development (Tardif and Sternberg, 1988).

A. The cognitive characteristics can be grouped into three sets: the traits, abilities and processing styles that creative individuals use and possess (Tardif and Sternberg, 1988). (i) Traits that are associated with creative individuals include relatively high intelligence, originality, articulateness and verbal fluency, and a good imagination. (ii) Cognitive abilities include the ability to think metaphorically, flexibility and skill in making decisions, independence of judgement, coping well with novelty, logical thinking skills, internal visualization, the ability to escape perceptual sets and entrenchment in particular ways of thinking, and finding order in chaos. (iii) The approach to problems (i.e. style) includes using wide categories and images, a preference for non-verbal communication, building new structures, questioning norms and assumptions in the domain, being alert to novelty and gaps in knowledge, and using existing knowledge as a base for new ideas.

B. The most commonly mentioned personality or motivational characteristics are a willingness to confront hostility and take intellectual risks, being open to new experiences, curiosity and growth (Barron, 1988; Torrance, 1988), discipline and commitment to one's work, high intrinsic motivation, being task-focused, a high degree of self-organisation and competence in meeting optimal challenges (Hennessey and Amabile, 1988). Some additional characteristics mentioned less often include tolerance for ambiguity, a tendency to play with ideas, valuing originality and creativity (Walberg, 1988), unconventionality in behaviour, experiencing deep emotions, intuitiveness, seeking interesting situations and some degree of conflict between self-criticism and self-confidence (Barron, 1988).

C. Environmental factors which stimulate home environment and provide diverse experiences.

Creativity as Product

Creativity is also conceptualized in terms of the actual product. These products should be novel, unique and useful. In this form of understanding, creativity is defined in terms of products. Product-oriented psychologists give primary importance to the product. If the product is considered creative, then the person who made it may be considered creative. The products of creativity can include behaviours, performances, ideas, things, and other kinds of output, through any channel or type of expression (Taylor, 1988). Parnes (1966) defined creative behaviour as that 'which demonstrates both uniqueness and value in its product'. Creativity may be defined quite simply as the ability to bring something new into existence (Barron, 1965).

Creative products can be solutions to problems, responses to creativity tests, or explanations for phenomena. The products are novel—they are not imitations, nor are they mass-produced (Perkins, 1988, Taylor, 1988; Torrance, 1988)

Many researchers see creativity as the ability to bring something new into existence (Drevdahl, 1956; Dehaan and Havighurst, 1957; Maslow, 1959; May, 1959; Stein, 1960; Barron 1969; Johnson-Laird, 1993).

Stein (1963) has made product as the basis of his definition of creativity and defined creativity as the process which results in a novel work that is accepted as tenable or useful or satisfying by a group at some point in time. This definition emphasizes both novelty and utility.

According to Isareli (1946), Drevdahl (1956) and Kavoli (1964) creativity is the capacity of the individual by which something new is produced. The product could be an idea or an object including a new form or arrangement of old elements.

National Advisory Committee on Creative and Cultural Education (NACCCE, 1998) defined creativity as 'imaginative activity fashioned so as to produce outcomes that are both original and of value' (Jubert, 2001).

Creativity refers to skill in generating ideas and products that are relatively novel, high in quality, and appropriate to the task at hand (Sternberg, 2003).

Creativity as Process

The orientation of process-oriented psychologists is towards understanding the process of thinking that leads to the emergence of creative products. If the creative process is understood, then efforts can be made to develop such thinking among children. Rogers (1954, 1959) defined the creative process "as the emergence in action of a novel relational product, growing out of the uniqueness of the individual on the one hand, and the materials, events, people or circumstances of his life on the other". According to Ghiselin (1952), creativity is a process of change and development in the psychic life of an individual leading to invention.

Mackinnon (1962) argues that creativity is "a process extended in time and characterized by originality, adaptiveness and realization". A number of authors outline steps in creative thinking. For instance, Graham Walls (1926) proposed four steps: preparation, incubation, illumination, and verification. Osborn (1948) proposed five stages which are similar to those of Walls: orientation; preparation; analysis and ideation; incubation and evaluation. Rossman (1931) proposed seven steps in creative activity: need or difficulty is observed; the problem is formulated; available information is surveyed; solutions are formulated; solutions are critically examined; new ideas are formulated and the new ideas are tested.

The process approach to creativity is concerned with what actually happens in producing something, or what processes are involved in the creative act. A number of psychologists have proposed definitions of creativity which centre on the process of creativity. Among these are Torrance, Khatena, Mednick, Kubic and Koestler.

Torrance (1988) in his research based definitions describes creative-thinking as the process of sensing difficulties, problems, gaps in information, missing elements; making guesses and formulating hypotheses about these deficiencies; evaluating and testing these guesses and hypotheses; possibly revising and retesting them; and finally communicating the results.

Another process based definition of creativity has been given by Khatena who has chosen to define originality rather than creativity. "Originality is the power of imagination to break away from perceptual set so as to restructure new ideas, thoughts and feelings into novel and meaningful associate bonds" (Khetna and Torrance, 1973).

Mednick in his definitions of creativity has emphasized the importance of remote association. According to him creative thinking consists of forming new combinations of associative elements, which either meet specified requirements or are in some way useful. The more mutually remote the elements of the new combination, the more creative are the process or solution (Mednick, 1964).

Wallach and Kogan (1966) have expressed agreement with Mednick and observed that creativity most appropriately refers to the ability to generate or produce, within some criterion of relevance, many cognitive associates and many that are unique.

Creativity as Press (or Places)

In the context of environment creatiity may be defined as environment or cultural influences that make a man creative. The process of manipulating the environment results in the production of new ideas, patterns or relationships through the interaction between persons and their environment. Creative places or environments include domains, fields and contexts.

Creative acts cannot be understood from a psychological perspective alone. The unit of analysis must be the individual as part of his or her cultural environment. According to the logic of part and whole structure, the primary focus must be on the cultural-historical context that makes the creative act possible and meaningful (Floistad, 1993). Particular social and historical contexts have been seen by some to be influential. Creativity can be viewed as an outcome of these (Csikszentmihalyi, 1988).

An analysis of concept of creativity based on the definitions of creativity reveals that there are four major trends in defining creativity viz. creativity as a process, as a product, as a person and as a consequence of environmental traits (Press). Thus the phenomenon of creativity is multi-dimensional and multi-splendoured. It can be understood as convergent-divergent process of self expression. The definitions whether given in terms of person, product, or environment indicate that creativity includes four things transformation, originality, adaptability and realization.

Approaches to Creativity

Different psychologist have attempted to explain the nature of creativity, creative functioning or creative behaviour as well as the process of creativity in different ways. These approaches are explained hereunder:

(i) *Associationistic Approach to Creativity:* Associative theory, as developed by Mednick (1962) defines the creative thinking process as "forming new combinations of associative elements which either meet specified requirements or are in some way useful". He proposes that creativeness is simply a process of arranging well-known facts into new relationships so that results may be achieved more effectively. Similarly Wallach and Kogan (1965) propose the associative basis of the creative process, suggesting that "creativity involves the ability to produce more associations and to produce more that are unique".

(ii) *Psychoanalytic Approach to Creativity:* Freud (1958) argues that the creative process depends mainly on defence mechanisms, because defence mechanisms prevent an accurate perception of the world and because they use up psychic energy. He believed that although most defence mechanisms interfere with the creative act, the mechanism he called sublimation is actually the primary cause of creativity. He strongly believed that "people are only motivated to be creative when they cannot directly fulfill their sexual needs". According to Freud creative activity is a form of daydreaming. A close associate of Freud, Jung (1928) also believed that the unconsciousness plays a vital role in high-level creativity.

Disagreeing with Freud and Jung, Adler (1927) developed the compensatory theory of creativity. He argued that the creative power was necessary in each individual as the third power. In addition to heredity and environment, the creative process combines the innate potentialities and environmental influences into a movement toward the overcoming of obstacles in one's life path. He says that creativity is "supremely useful, and those who are more creative are more useful for purposes of serving a social function".

The psychoanalytic position as developed by Kris (1952) emphasized the role of the preconscious during the creative process, in particular the degree of preconscious elaboration of ideas from which a sudden "solution" or "inspiration" may emerge into conscious. Kris asserted that the defence mechanism of regression is involved in the creative act. May

(1975) asserted that, "creativeness is the unconscious (i.e. mindful awareness) breaking through into consciousness (i.e. mindful understanding)". Kubie (1958) viewed creativity as a healthy process. According to him, creativity is the result of preconscious rather than unconscious thought. He believed that the preconscious is the wellspring of creative thought.

Psychoanalytic theorists have emphasized the unconscious rather than the conscious in their conceptualization of the process of creativity. They suggest that creative people tend to suffer from emotional imbalances. Some of them argue that *"creative is next to madness"* (Dacey, 1989). Another point that can be made is that though the source of creative thought may be the unconscious, it is necessary for these thoughts to become conscious, otherwise they remain unrecognized and incommunicable (Kris 1952; Kubie, 1958 and May, 1975).

(iii) *Humanistic or Holistic Approach to Creativity:* In contrast to those adopting psychoanalytic approaches, humanistic psychologists feel that a creative person is emotionally healthy and sensitive to the needs and the capabilities of his/her unconscious which enables him to produce creative ideas. These psychologists equate creativity with mental health. "They give least importance to unconscious drives and compensation for deficits in the personality and much more credit to positive, self-fulfilling tendencies" (Dacey, 1989). According to them, creativity evolves throughout life and can be cultivated throughout the life span.

Maslow (1957) believed that human beings have six basic instincts, which manifest themselves as needs. At the highest level, the process of self-actualization is closely analogous to creativity. Self-actualization is seen as a manifestation of the life forces, which govern the creative process of nature. Personality itself is regarded as an emerging creative product. Free of neurosis, self-actualizing people are more likely to be creative. They are likely to achieve peak experiences and moments of unselfish ecstasy.

A creative act was seen by Rogers (1954) as motivated by the individual's desire to expand and grow, and hence 'form new relationships with the environment'.

Rogers and Maslow take a holistic approach, since they see the creative product as the result of an interaction between the creative person and his/her situation. "They see creativity as more conscious, cognitive and intentional than do the psychoanalysts" (Dacey, 1989). The humanistic concept mainly contends that creativity is born through a striving for the highest possibilities in life, rather than as a defence against neurosis.

(iv) *Boden's Impossibility Theory:* Boden (1994) distinguishes two senses of creativity. One is psychological (P-creativity), the other historical (H-creativity). A valuable idea is P-creative if the person in whose mind it arises could not have had it before; it does not matter how many times other people have already had the same idea. By contrast, a valuable idea is H-creative if it is P-creative and no one else, in all human history, has ever had it before.

(v) *Convergent-Divergent Thinking and Creative Thinking:* The work of Guilford is usually seen as the starting point for deliberate and explicit research on creativity. Guilford (1950, 57, 61, 67, 68, 86) has viewed creativity in terms of the theory of the structure of the intellect. His theory of creativity is derived from factor analytic procedures (five intellectual operations-cognition, memory, convergent thinking, divergent thinking and evaluation). Creativity is not seen as a unitary trait, but rather a collection of interacting and complementary, component abilities, all of which may enter into creative thinking. All genuine problem solving is creative and most, if not all, creative thinking is problem solving. Both problem solving and creativity are modes of productive thinking, which include both convergent and divergent abilities. Divergent thinking abilities can be defined as the means the individual has for expressing whatever creativity he possesses. He maintains that these abilities are somewhat general and can be applied to a variety of tasks. They are not associated with particular subject matter or disciplines. According to him these abilities together constitute creative thinking. The distinctive aspect of creative thinking is divergent thinking, which is characterized by, among other things, flexibility, originality and fluency.

(vi) *Lateral Thinking and Creativity:* According to De Bono (1992) lateral thinking is directly concerned with two senses, one of which is specific and the other one general. He argues that creativity has a very wide and confused meaning. There are elements of "newness" and of "bringing something into being" and even elements of "value". There may be several entirely different processes involved in this wide definition of "creativity", the term "lateral thinking" is, however, very precise. Lateral thinking is concerned with changing concepts and perceptions. Divergent thinking is but one aspect of lateral thinking. Divergent thinking is interested in multiple possibilities, just like lateral thinking, but that is only one aspect of lateral thinking. The relationship between lateral thinking and creativity is overlapping. The term "lateral thinking" is reserved for the specific techniques and tools that are put forward as a systematic way of getting new ideas and new concepts. Creative thinking is concerned with new concepts and new ideas.

All the approaches discussed above getting articulated around the factors that influence creativity like unconscious drives, unusual drives, unusual associations between stimulus and response, divergent thinking, motivation, rewards and positive environment which is open and democratic. The logic of these positions on the faculty of creativity posits that these factors positively contribute for creativity.

Interrelationship of Creativity and Intelligence

Relationship between creativity and intelligence can be described in following ways:

(i) Creativity as Subset of Intelligence: Guilford in his Structure of the Intellect (SI) Model (1967) suggested three basic dimensions of intelligence, which form a cube. By crossing 5 operations (cognition, memory, divergent production, convergent production, and evaluation), 4 contents (Figural, symbolic, semantic, behaviour), 6 products (units, classes, relations, systems, transformations, implications) one can get 120 factors. Divergent production is just one of the 5 operations of the intellect, thus creativity can be seen as subset of intelligence. Guilford (1968) clearly distinguishes between the intellectual operations of 'divergent thinking' (creative process) and convergent thinking (which represents intelligence). Generally it is accepted that the path to creativity lies through intelligence

Cattel (1971) believed that real-life creative performance is determined by one's general intelligence first, particularly fluid intelligence (reasoning ability) as opposed to crystallized intelligence (knowledge or learned material) and then by personality factors.

Howard Gardner's (1983, 1993, 1995) theory of multiple intelligence (MI), intelligence is a collection of eight distinct intelligences. Creativity can be understood in terms of the uses of multiple intelligences to generate new and even revolutionary ideas.

(ii) Intelligence as a Subset of Creativity: In this view intelligence can be viewed as a subset of creativity. Sternberg and Lubart (1995) argue that there are six main elements that coverage to form creativity. These are intelligence, knowledge, thinking styles, personality, motivation, and the environment. Intelligence is thus just one of the six forces that influence and generate creative thought and behaviour. According to the theory, these aspects of intelligence are of central importance for creativity, synthetic, analytical and practical abilities. These three aspects are drawn from Sternberg's triarchic theory of human intelligence. They are viewed as interactive and as involved in creative functioning. In Sternberg's (1985) "Triarchic Theory of Intelligence", it is argued that effective adaptation to the environment, and hence successful use of intelligence, involves combining analytic intelligence with practical intelligence and creative intelligence. Creative work requires applying and balancing the three intellectual abilities—creative, analytic, and practical all of which can be developed.

Leon Smith (1970) in Bloom's Taxonomy of Educational Objectives viewed intelligence as a subset of creativity. The basic assumption of the taxonomy is that cognitive processes can be placed along a cumulative and hierarchical continuum, viz: comprehension, application, analysis, synthesis, and evaluation. Intellectual ability is required in the first three and creative ability is required for the last two i.e. syntheses and evaluation.

(iii) Creativity and Intelligence as Overlapping Sets: The concept of creativity and intelligence as overlapping sets implies that in some ways creativity and intelligence are similar, but.in other ways they are different. The relationship between intelligence and creativity has been reported to be highly significant. However, at the same time this is highly controversial

The problem solving ability manifestation of intelligence will also be a manifestation of originality (Barron, 1963); it was also concluded that creative people tend to show above average IQ, often above 120 (Renzuli, 1986). Creativity may be more highly correlated with IQ below an IQ of 120, but it correlates only weakly or not at all with IQ of 120 and above (This relationships is called threshold theory). Hudson (1966) has explored the statistical relation between measures of divergent and convergent thinking (or of 'creativity' and 'intelligence') and of the circumstances in which the two traits are more or less independent, with special reference to the 'threshold' theory. Another view point is that the correlation between IQ and creativity is variable, usually ranging from weak to moderate (Flescher, 1963; Getzels and Jackson, 1962; Guilford, 1967; Herr *et al.* 1965; Torrance, 1962; Wallach and Kogan, 1965; Yamamato, 1964). Mednick (1962) suggests that creativity and intelligence are closely related. The correlation is 0.55, 0.43 and 0.41 between RAT and WISC, SAT verbal and Leorge-Thorndilce verbal intelligence respectively (Mednick and Andrew, 1967). When people were asked to rate hypothetically described individuals in terms of their creativity and intelligence Sternberg (1985) found a correlation of 0.69 between their ratings of creativity and intelligence. Hensly and Reynolds (1989) argue that creativity and intelligence should be viewed as a "unitary phenomenon". That is, as a conjoint set. They proposed that creativity is an expression of intelligence.

Empirical findings suggest that intelligence and creativity are statistically significant and positively correlated (Sharma, 1972; Bedi, 1974; Dhailwal and Saini, 1976; Patel and Joshi, 1978; Gupta, 1979; Gulati, 1979; Qureshi, 1980; Muddu, 1982; Srivastava and Thomas, 1991), but some researchers have reported that there is no significant relationship between creativity and intelligence (Sansanwal and Jarial, 1979; Yamamato, 1964; Mehdi, 1977; Sharma, 1979; Chadha and Sen, 1981). The bulk of the evidence points to the independence of creativity from conventional measures of intelligence (Gakhar and Kaur, 1976-77; Cropley, 1966). More accurately, there is a marked discontinuity between lower and higher IQ, so that little or no creativity occurs at levels below a higher average (say, IQ 120) and above that point the correlation is negligible (Barron, 1963). That is although highly creative people are typically high in intelligence, the reverse does not necessarily hold true. Sharma (1971), in his study of both rural and urban high schools, reported some rise in creativity with intelligence. Further, he reported a consistent rise in creativity of the lower IQ level but after 120 IQ the relationship demonstrated inconsistent fluctuations. Similar findings have been reported by MacKinnon (1962), Venkatarami and Balakrishna (1983), Fuchs-Beauchamp, Karnes and Johnson (1993). However, the kinds of correlation outlined would occur even if the correlation between IQ and creativity were high, as a result of the restriction of range resulting from concentrating on those with IQs over 120. Torrance (1966) reported that the correlation of creativity scores with IQ was 0.50 for children with IQ scores below 120, but only 0.20 for children with IQs above 120, if correlations across the whole ability range were in reality 0.80. Dutt, Bountra and Sabhrawal (1977) showed a curvilinear relationship between creativity and intelligence. To a certain extent they go together but thereafter take different directions. As such, highly creative students need not necessarily be highly intelligent as well. As McNemar (1964) pointed out, high IQ is no guarantee of creativity, but a low IQ means that it is impossible.

(iv) Creativity and Intelligence as Disjoint: Many investigators show that creativity is different from intelligence. Or, that they are disjoint sets (Getzels and Jackson, 1962; Torrance, 1975; Wallach and Kogan, 1965). Creativity as measured by divergent thinking tests correlates moderately with measures of IQ measured by conventional intelligence tests. A certain basic level of analytical intelligence is essential for creativity, but beyond that critical base level, creativity and IQ are relatively independent sets of abilities.

At the very least, creativity seems to involve synthetic, analytical and practical aspects of intelligence. Synthetic aspect of intelligence implies the ability to come up with ideas, analytical to evaluate the quality of those ideas, and practical to formulate a way of effectively communicating those ideas and of persuading people of their value.

Creativity is a rare trait. It requires the simultaneous presence of a number of traits (e.g. intelligence, perseverance, unconventionality, the ability to think in a particular manner) (Martindale, 1999). Creativity is the hallmark of all progress. A search for new methods, ways, alternatives, possibilities approaches, processes and products has led to change and advancement in all fields. Clarkson (2005) has mentioned that there are many traits which have been associated with creativity, such as divergent thinking, introversion, self esteem, tolerance, willingness to take risks, behavioural flexibility, emotional variability, ability to absorb imagery and even the tendency to neurosis and psychosis. Torrance (1975), Sternberg (1986) and Barron (1988) hold the view that characteristics and abilities that are associated with creative personality are imagination, independence and divergent thinking. In addition, abilities such as critical thinking, analogical reasoning and problem finding ability have been associated with creativity (Nickerson *et al.* 1985; Weisberg, 1986; Torrance, 1988).

Characteristics of creative person as described by Taylor (1963) are divergent thinking, especially in production of ideas, fluencies, flexibility, and originality, humor, fantasy and playfulness with ideas. Other traits that have been linked to a creative person include curiosity, manipulation, questioning, ability and restructuring of ideas, curiosity, manipulation, questioning ability and restructuring of ideas. Personality characteristics that are normally linked with creativity are autonomy, independence, and femininity of interests, dominance, self-assertion, self-acceptance, resourcefulness, radicalness and complexity of personality. Mackinnon (1962-63) has summarized the characteristics of creative person as follows: They are intelligent, original, and independent in thought and action, open to experience both of the inner self and outer world, intuitive, esthetically sensitive and free from crippling restraints. They also have high energy level, and persistent commitment to creative endeavour.

General, Social, Emotional Intelligence and Creativity of Effective Teachers

The characteristics of teacher effectiveness are very different for different people. Their approaches to presenting this concept are also very different. Some researchers have focused on teacher personalities, traits, behaviours, attitudes, values, abilities, competencies in addition to several other personal characteristics. Some other researchers are more concerned with the teaching process (including such factors as teaching styles, teacher-student interactions, classroom climate, etc) or the teaching outcomes (including such factors as students' academic achievements, personal developments, learning experiences, etc). Educational administrators in the study of Bagley and Keith (1924) have enumerated that the qualities of an effective teacher are personal appearance, health (vitality, physical control); social intelligence (address, tact, sympathy, leadership); moral qualities (sincerity, loyalty).

Panton (1948) opines that the qualities correlated with teacher efficiency are leadership, capacity for self-criticism and that of others besides carefulness, initiative, persistence, sociability and sense of humour. Raja Gopalan (1976) identifies and lists qualities of effective teachers such as mastering of subject matter, proper professional training, love for profession and children, knowledge of psychology, good conduct, honesty, politeness and sincerity, patience and tolerance, optimistic outlook, sense of humour, patriotism, sympathy, the ability to be friend, philosopher and guide, sound physical health and mental health.

General, social, emotional intelligence are significant in that they generate interpersonal and intrapersonal skills that help a teacher in understanding performance at work. These all are predictors of job performance. Campbell (1990) explored the relationship between general mental ability and emotional intelligence. He found general mental ability to be closely related to the cognition domain of the human mind and it is primarily related to declarative knowledge (knowledge about fact, principle, self knowledge, goals) and parts of procedural knowledge and skills (cognitive skills, psychoticism skills, physical skills, self-management and interpersonal skills) in the job content (*see* Fig. 1.8).

There is no doubt that both types of intelligence are important, but they are important in different ways. Research shows that IQ accounts for only about 20 per cent of a person's success in life. The balance can be attributed to EQ (80%). Goleman's initial publication claimed—that emotional intelligence could be "as powerful, and at times more powerful, than IQ." (Goleman, 1995) Much of this claim was based on past research revealing that IQ had little relation to work place and personal success. Emotional intelligence is more important in determining success. Emotional intelligence can be understood as the ability to handle

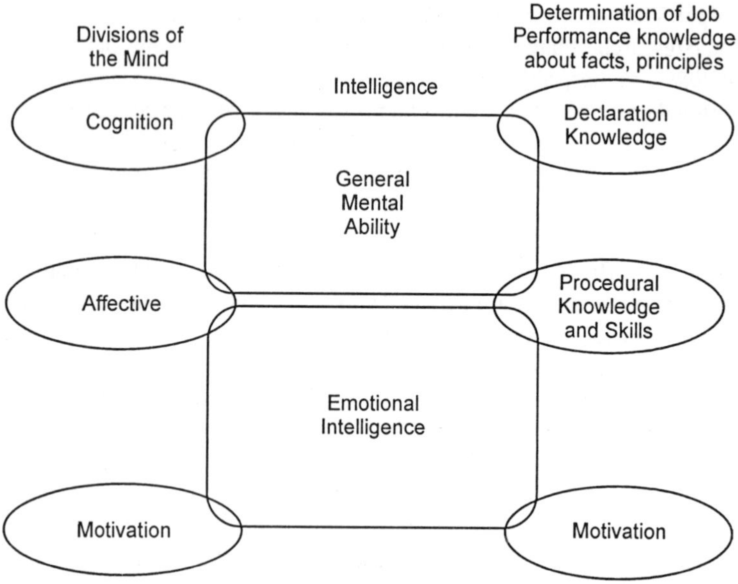

Fig. 1.8: The Relationship between General Mental Ability and Emotional Intelligence (Campbell, 1990)

frustration, control emotions and get along with others (Snarey and Vaillant, 1985). There are many ways in which a person's destiny depends on possessing the skills that make up emotional intelligence (Neil, 1996). If a teacher has these emotional competencies he/she can recognize the emotions, emotional patterns, and tendencies and also devise ways to generate and use emotions which will create joy and enthusiasm to motivate learning in themselves and others. As a result realistic understanding of capabilities and recognition of emotional strengths and weaknesses can be achieved.

Social and emotionally competent teachers also have high social awareness. They know how their emotional expressions affect their interactions with others. Such teachers also recognize and understand the emotions of others. They are able to build strong and supportive relationships through mutual understanding and cooperation and can effectively negotiate solutions to conflict situations. Socially and emotionally competent teachers are culturally sensitive. They understand that others may have different perspectives than they do, and take this into account in relationships with students, parents and colleagues (Jennings and Greenberg, 2009). When teachers experience mastery over these social and emotional challenges, teaching become more enjoyable and efficacious (Goddard *et al.* 2004).

Alan Mortiboys (2005) in his book, 'Teaching with Emotional Intelligence" has discussed the role of emotional intelligence in a teacher's work (*see* Fig. 1.9).

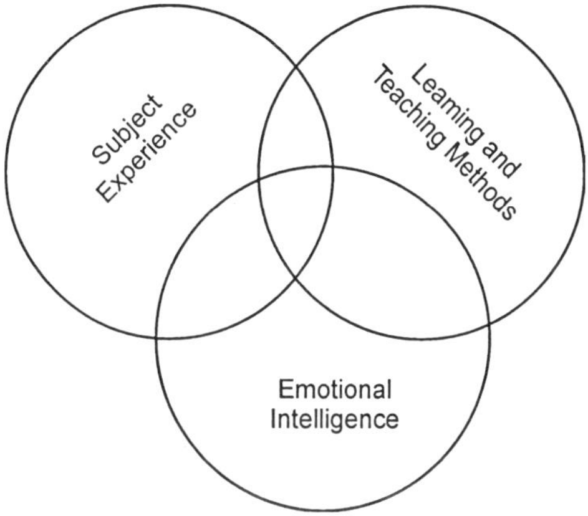

Fig. 1.9: Role of Emotional Intelligence in Teaching

Conventionally a teacher brings two things to the classroom that are of value to the learners—one is knowledge of subject matter and the other is knowledge of learning and teaching methods which includes teacher's pedagogy. In the contemporary context emotional intelligence is a third component which will complement the subject expertise and pedagogical skills. The transmission of knowledge of subject matter and pedagogical skills can be facilitated through the use of emotional intelligence. Emotional intelligence has potential to affect several aspects of teachers/teaching like handling problems with learners, relationship with teachers, class room experience, likelihood of learners being engaged, motivated, ready to take risks in their learning, approach in learning, apart from collaborative and creative attitudes.

Emotionally healthy behaviour is reflected in characteristic ways of thinking, identifying, managing, and expressing feelings and choosing effective behaviours. Becoming an emotionally intelligent teacher is a journey and process, not an arrival, state or end result. Emotionally intelligent teachers are active in their orientation to students, work and life. They are resilient in response to negative stress and less likely to overwhelm themselves with pessimism and strong, negative emotions. An emotionally intelligent teacher learns and applies emotional intelligence skills to improve interpersonal and healthy relationships, personal leadership, and self-management. A teacher who consciously develops emotional skills and models emotionally intelligent behaviour on a daily basis experiences more success and satisfaction in his/her professional career and life (Nelson *et al.* 1999).

Creativity is a powerful force for lifting man to higher levels of intellectual functioning, human dignity and achievement. Research has continued to a accumulate evidence (Torrance, 1965) that creative thinking is important in mental health, educational achievement vocational success and many other important areas in life. An imaginative and inventive teacher can manage classroom behaviours and produce ingenious ideas for teaching. A creative teacher can recognize desirable behaviour which may indicate valuable potentialities which if properly guided and developed, may lead to socially valued achievements. By arranging different activities teacher can get better understanding of children behaviour (Torrance, 1965). The NACCE (1998) proposed that teaching for creativity involves three key tasks or principles: encouraging certain beliefs and attributes in pupils, identifying creative talents and fostering creative potential.

Creativity is the Hallmark of an effective teacher. Creative teachers use imaginative approaches to make learning more interesting and exciting. The goal of effective teaching cannot be achieved without creative teaching which is the key component of good teaching. An effective teacher creates a conducive atmosphere in classroom, presents the subject matter in interesting way, encourages students to speak, accept mistakes and criticism in positive manner and accepts the pupil's right to be different. All these things greatly enhance creativity among children. It is true that creativity cannot be produced but it can be nourished by appropriate education and environment. Students should be placed in the most appropriate environment and responsibility of educating them should be entrusted to creative teachers. A creative teacher can make an activity better, richer, more productive, fruitful and aesthetically satisfying. Mackinnon (1967) has discussed that the determinatives of effective individuals are emotional stability or personal soundness and originality or creativity of thought and action.

Cognitive characteristics of creative teacher refer to the traits, abilities and styles of information processing. Originality, relatively high intelligence, good imagination and verbal fluency are often the traits associated with creative teachers. The abilities of the creative teachers include flexibility, skill in decision-making, coping with novelty, visualization, the ability to breakaway from the fixed set of ideas and rigid thinking, sensitivity to problems and finding order in chaos. There is a range of personality characteristics associated with creative teachers. The most commonly mentioned personality characteristics include willingness to face and take risks; perseverance, being open to new experiences, commitment to work; high internal motivation; competence in meeting challenges; reflectiveness, independence of judgement; display of courage; excellent work habits; capacity of sustained effort; persistence; liking to think, manipulation of ideas; and a desire to improve upon currently accepted systems.

Thus, it can be concluded that creative teacher may be described as an individual who introduces changes and novelties into day-to-day teaching and learning activities making education meaningful, enjoyable, useful, and explorative experience to children. A creative teacher is seen as an information-processor, a problem-finder, a problem-poser and a problem-solver. Teaching is regarded by the creative teacher as an exercise of imagination to generate fluent and novel ways of organizing ideas, content and materials for solving problems.

Education can achieve its aim if its product the students can achieve their goals successfully. Many factors effect the achievement of students. Most important of these are effectiveness of the teacher. It is concluded a teacher who has these cognition and affective abilities that is general, social, emotional intelligence and creativity can impart education that help the students to grow in the most efficacious and meaningful ways.

Teacher Effectiveness and its Psychological Correlates: Research Evidence

Survey of the related literature for the present problem has been done from various sources like research articles published in educational journals, published books, unpublished M.Phil./Doctoral dissertation, surveys of educational research, published by NCERT, New Delhi, the websites related to educational research and the encyclopedias of education. Teacher effectiveness and emotional intelligence are the two areas in which work has been done by researchers. A plethora of studies do exist in these areas. Studies have highlighted the areas in which teachers are effective and have emphasized the attributes of emotional intelligence. A little work is done in the area of general intelligence and social intelligence in case of secondary school teachers. After reviewing the studies related to social intelligence it is felt that much work could not found out related to social intelligence of teachers specifically in India.

International studies give more importance to people's implicit concepts of social intelligence, socially competent behavior. Moreover emotional intelligence which is comparatively a new concept has not been studied as a related variable with social or general intelligence.

Teacher effectiveness was studied in terms of socio-demographic variables i.e. gender, income level, locality of residence, marital status, qualification, caste, designation, nature and management of schools and other psychological variables i.e. self-efficacy, job satisfaction, life satisfaction, locus of control, burnout, stress, school organizational climate, administrative behaviour etc.

Intelligence is a type of mental ability that concerns the handling of and reasoning about—information of various sorts (Carroll, 1993; Spearman, 1927; Sternberg and Detterman, 1986). While emotional intelligence concerns the ability to carry out accurate reasoning about emotions and ability to use emotions and emotional knowledge to enhance thoughts. In this study intelligence has been studied by its three types i.e. general, social and emotional. These variables are studied in terms of socio-psychological variables i.e. adjustment, proficiency in teaching, work success, job satisfaction, teacher efficacy, leadership behaviour, personality alongwith some demographic variables. Creativity of teacher has been studied with teaching experience, creative classroom behaviour, teacher student relationships, sex, self-esteem, job satisfaction, socio-economic status, age, teaching at different levels, values and socio emotional climate of school.

1. Effective teacher possess certain qualities like well balanced personality, self confidence, good character, favourable attitude towards teaching, higher level of motivation, self actualization, patience, cheerfulness, empathy, high moral and social values, good explanation of subject matter, problem solving ability, competent and favourable attitude information technology than ineffective teachers (Arora, 1978; Baacke, 1985; Pandey and Maikhuri, 1999; Raj, 2000; Katoch, 2001; Singh, 2002; Newa, 2007; Kaur, S. 2008).
2. Teacher effectiveness was studied in terms of gender, professional knowledge training, nature of schooling, income level, locality of residence, management of schools, interpersonal relationships, marital status, designation, achievement motivation, self efficacy, job satisfaction, life satisfaction, locus of control, burnout, stress, educational qualification, caste, etc. (Krishnan and Singh, 1994; Biswas and Tinku, 1995; Raja and

Thiagarajan, 1998; Kumar, 1999; George, 2002; Kagathala, 2002; Singh, 2002; Agrawal, 2003; Vijaylaksmi and Mythill 2004; Amandeep and Gurpreet, 2005; Arokidass 2005; Cheung, 2006; Williamson, 2006; Gupta and Jain, 2007; Newa, 2007; Roul, 2007; Duckworth, 2009; Kalara, 2010; Goyal and Duggal, 2011; Kauts and Mittu, 2011).

3. Perceptions related to characteristics of effective teachers are mostly cited are student centeredness, ethical, enthusiastic, behavioural manager, competent instructor, individual report, communication skills, sense of humor, caring, flexible instructional style etc. (Allington and Johnson, 2000; Selsor, 2003; Ayres, 2004; Malikow, 2005; Schulte et al. 2008; Onderi and Croll, 2009; Aregbeyen, 2010).
4. Intelligence promoted proficiency in teaching and positively related to success in teaching (Jain, 1977; Sharma, 1977; Kaur, Charanjeet, 2010). Teacher effectiveness is correlated with intelligence and adjustment (Kaur, 1993 and Hiremath, 2012). General intelligence, creativity, academic achievement have positive relationship with emotional intelligence (Manhas, 2004). People with high intellectual ability are more confident, satisfied, achievement oriented and open to others (Ackerman and Heggested, 1997).
5. Emotional Intelligence has significant role in effective teaching-learning, school success, integrated curriculum, work success, teaching motivation and job satisfaction (Aggarwal, 1998; Nelson et al. 1999; Stein and Book, 2001; Zembylas, 2004; Bardoch, 2008; Upadhaya, 2008; Ghoniem et al. 2011). Indian view attach greater importance to competency in displaying pro-social values and social sensitivity (Sibia and Misra, 2004).
6. Emotional intelligence is positively correlated with career success, teacher efficacy, personality, life satisfaction, academic achievement, coping resources, self concept, self actualization, self confidence, work motivation and negatively correlated with academic stress, achievement motivation, leadership behaviour, conflict management style (Witte, 2004; Punia, 2005; Singh and Koteswari, 2006; Upadhyaya, 2006; Kamboj, 2007; Kaur, 2007; Penrose et al. 2007; Sharma, 2007; Annm, 2008; Kaur, D. 2008; Deshmukh and Sawalakhe, 2010).
7. Effect of locality of residence, socio-economics status, management of school, teaching experience, teachers

qualification, age, gender, faculty, religion, family occupation and marital status are seen on emotional intelligence (Chouhan and Bhatnagar, 2003; Tyagi, 2004; Wu, 2004; Punia, 2005; Srinivason, 2005; Amritha and Kadhiravan, 2006; Patil and Kumar, 2006; Neelkandon, 2007; Singravalu, 2007; Jarmali et al. 2008; Gowdhaman and Murugan, 2010; Indu, 2009; Bhagnagar and Mittal, 2010; Kauts and Chechi, 2011; Begum, 2014).

8. Social consciousness, curiosity, sensitivity, honesty (Sternberg et al. 1981), pro-social skills, emotionally supportive, leadership skills, self efficiousness (Ford and Miura, 1983), understanding of people's feelings, knowledge of human relations and caring (Kosmitzki and John, 1993) are the characteristics of which make up people's implicit concept of ideally social intelligent persons.
9. Socio-economic status, home environment, locale, gender, religion, caste, mothers' education and parental income, stream have an effect on social intelligence and social maturity of adolescents (Jain, 1998; Kaur and Kalaramna, 2004; Vasilova and Baumgartner, 2004; Babu, 2007; Kumar and Rao, 2009; Ramalingam and Mahi, 2009; Gakhar and Bains, 2010; Nikose, 2010; Gnanadevan, 2011). Social knowledge is an important aspect of social competence (Jones and Day, 1997). Academic and social intelligence represent separate although overlapping concepts (Brown and Autnony, 1990; Riggio et al. 1991).
10. Significant relationship exists between teacher effectiveness and social skills (Hamann et al. 1998). Personality dimensions are closely related to social competence as compare to cognitive ability (Scheider et al. 1996). Teacher effectiveness and social intelligence of teachers are significantly effect by gender, age educational qualification, marital status, category, teaching experience, discipline, administrative set-up, locale and board of education (Agrawal, 2003). Whereas Suresh and Bhaskar Rao (2009) concluded that student teachers possessed high level of social intelligence. Gender, qualification, methodology of teaching, background of the student teachers has no significant impact on social intelligence with no significance between them. Social intelligence is positively and significantly related with job satisfaction, mental health and with use of classroom strategies (Jelouder, 2011; Jeloudar and Lotfi-Goodarzi, 2012; Parithma and Kulsum, 2013).

11. Social intelligence promotes relationship with teachers and academic achievement in elementary schools. Teachers give more importance to self regulation and social intelligence for success in school (Valeski, 2000; Harkeness et al. 2007).
12. Attitude of creative learning and teaching is determined by gender, teaching level, training of teachers, teaching experiences (Singh, 1985; Das, 1986; Mathur, 1988; Singh and Dass, 1989; Saini, 1998; Pal, 2001; Roy, 2005).
13. Creativity of teacher is correlated with teaching experience, creative classroom behaviour, teacher student relationships, sex, self-esteem, job satisfaction, socio-economic status, age, teaching at different levels, values and socio emotional climate of school (Raina, 1970; Tafuri, 1995; Singh, 1996; Kaur, 1998; Saini, 1998; Reddy et al. 1999; Kaur, 2001; Noor, 2001; Jayanthi and Agarwal, 2005; Christine et al. 2008).
14. Qualities of creative teacher or beliefs which as associated with creative behaviour are imagination, intelligent, divergent thinking, sociability or interpersonal aspects (Choadhary, 1989; Raina, 1990; Fryer and Collings, 1991; Diakidoy and Kanori, 1999; Panda and Yadva, 2005; Seng et al. 2008). Creative teachers have adequate mastery over the subject and strong desire to acquire more learning continuously (Khan, 2008).
15. Intelligence and creativity are studied with teacher effectiveness and teaching competence. Creativity and intelligence are taken jointly are better predictor of teacher effectiveness (McElvain et al. 1963; Nair, 1974; Singh, 1987; Gupta, 1988; Singh, 1991; Vesanthi and Anandi, 1997; Panda, 2004). Teacher effectiveness is related to personality, attitude, intelligence, adjustment, experience and educational qualification of teacher (Singh, 1987; Gupta, 1988). Effective teacher shows high emotional maturity and teachers with high I.Q. are found effective than low and average I.Q. teachers (Kaur, 1989; Phaewsakul, 1989; Dass, 1995).
16. Intelligence and creativity are positively related with each other (Chadha and Sen, 1981; Sofaya, 1981; Gupta, 1988; McCabe, 1991; Goyal and Singh, 2010). I.Q. significantly predicts each component of creativity (Olatoye and Oyundoyin, 2007). There is positive relationship between intelligence and emotional intelligence but this relationship is not strong (Sitaram, 2005). There is no significant relationship between emotional

intelligence and general intelligence (Jadhav and Patil, 2010) while emotional stability and intelligence are positively related (Bansal and Kaur, 2011).

17. There is significant relationship between teacher effectiveness, creativity and interpersonal relationships (Rao, 1995; D'costa and Deshmukh, 2010). Emotional intelligence effect certain aspects of effective teaching like teachers sense of humour, and mastry in the subject (Latha and Ananthasayanam, 2005). The teaching of emotionally mature teachers is more effective than those of emotionally immature teachers (Bansibihari and Surwade, 2006). Effective teachers demonstrated effective social skills (Juchniewicz, 2010). Emotional intelligence and attitude towards teaching are found to be good predictor of teacher effectiveness (Puri, 2008). Understanding of emotions is related with verbal creativity (Kumar and Sharma, 2009). Emotional intelligence was positively associated with social competence (Mavroveli et al. 2007 and Srivastva & Mallick, 2010). Significant and positive correlation was found between emotional intelligence and work place performance (Mishra and Mohapatra, 2010). There is positive and significant relationship between emotional intelligence and teacher effectiveness (Ghosh, 2015; Hassan, 2015). Emotional intelligence and teaching experience matters in making a teacher to be effective (Kauts and Cheechi; 2014)

Summarizing the review of related studies on the variable of teacher effectiveness it can be concluded that teacher effectiveness is extensively studied with number of social psychological variables. As stated in forgoing pages many studies explored relationship of emotional intelligence, social intelligence, general intelligence and creativity with many factors, but a very few studies have been done to find out the relationship of general, emotional, social intelligence and creativity with effectiveness of the teachers at different level of education. This emphasizes the need of the study.

Significance, Objectives, Hypotheses and Delimitations

Development of any country depends upon its people. If the people are well developed physically and mentally, are literate and educated then they can contribute directly to the national development. For this purpose every nation frames a structure of education from nursery class to higher education. In India at present there are 384 universities, 17,062 colleges, 11,89,695 schools in which 46,23,89,880 children and students are getting education from 60,48,367 teachers (Statistical Abstract of India, 2007). In Punjab there are 10 universities, 989 colleges and 30376 elementary, high and secondary schools in which 5,853,508 students are getting education from 2,52,214 teachers (Statistical Abstract of Punjab, 2013). Society looks at these schools and colleges for harmonious development of its members. It has been always expected that a teacher must excel in various positive aspects academic and non-academic because his abilities are going to affect children's' behaviour positively. In academic qualities his intelligence level, knowledge of the subject matter and methodology of teaching and learning are important and in non-academic area disciplined behaviour, healthy relationship with others and qualities of head and heart are important. Above all most important is to be a good human being.

The usefulness and effectiveness of the education system largely depends upon the active, resourceful and competent teachers. Teacher's competence, capability and effectiveness make school good or bad, flourishing or deteriorating. So quality of teaching depends upon the efficiency of the teacher. One can say that teacher effectiveness is the capability of teacher to teach in such a manner that he gets success to bring the desirable change in the students' behaviour. It is assessed not only from the academic pursuits and classroom teaching of the teacher but from the sum total influences exerted by the teacher upon the students. Effective teaching results into positive outcomes. Unfortunately before a teacher is recruited no effort is made to judge how effective the teacher will be and how effectively he will convey his abilities. Likewise before giving him job his personality traits like honesty, emotionality, social abilities and resourcefulness are not studied or evaluated. It is always recognized that the personality of the teacher and healthy attitude towards his work contributes to effective and efficient teaching. The effectiveness of the teacher lies not only in the presentation of the subject matter in an effective way but it is to make the whole environment of the classroom conductive for the all round development of child. So there is need to know the incidence of general intelligence, social intelligence, emotional intelligence and creativity of effective teachers.

In Punjab we have two type of educational institutions among them one which are run by government and others by private authorities. Recent years have seen that parents are sending their children in private schools and society feels that better and quality education is being provided to the students in these schools. Private schools are going more attractive and showing better results than government schools. There can be many reasons for the better results but the quality of the teacher in the institution can be one of the reason for better results. Quality of teacher undoubtfully depends upon the academic potentialities and psychological abilities of teachers. The selection of the teachers in government schools is strictly done as per merit and the selection in private schools is done by the managements depending upon the criterion laid down by them from time to time. Hence there is need to see whether there is difference in psychological variables such as general, social, emotional intelligence, creativity of effective teachers of private and government schools.

In knowledge based society the role of the teacher is now much wider than teaching the contents of a subject and or subjects. In the present scenario teacher is the one who should know the content, methodology of teaching and guides students about sources of knowledge and get imbibed different skills through teaching. His role as recognized by educational resources and contemplated by educationists is not only to impart instruction but make an effort to develop the child fully academically, socially and emotionally besides other such attributes. A teacher can size up to this expectation if he is possessing of these abilities. Moreover, a teacher if possesses all these then only he can inculcate these in the students. It is hence very important to study in what proportion a teacher himself possesses these qualities.

Creativity is other factor which is surely related to intelligence of an individual. Teacher's behaviour such as willingness to welcome, accept and reward or praise students' independent thinking and new ideas, formulating positive classroom climate are known to be creative aspects of teachers' personality. If a teacher is creative then he can nurture creativity among students. Many studies have shown that creativity and intelligence (Jain, 1977; Chadha and Sen1981; Gupta 1984; Singh, 1991; Aggarwal and Aggarwal, 1999) are related to each other. Through this study investigator will try to find out what is the relationship of these variables with effectiveness of teachers.

The results of the present study will through light on the intellectual and creative dimensions of effective teachers in terms of psychological characteristics i.e. general, social, emotional intelligence, creativity of effective teachers' along with their type of school and gender differences.

The results of study in hand would be significantly useful for educational administrators in matters of organising various programmes like: refresher courses, orientation courses, seminar etc. to improve the teacher effectiveness.

Objectives

1. To study the *incidence* of teacher effectiveness, general intelligence, emotional intelligence, social intelligence, creativity of secondary school teachers.
2. To *identify* more and less effective secondary school teachers.
3. To study the *incidence* of general intelligence, emotional intelligence, social intelligence, creativity of more and less effective secondary school teachers.
4. To *compare* general intelligence, emotional intelligence, social intelligence, creativity of secondary school teachers across teacher effectiveness, gender and type of school.
5. To study *relationship* of general intelligence, emotional intelligence, social intelligence and creativity with teacher effectiveness among secondary school teachers.
6. To study *inter-correlation* of general intelligence, emotional intelligence, social intelligence and creativity among secondary school teachers.
7. To *determine* the predictors of teacher effectiveness among secondary school teachers in terms of general, emotional, social intelligence, and creativity.
8. To examine the *relative effects* of general intelligence, emotional intelligence, social intelligence and creativity on teacher effectiveness among secondary school teachers.
9. To *determine* which variable among given set of variables i.e. general intelligence, emotional intelligence, social intelligence and creativity will discriminate more and less effective secondary school teachers.

Hypotheses

1. There is significant mean difference in general intelligence of more and less effective secondary school teachers across gender and type of school.
2. There is significant mean difference in emotional intelligence of more and less effective secondary school teachers across gender and type of school.
3. There is significant mean difference in social intelligence of more and less effective secondary school teachers across gender and type of school.
4. There is significant mean difference in creativity of more and

less effective secondary school teachers across gender and type of school.

5. There is significant relationship between general intelligence, emotional intelligence, social intelligence and creativity with teacher effectiveness of secondary school teachers.
6. There is significant inter-correlation between general intelligence, emotional intelligence, social intelligence and creativity among secondary school teachers.
7. General intelligence, emotional intelligence, social intelligence and creativity will be significant predictors of teacher effectiveness of secondary school teachers.
8. General intelligence, emotional intelligence, social intelligence and creativity will directly or indirectly effect teacher effectiveness of secondary school teachers.
9. General intelligence, emotional intelligence, social intelligence and creativity will significantly discriminate more and less effective secondary school teachers.

Delimitations

1. The study was confined to only seven districts of Punjab namely Ludhiana, Ferozpur, Sangrur, Patiala, Moga, Mansa and Muktsar and more and less effective teacher has been selected from these districts.
2. This study was delimited to those teachers working in schools which are recognized by Punjab School Education Board.
3. In this study residential background of school teachers has not been undertaken.
4. The assumptions of normalcy was not tested in the light of Norton's and Box's findings that F is rather insensitive to variations in the shape of population distributions may be leptokurtic, rectangular, markedly skewed, and even J-shaped (Guilford and Fruchter, 1981).

2
Research Methodology

Research can be described as an orderly investigation of a subject matter for the purpose making meaningful and constructive contribution to the existing literature on the subject. There are number of ways or methods which are used to conduct research. For the present study which aims to explore how general intelligence, emotional intelligence, social intelligence and creativity are related to teacher effectiveness among secondary school teachers the descriptive method of research has been employed. It requires sample and certain research tools for conduct of the study. The description of tools and sampling is given below.

Research Tools

For any type of research specific tools that can facilitate research and investigation are required. These help in exploring new fields and relationships, which act as "means" for data collection. The success of any research partly depends upon the tools which are used for data collection. The tools selected and used are—.

- Teacher Effectiveness Scale by Kumar and Mutha (1999)
- The Standard Progressive Matrices (SPM) (1958)
- Emotional Intelligence Scale by Anukool Hyde and Sanjyot Pethe and Upindhar Dhar (2002)
- Social Intelligence Scale (2004) by N.K. Chadha and Usha Ganesan
- Divergent Production Abilities by K.N. Sharma (2006)

Teacher Effectiveness Scale by Kumar and Mutha (1999)

In order to elicit information about the effectiveness of teachers, the Teacher Effectiveness Scale by Kumar & Mutha (1999) was employed. The TES (Teacher Effectiveness Scale) is a self-administering scale. The subjects were requested to read instructions carefully and ask the tester if there was any difficulty in the understanding of the instructions. It was emphasized that no item should be omitted and there was nothing 'right' or 'wrong' about these questions. There was no time limit for the scale. The Scale (TES) consists of 69 highly discriminating items. The area wise distribution of items of the scale is given in the table 2.1 (*see*, page 70).

Reliability: The split-half reliability of the scale, is 0.67 (N = 100) with an index of reliability of 0.82. The author also claims that test-retest reliability of the scale is 0.75 (N = 60) with an index of reliability of 0.85 with two months interval of time.

Validity: The scale has been validated against principal's rating. The correlation between principal's rating and self-rating is 0.77 (N = 50) with an index of reliability of 0.87.

The Standard Progressive Matrices (SPM) (1958)

For the purpose of studying general intelligence of the subjects Raven's Standard Progressive Matrices SPM (1958) was used. It was constructed on the priory assumption that, if Spearman's (1927) principles of neo-genesis were correct, it should provide a test suitable for comprising people with respect to their immediate capacities for observation and clear thinking.

The Standard Progressive Matrices (Sets A, B, C, D and E) or SPM, is a test of a person's capacity at the time of the test to apprehended meaningless figures presented for his observation, see the relation between them, conceive the nature of the figure completing each system of relations presented, and by so doing, develop a systematic method of reasoning. The scale consists of 60 problems divided into five sets of 12. In each set the first problem is nearly as possible self-evident. The problems which follow become progressively more difficult. The order of the items provides the standard training in the method of working. The five sets provide five opportunities for grasping the method and five progressive assessments of a person's capacity for intellectual activity. To ensure sustained interest and freedom from fatigue, the figures in each problem are boldly presented accurately drawn and, as far as possible, pleasing to look at. SPM was designed to cover the widest possible range of mental ability and to be equally useful with persons of all ages, whatever their education, nationality or physical conditions.

The scale is intended to cover the whole range of intellectual development from the time a child is able to grasp the idea of finding a missing piece to complete a pattern and to be sufficiently long to assess a person's maximum capacity to form comparisons and reason by analogy without being unduly exhausting. The scores obtained by adults tend to cluster in the upper half of the scale, but there are enough difficult problems to differentiate satisfactorily between them.

Everyone, whatever his age, is given exactly the same series of problems in the same order and is asked to work at his own speed, without interception from the beginning to the end of the scale. As the order of the problems provides the standard training in the method or working, the scale can be given either as an individual, a self-administered or as a group test. A person's total score provides an index of his intellectual capacity with relatively little influence from the cultural environment to which the individual grew up or his education.

Reliability: Over forty studies dealing with reliability of the SPM have been reported in the existing literature. Both internal consistency and test-retest reliability have been computed and found highly satisfactory. The test-retest reliability and inter-correlation of the progressive matrices and Mill Hill Vocabulary (MHV) scales at different ages have been given in table 2.2 (*see* page 71).

Validity: The criterion oriented validity, context validity and factorial construct validity have been estimated for Raven's Progressive Matrices and reported highly satisfactory.

Emotional Intelligence Scale by Anukool Hyde and Sanjyot Pethe and Upindhar Dhar (2002)

For the purpose of measuring emotional intelligence of teachers emotional intelligence scale by Anukool Hyde, Sanjyot Pethe and Upinder Dhar (2002) has been used. It is eminently suitable for group as well as individual testing. It is a self-administering scale and contains 34 items. Factor wise number of items of scale is shown in the table 2.3 (*see*, page 71).

Before administering the scale, the subjects were advised orally that responses would be checked as quickly as possible and sincere cooperation was sought for the same. It was further clarified that the responses would be kept confidential. It was also emphasized that there was no right or wrong answer to the statements. The statements were designed to understand the differences in individual reactions to various situations. The scale was meant to assess the difference between individuals and not meant to rank them as good or bad. It was duly emphasized that all statements have to be responded to and no statement should be left unanswered. It was not considered desirable to reveal to the subjects the exact purpose for which the scale was being used. Though the scale is self-administering, it was found useful to read out the instructions printed on the response sheet to the subjects. Moreover, it was felt that no time limit should be given for completing the scale. However, it was estimated that most respondents would complete it in about 10 minutes.

Reliability: The reliability of the scale was determined by calculating reliability coefficient on a sample of 200 subjects. The split-half reliability coefficient was found to be 0.88.

Validity: Besides face validity, as all items were related to the variable under focus, the scale has high content validity. It is evident from the assessment of judges/experts that items of the scale are directly related to the concept of emotional intelligence. In order to find out the validity from the coefficient of reliability (Garrett, 1981), the reliability index was calculated, which indicated high validity on account of being 0.93.

Social Intelligence Scale by N.K. Chadha and Usha Ganesan (2004)

Social intelligence of teachers was measured by social intelligence scale of N.K. Chadha and Usha Ganesan (2004). The initial selection of the dimensions that measure social intelligence was determined on the basis of the judgement of 25 experts in the field of behavioural sciences. In order to construct the scale the dimensions of social intelligence were selected in a scientific manner. Accordingly, sixteen relevant and meaningful dimensions of social intelligence were selected and defined. An initial pool of 140 items was constructed for the whole scale. The six dimensions (Patience, Recognition of Social Environment, Confidence, Sensitivity, Sense of Humour and Co-operativeness) were constructed using the multiple choice technique. In the tactfulness dimension, responses were elicited in terms of 'Yes' or 'No'. In the last dimension, that of 'Memory' a set of 30 pictures was presented for recognition. The entire set of 140 items was given to 5 experts and the necessary changes introduced. 91 items which met with 100 per cent approval amongst the judges were retained. These items were then tested for social desirability with the help of five experts. The items were rated on a 9 point rating scale ranging from "extremely desirable", through "Neutral" to "extremely undesirable". All the items were retained and subjected to item analysis. Distribution of final 66 items is shown in the table 2.4 (*see*, page 71).

Social intelligence scale is a self-administering scale. The subjects were given a choice of three alternatives for each item and were asked to choose in the case of 6 dimensions such as patience, confidence, cooperation, sensitivity, sense of humour and recognition of social environment. In case of the tactfulness dimension the responses were in the form of 'Yes' or 'No'. In the last dimension, that of 'Memory' a set of 12 pictures was presented for recognition

Reliability: In the present scale test-retest and split half techniques were employed to find the reliability co-efficient. For finding the split-half reliability a sample of 150 (75 males and 75 females) was taken. In order to determine the test-retest reliability the previous sample used for split half was administered the scale after a period of 15 days. The Test-Retest reliability came out to be 0.857 which is significant at 0.01 level (2-Tailed). The coefficients obtained are shown in the table 2.5 (*see*, page 72).

Validity: In order to test the empirical validity a sample of 50 individuals was taken. The external criterion used was the 'Social Intelligence Test' by F.A. Moss, T. Hunt, K.M. Omwaka and L.G. Woodward (1949), George Washington University series. The present scale and the Social Intelligence Test by Moss and Hunt were administered and scored accordingly. The data obtained were subjected to 'Pearson Product Moment Correlation' for testing the validity. The total score of the present scale is highly and significantly correlated with the Social Intelligence Test of Moss and Hunt. ($r = 0.70 < 0.01$). Henceforth, the present scale has a validity coefficient of 0.70.

For the purpose of cross validation a sample of 50 individuals was taken. The data obtained on the first sample and second sample was correlated to test the validity of the scale (Overall cross validation $r = 0.80$). The co-efficients of cross validation between two groups of social intelligence scale turned out be 0.82 (Patience), 0.91 (Cooperativeness), 0.86 (Confidence), 0.75 (Sensitivity), 0.91 (Recognition of Social Environment), 0.75 (Tactfulness), 0.95 (Sense of Humour), 0.94 (Memory) respectively.

Divergent Production Abilities by K.N. Sharma (2006)

For measuring creativity of secondary school teachers the battery of Divergent Production Abilities by K.N. Sharma (2006) was used. It contains six tests in Hindi for measurement of the eight abilities given in the table 2.6 (*see*, page 72).

From the table it is clear that broadly speaking there are only four abilities: fluency, flexibility, originality, and elaboration. However, each sub-ability is measured separately. In the present battery two tests can measure two abilities each through a psychometric variation. For example, second test of uses of things can measure ideational fluency as well as spontaneous flexibility, and the Titles test can measure adaptive flexibility as well as originality. Therefore, only six tests are required to measure eight abilities. The battery can be used on children, adolescents and adults.

1. *Word Production Test (WPT):* It contains five items indicating the subjects to write more and more words starting or ending or both with a given letter, or using a particular letter of Hindi and English language. Items 1 and 4 require the subject to write words starting with a given letter and item 3 requires the subject to write words ending with a given letter. Item 2 requires use of a given letter, at the start and end of each word, and item 5 requires use of a letter at any place of the word.

2. *Uses of Things Test* (*UTT*): The test contains five items in Hindi and English in the form of names of common things. The subjects were required to write more and more, in the form of words, phrases and short sentences diverse uses of those things. The two instructional phrases "more and more" and "diverse" are necessary to extract ideational fluency and spontaneous flexibility respectively.

3. *Similarities Test* (*ST*): The test contains six words in Hindi and English denoting names of things and qualities to which the subjects are required to write synonyms or related words as many as he/she can. As we were interested more on positive relations rather than negative, only synonyms have been used.

4. *Sentence Construction Test* (*SCT*): The test contains five items in Hindi and English. In first four items four Hindi letters were placed at little distance and five in the fifth, which indicate the first letters of words to make sense sentences. Such items were used in other countries also. The subjects were asked to write sentences using those letters as many as he/she can.

5. *Titles Test* (*TT*): The test contains three short stories of three or four lines in Hindi and English. The subjects were required to give different titles, as many as he/she can, to each story. Two factors can be scored from the title responses: adaptive flexibility and originality.

6. *Elaboration Test* (*ET*): The test contains three items in Hindi and English: the first two give some common problems, and the third gives an incomplete story. The subjects were asked to suggest more and more solutions, to the two problems and complete the story and make it as long as he/she can. The total number of the three shall be the 'elaboration score'.

Reliability: The test-reliabilities of the battery are given in the table 2.7 (*see*, page 73).

Validity: To ensure content validity, a consistent and deliberate effort has been made to use the test stimuli, test tasks, instructions and scoring procedures based on the Test Theory and researches available on creativity or divergent production abilities, or creative thinning abilities. The following table 2.8 (*see*, page 73) shows the correlations of the Battery with Baqer Mehdi's Test of Creative Thinking.

Universe and Sample

The universe of the study is 62870 (Now 98578) high and senior secondary school teachers teaching in 4128 (Now 5657) schools in 17 (Now 22) districts in the state of Punjab (Statistical Abstract of Punjab, 2008, 2011). The number of schools varies in each district. The variation ranges from a minimum of 45 schools in Mansa to 206 schools to Ludhiana. In the present research stratified random sample technique was followed.

The State of Punjab has been divided into three parts depending upon the literacy rate of the State. In first group high literacy districts, in second group average literacy districts and in third group lower literacy districts have been placed. So out of 17 districts of Punjab three strata were made according on the basis of the overall literacy rate of Punjab 69.95 per cent (Now 76.70%). Districts with literacy rate above 68 per cent were considered as educationally advanced districts, districts with literacy rate of 60 per cent-67 per cent were considered as educationally average and districts with literacy rate below 59 per cent were considered as educationally backward districts. Among these three strata 2-3 districts were selected randomly. Accordingly Ludhiana and Patiala from educationally advanced districts, Moga, Ferozpur and Sangrur from educationally average districts, Muktsar and Mansa from educationally backward districts were selected. Further selection of schools from each of the seven districts was made on the random basis giving due weightage to government and private schools situated both in urban and rural areas (Fig. 2.1).

From total schools (4128), a total number of 172 schools were selected which constitute nearly 4.16 per cent of the total schools. From these schools all the teachers who teach 9th and 10th classes were selected for the conduct of study.

172 schools from 7 districts of Punjab were included in the sample. District wise distribution of government and private schools and teachers is shown in the table 2.9 (*see*, page 73).

Data Collection

The purpose of the present study, given in this chapter was to study the general, social, emotional intelligence and creativity of effective secondary school teachers. Accordingly representative sample of 850 senior secondary school teachers was selected from seven districts of Punjab.

All the five tools selected in the study were administered to the subjects. The data for the present research were personally collected by

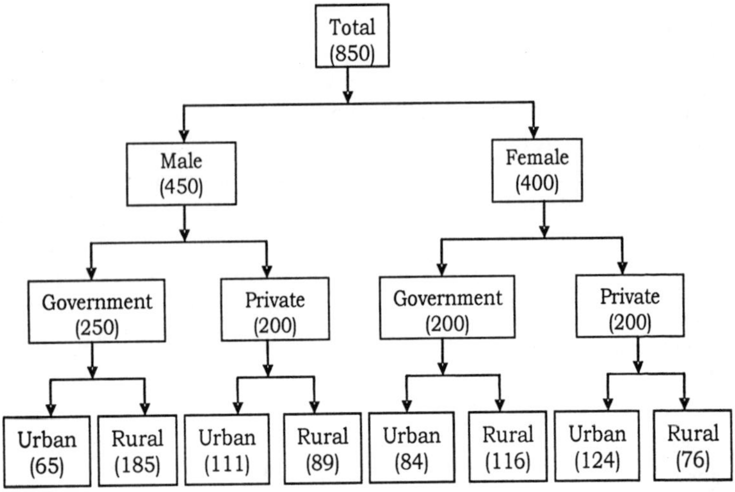

Fig. 2.1: Distribution of Sample

the investigator from the teachers of secondary schools selected for the collection of data.

Nearly 1500 test booklets were distributed to the secondary school teachers for data collections. Only 850 test booklets were received back with response rate of 56.6 per cent. Not surprisingly there was strong tendency of secondary school teachers to use the positive end of the teacher effectiveness scale. The teachers tended to rate themselves between agree to strongly agree.

Teacher effectiveness of the secondary school teachers was studied by using the teacher effectiveness scale by Kumar and Mutha. According to the objectives of the study the identification of the more effective and less effective teachers was made in following way.

The manual of the teacher effectiveness scale shows that score of teacher effectiveness ranges from 69 to 345 or from less effective to more effective scores. So, percentile norms of scale show that the teachers having 309.75 to 328.90 are effective and very effective which is between 70th to 90th percentiles and teachers having score between 253-278.07 are less effective and very less effective which is between 10th to 30th percentiles. In this study mostly secondary school teachers used positive end of the scale. Therefore, the class intervals and distribution of scores of 850 teachers was plotted and Q_1 (P_{25}) and Q_3 (P_{75}) were calculated. On the basis of P_{25} and P_{75} cut points the number of secondary school teachers were identified as being more effective (200) or less effective (200) teachers because scores lying above or below cut points have different numbers. The teachers scoring 331 and above (i.e. >331) were treated as more effective and these scoring 290 and below (i.e. <290) were treated as less effective secondary school teachers. By employing this method 200 more effective and 200 less effective teachers were selected to get required information relating to variables such as general intelligence, emotional intelligence, social intelligence and creativity of these teachers.

The environment, testing situations and procedure for all the subjects were kept as uniform as possible in order to obtain true, correct and required information. In this way, data were collected from all the subjects selected from secondary schools of Ludhiana, Patiala, Moga, Ferozepur, Sangrur, Muktsar and Mansa districts of Punjab.

The filled-in test booklets/answer sheets collected from each teacher were grouped in their respective category for scoring. The scoring of the answer sheets was done strictly according to the directions and instructions given in the respective test manuals.

Scoring and Tabulation

The scoring of research tools is done as under

1. Teacher Effectiveness Scale: All the 69 items of the scale are positively worded. Items are given a score of 5, 4, 3, 2 and 1 for strongly agree, agree, undecided, Disagree and strongly disagree respectively. The sum of these values gives the teacher effectiveness score for the subject. The total score values from 69 to 345 show least teacher effectiveness to highest teacher effectiveness.

2. The Standard Progressive Matrices: The scoring of the answer sheets of SPM was done with the help of scoring key provided in the manual. A person's score on the scale is the total number of problems he solves correctly when he/she is allowed to work quietly through the series from the beginning to the end. Accordingly, a subject's total score was found out. In case of more than two responses, only the number on the extreme right was considered, irrespective of whether the other numbers were right or wrong.

3. Emotional Intelligence Scale: The scoring of emotional intelligence scale is done manually. Hence no scoring key is provided. Each item or statement can be scored 5 for strongly agree, 4 for agree, 3 for neutral, 2 for disagree and 1 for strongly disagree. The total score values range from 34-170

4. Social Intelligence Scale: Scoring of the SIS was done manually. Proper scoring key was provided for all dimensions. In the case of first four dimensions (Patience, Cooperativeness, Confidence, and Sensitivity) scores of 1, 2 and 3 were given to the three response alternatives. For e.g. in the confidence dimension a score of 3 would indicate a high degree of confidence, a score of 1 a lack of confidence and a score of 2 would reveal moderate confidence. In the other two dimensions (Sense of Humour and Recognition of Social Environment) one of three alternatives given is the appropriate response. This response when given was allotted of scores of 1. In case of the tactfulness dimension the responses were in the form of 'Yes' or 'No' and appropriate response was awarded a score of '1'. The last dimension that of 'Memory was scored '1' or '0' depending on whether or not the subject's response was 'right' or 'wrong'. The total score ranges from 36-138.

Divergent Production Abilities: The scoring of six sub sets is given below

(i) *Word Production Test* (*WPT*)*:* It contains five items indicating the subjects to write more and more words starting or ending or both with a given letter, or using a particular letter of Hindi and English language. The wrong words were deleted, and the total response words counted, which indicates the 'word fluency score'.

(ii) *Uses of Things Test* (*UTT*)*:* The test contains five items in Hindi and English in the form of names of common things.
The total number of appropriate answers, to all the five items gives the "ideational fluency score". The number of classes or trains of thought to all the five items can give us the 'spontaneous flexibility score' as (1) to make chair, (2) to make table, (3) to make cot, (4) to burn, (5) to beat, the first 3 responses shall be scored as 1 since they all indicate one train of thought, i.e. to make furniture, whereas the fourth and fifth responses shall also get 1 score each since they are of different ideas. Thus to the above examples of responses, the ideational fluency score shall be 5, while the spontaneous flexibility score shall be only 3.

(iii) *Similarities Test* (*ST*)*:* The test contains six words in Hindi and English denoting names of things and qualities to which the subjects are required to write synonyms or related words as many as he/she can. The total number of appropriate response words to all the items shall indicate 'associational fluency score'.

(iv) *Sentence Construction Test* (*SCT*)**:** The test contains five items in Hindi and English. In first four items four Hindi letters were placed at little distance and five in the fifth, which indicate the first letters of words to make sense sentences. The total number of appropriate sentences shall indicate the 'expressional fluency score'.

(v) *Titles Test* (*TT*): The test contains three short stories of three or four lines in Hindi and English. Two factors can be scored from the title responses: adaptive flexibility and originality, irrelevant title, if any, may be ignored. Since all the titles may be different, being of different trains of thoughts their total number will indicate 'adaptive flexibility score'. If some titles appear to be very similar, all of them must be scored only once. For scoring originality, the unusualness of responses is to be found out. The response unusualness and their weights are given in the table 2.10 (*see*, page 73).

Less the number of occurrence of a response more the weight it gets. Responses that occur more than 95 per cent times are called common or usual and do not get any score. If in a group of 100 subjects one response was given by a subject only once, it will get a weight of 5 scores; and if a title response was given by five subjects out of a group of 100 subjects, it will get only 1 score. This inverted weightage of originality score can be calculated by the test user separately for separate type of groups. Since originality can vary from group to group according to the experiences of the subjects or of the groups, this suggestion is made.

(vi) *Elaboration Test* (*ET*): The test contains three items in Hindi and English: the first two give some common problems, and the third gives an incomplete story. The total number of relevant solutions suggested for the first two items were counted. The number of ideas given in the completed part, whether they be in the form of phrase or sentence, should also be added to the scores of the first two items. The total number of the three shall be the 'elaboration score'.

Creativity is the sum total of fluency, flexibility, originality and elaboration. The raw score of all the tests cannot be added directly to get creativity scores because of greater variations in the score incomparability: their domains and approaches are different. The raw scores of different dimensions were converted into standard scores (T-scores) by using following formula.

$$T = X - M/SD \times 10 + 50$$

Therefore, the raw scores received for all the dimensions were converted into standard scores. The respective standard scores of the raw scores of all the dimensions can be added to get creativity score, or the mean values of those standard scores of all the eight dimensions were added to get the creativity score

Statistical Treatment of Data

According to the objectives of the investigation, the data so collected, were recorded in tabular form for statistical analysis. This interpretation has been done in different sections.

Mean, median, mode, standard deviation, skewedness, kurtosis of all the variables, teacher effectiveness, general intelligence, social intelligence, emotional intelligence and creativity were calculated. Three-way ANOVA along with t-test was used to find the statistical significance of the difference between means for all the variables separately. Correlation analysis following triangulation approach with the help of zero order correlation, step wise multiple regression analysis along with path analysis and discriminant analysis were corroborated to determine teacher effectiveness among secondary school teacher from general intelligence, emotional intelligence, social intelligence and creativity. Data analysis was done by using SPSS programme.

TABLES

Table 2.1: Area Wise Distribution of Items in Teacher Effectiveness Scale

Area	*Sub-Areas*	*Items*	*Total*
1. Academic	1. Information source	2, 3, 24, 57	4
	2. Motivator	5, 6, 44, 68	4
	3. Teaching Skills	41, 42, 43, 45, 47, 50, 51	7
2. Professional	4. Co-curricular Activities	29, 30, 31	3
	5. Professional Knowledge	1, 32, 33, 34, 40, 55	6
	6. Class room management	16, 52, 54, 58	4
3. Social	7. Relationship with pupils, fellow teachers Principals and Parents	7, 9, 11, 12, 15, 21, 22, 23, 25, 26, 28	11
4. Emotional	8. Advisor and Guide	4, 8, 19, 27, 46, 48, 49, 56	8
5. Moral	9. Disciplinarian	10, 13, 17, 20, 60, 61, 62, 64, 65, 69	10
6. Personality	10. Personality Characteristics	14, 18, 35, 36, 37, 38, 39, 53, 59, 63, 66, 67	12
	Total		**69**

Table 2.2: Test-Retest Reliability and Inter-Correlation of the Progressive Matrices and Mill Hills Scales at Different Ages

Age Range (Years)	*RPM*		*MHV*		*'r' RPM and MHV Scores*
	Mean Score	*Test-Retest Reliability*	*Mean Score*	*Test-Retest Reliability*	
13+1	41	0.88	34	0.87	0.57
Under 30	48	0.93	41	0.97	0.60
30-39	37	0.88	33	0.91	0.51
40-49	35	0.87	31	0.98	0.45
50 and Above	29	0.83	31	0.90	0.44

Table 2.3: Factors Wise Distribution of Emotional Intelligence Scale

Dimensions	*Item Number*	*Total*
A. Self-Awareness	6, 12, 18, 19	4
B. Empathy	9, 10, 15, 20, 25	5
C. Self-Motivation	2, 4, 7, 8, 31, 34	6
D. Emotional Stability	14, 19, 26, 28	4
E. Managing Relations	1, 5, 11, 17	4
F. Integrity	16, 27, 32	3
G. Self-Development	30, 33	2
H. Value Orientation	21, 22	2
I. Commitment	23, 24	2
J. Altruistic Behaviour	3, 13	2
Total		**34**

Table 2.4: Distribution of Dimensions in Social Intelligence Scale

Dimension	*Item Number*	*Total*
A. Patience	4, 8, 15, 16, 20, 27, 33, 36	8
B. Co-operativeness	1, 5, 9, 14, 17, 21, 25, 26, 28, 31, 32	11
C. Confidence	3, 7, 11, 12, 19, 23, 30, 33	8
D. Sensitivity	2, 6, 10, 13, 18, 22, 24, 29, 34	9
E. Recognizing of Social Environment	37, 38, 39	3
F. Tactfulness	40, 41, 42, 43, 44, 45, 46	7
G. Sense of Humour	47, 48, 49, 50, 51, 52, 53, 54	8
H. Memory	55, 56, 57, 58, 59, 60, 61, 62, 63, 64, 65, 66	12
Total		**66**

Table 2.5: Split-Half Reliability and Test-Retest Reliability Coefficients of Social Intelligence Scale

	Areas	*Split-Half Reliability Coefficients*	*Test-Retest Reliability Coefficients*
A.	Patience	0.93	0.94
B.	Cooperativeness	0.91	0.91
C.	Confidence	0.89	0.90
D.	Sensitivity	0.90	0.93
E.	Recognition of Social Environment	0.95	0.95
F.	Tactfulness	0.91	0.84
G.	Sense of Humour	0.90	0.92
H.	Memory	0.96	0.97

Table 2.6: Divergent Production Abilities and their Test Names

S. No.	*Divergent Production Ability*	*Name of the Test*
1.	Word Fluency	Word Production
2.	Ideational Fluency	Uses of Things
3.	Associational Fluency	Similarities
4.	Expressional Fluency	Sentence Construction
5.	Spontaneous Flexibility	Uses Test
6.	Adaptive Flexibility	Titles
7.	Originality	Titles
8.	Elaboration	Solutions/Completion

Table 2.7: Test-retest Reliabilities of Divergent Production Abilities

Sr. No.	*Name of Test*	*Reliability*
1.	Word Production	.67
2.	Uses of Things	.80
3.	Similarities	.68
4.	Sentences Constructions	.84
5.	Titles	.85
6.	Elaboration	.82

Table 2.8: Product Moment Correlations between Divergent Production, Abilities and Baqer Mhedi's Test of Creative Thinking (verbal) (N = 40)

Divergent Production Abilities	*Baqer Mehdi's Test Dimensions*					
	Fluency	*Flexibility*	*Originality*	*Elaboration*		*Creativity*
				N.V.	*V.*	
Word Fluency	0.48	0.32	0.36	0.31	0.40	0.50
Ideational Fluency	0.58	0.40	0.40	0.42	0.52	0.43
Associational Fluency	0.66	0.51	0.38	0.36	0.48	0.33
Expressional Fluency	0.63	0.36	0.51	0.38	0.47	0.37
Spontaneous Flexibility	0.47	0.58	0.40	0.43	0.50	0.39
Adaptive Flexibility	0.43	0.60	0.42	0.42	0.45	0.48
Originality	0.31	0.35	0.58	0.33	0.32	0.43
Elaborations	0.46	0.35	0.32	0.41	0.50	0.44
Creativity	0.44	0.48	0.39	0.40	0.44	0.48

Table 2.9: District wise Number of Schools and Teachers Covered in Sample

Districts	*Schools*			*Teachers*				*Total*
				Male		*Female*		
	Govt.	*Private*	*Total*	*Govt.*	*Private*	*Govt.*	*Private*	
Ludhiana	38	16	54	101	31	106	47	285
Ferozpur	13	13	26	30	17	20	35	102
Sangrur	10	9	19	26	32	24	24	106
Patiala	7	10	17	17	20	6	20	63
Moga	7	10	17	8	23	17	46	94
Muktsar	7	8	15	30	26	10	21	87
Mansa	12	12	24	38	51	17	7	113
Total	**94**	**78**	**172**	**250**	**200**	**200**	**200**	**850**

Table 2.10: Weightages for Unusuality of Responses of Divergent Production Abilities

Weight	*Percentage of Unusualness*
1.	95-95.99 percent occurrence
2.	96-96.99 percent occurrence
3.	97-97.99 percent occurrence
4.	98-98.99 percent occurrence
5.	99-99.99 percent occurrence

3

Analysis and Interpretation of Data

The present study aimed at explored psychological dimensionality of effective teachers. For this purpose data collected, quantified and processed and has been prevented in this chapter in the form of tables pertaining to different variables. The analysis and interpretation of data has been done by following descriptive and multivariate analysis approaches. Hence this chapter has been divided into two sections. Detailed description of teacher effectiveness and its psychological dimensionality has been explained below.

SECTION (A)

Teacher Effectiveness and its Psychological Dimensionality: Descriptive Analysis

With the aim of realizing the first three objectives of the study: "*To study the incidence of teacher effectiveness, general intelligence, emotional intelligence, social intelligence, creativity of secondary school teachers*," "*To identify more and less effective secondary school teachers*". "*To study the incidence of general intelligence, emotional intelligence, and social intelligence, creativity of more and less effective secondary school teachers*" data were collected using techniques and methods explained in chapter II of the present study. The first section of this chapter deals with above three objectives.

Descriptive Analysis of Teacher Effectiveness, General Intelligence, Emotional Intelligence, Social Intelligence and Creativity of Secondary School Teachers (N = 850)

This section deals with descriptive analysis of different variables under study namely teacher effectiveness, general intelligence, emotional intelligence, social intelligence and creativity. In the first part of this section teacher effectiveness, general intelligence, emotional intelligence, social intelligence and creativity of the total sample of secondary school teachers (N = 850) has been studied through descriptive statistics. Descriptive measures such as mean, median, mode, SD, skewness, kurtosis have been used to describe characteristics of the sample. The detailed description of descriptive analysis of different variables is given in table 3.1 (*see*, page 122).

Teacher Effectiveness

Teacher effectiveness of secondary school teachers was studied by administering the teacher effectiveness scale by Kumar and Mutha (1999). The scoring of the response sheets has been done as per manual. The scores of all the 69 items in teacher effectiveness scale obtained from each of the 850 teachers were summated. The scores range from 69-349. In order to understand the nature and incidence of teacher effectiveness among secondary school teachers' descriptive statistics was worked out (*see* table 3.1, p. 122).

Table 3.1 shows that the mean teacher effectiveness scores of total group of secondary school teachers is 308.78 with SD 27.07, median and mode turned out to be 312.86 and 320.98. The range of scores turned out to be 220-345 with skewness -0.450 and kurtosis 0.280 respectively. The value of median is greater than mean, so distribution is negatively skewed. The value of kurtosis 0.280 is greater than 0.263 which is platykurtic because it is flatter than normal. On the basis of these statistics, it may be stated that secondary school teachers fall in effective category and lie at 70th percentile of norms given in teacher effectiveness scale by Kumar and Mutha.

From these results, it can be concluded that secondary school teachers are generally positive about their effectiveness. They possess a strong sense of classroom competence and appropriate personal and professional qualities. As regards their self-perception, they believe that they know their subject well, manage their class effectively, arrange co-curricular activities, work with their colleagues in a co-operative spirit and are always supportive towards students as advisors, guides and counselors. It needs to be stated, that these findings do not corroborate the findings of Arokiadoss (2005), Kagathala (2002) and Kaur, S. (2008) which show that mostly teachers possess average or moderate level of teacher effectiveness.

General Intelligence

General intelligence of secondary school teachers was studied by administering the standard progressive matrices (1958) as detailed in chapter II. The scoring of the response sheets has been done as per manual. The scores of all the 60 items in standard progressive matrices obtained from each of the 850 teachers were summated which range from 0-60. In order to understand the incidence of general intelligence among secondary school teachers descriptive statistics was given in table 3.1. Table 3.1 also shows that the mean general intelligence value of the total group of secondary school teachers is 44.95 with S.D. 7.30. The median and mode values are 45.50 and 46.60 respectively. The scores range from 27 to 60 and value of skewness is -0.226. The value of median is slightly higher than mean value. So frequency distribution is negatively skewed. The value of kurtosis is 0.250 which is less than 0.263, so distribution curve is leptokurtic in shape. It is more peaked than normal.

Emotional Intelligence

Emotional intelligence of secondary school teachers was studied by administering emotional intelligence scale by Hyde, Pethe and Dhar (2002). The scoring of the answer booklets has been done as per manual. The scores of all the 34 items in emotional intelligence scale obtained from each of the 850 teachers were summated. The scores range from 34-170. In order to understand the nature and incidence of emotional intelligence among secondary school teachers descriptive statistics has been given in the table 3.1. Table 3.1 further shows that mean value scores of emotional intelligence in the entire group of secondary school teachers is 140.70 with SD 16.12. The median and mode values are 142.82 and 148.06 respectively. The range of scores is 80-170. The value of skewness score is -0.390. The value of median is greater than the mean, so frequency distribution is skewed to negative side. The value of kurtosis is 0.250 which is less than 0.263. So it is leptokurtic in shape and more peaked than normal. These results are compared with norms given in Emotional Intelligence Scale by Hyde, Pethe and Dhar (2002). Hyde, Pethe and Dhar interpreted that subjects scoring 85 and above have higher level of emotional intelligence. Hence, it can be deduced that secondary school teachers possess high levels of emotional intelligence. From the above results, it may be concluded that secondary school teachers are highly intelligent in emotional behaviour. The results are significant as it is a basic premise that in one of its foremost pre-requisites teaching profession requires high levels of E.Q. (Singh 2003). It has been commonly opined and reiterated that emotionally intelligent teachers help students with improved motivation, increased performances, effective use of time and resource and improved leadership qualities. Emotionally intelligent teachers can also provide better guidance and motivation for team work (Amirtha and Kadhirawan, 2006).

Social Intelligence

Social intelligence of secondary school teachers was measured by administering social intelligence scale by Chatha and Ganesan (2004). The scoring of answer booklets was carried out through the means of scoring key given in the manual. The scores of all the 66 items in social intelligence scale obtained from each of the 850 secondary school teachers were arranged systematically. The scores range from 36-138. Table 3.1 shows that mean social intelligence scores for the entire group of secondary school teachers is 108.65 with SD 8.43. The median and mode values are 110.30 and 113.60 respectively. The range of scores is 73 to 138. The value of skewness is -0.587 and value of median is greater than mean so this distribution is negatively skewed. The value of Krutosis is 0.270 which is greater than 0.263. So the frequency distribution is platykurtic in shape.

On the basis of these statistics it may be stated that the total group of secondary school teachers falls in the category of 75th percentile of Social Intelligence Scale. This shows that secondary school teachers are having appreciably high levels of social intelligence. These secondary school teachers seem to possess the qualities of co-operation, sense of humour, recognition of social environment, memory, tactfulness, confidence and sensitivity. It is surely a positive sign because social intelligence carries immense importance for self-regulation and success of school and the overall education system (Harkeness *et al.* 2007). Other studies like those of Suresh and Rao (2009) and Kasture and Bhalerao (2014) have also conducted studies of the levels of social intelligence among pupil and teachers. They have also arrived at the conclusion that majority of teachers possess high levels of social intelligence.

Creativity

Creativity of secondary school teachers was studied by administering Divergent Production Abilities (DPA) by Sharma (2006). This test contains 8 subsets: word association test, uses of things test, similarities test, sentence construction test, uses test, title test and story completion test. These subsets measure fluency (word fluency, ideational fluency, associational fluency, and expressional fluency), flexibility (spontaneous flexibility, adaptive flexibility), originality and elaboration. The raw scores obtained from these answer booklets were converted into standard scores by common mean 50 and SD 10. Then standard scores are added to get total creativity score. Table 3.1 shows that mean creativity score for the total group of secondary school teachers is 398.50 with S.D. 52.86. The median and mode values for creativity scores of secondary school teachers are 391.76 and 378.28 respectively. The range of scores for secondary school teachers is 301.85-574. The value of skewness is 0.383 and value mean is greater than median. So this curve is positively skewed to the right. The value of Kurtosis is 0.260 which is less than 0.263. So it is leptokurtic and more peaked than normal.

Identification of More and Less Effective Secondary School Teachers

One of the objectives of the present investigation is the identification of more and less effective secondary school teachers. Hence, second part of this section deals with identification of more and less effective secondary school teachers. More effective and less effective teachers are identified on the basis of Q_1 and Q_3 criterion.

The manual of the teacher effectiveness scale shows that the score of teacher effectiveness ranges from 69 to 345. As is evident the range extends from less effective to more effective scores. So, the percentile norms of the scale show that the teachers having scores of 309.75 to 328.90 are effective and very effective i.e. between 70th to 90th percentiles. Besides this, teachers having scores from 253 to 278.07 are less effective and very less effective i.e. between 10th to 30th percentiles. In the present study most of the secondary school teachers used the positive end of the scale. Therefore, the class intervals and distribution of scores of 850 teachers was plotted and Q_1 (P_{25}) and Q_3 (P_{75}) were calculated. On the basis of P_{25} and P_{75} cut points the number of secondary school teachers were identified as being more effective (200) or less effective (200) teachers because scores lying above or below cut points have different numbers. The teachers scoring 331 and above (i.e. >331) were treated as more effective and those scoring 290 and below (i.e. <290) were treated as less effective secondary school teachers. By employing this method 200 more effective and 200 less effective teachers were selected in order to get the required information relating to variables such as general intelligence, emotional intelligence, social intelligence and creativity of these teachers.

The reason of secondary school teachers using positive end of the teacher effectiveness scale could be that measurement artifacts such as over estimation of ability on the part of secondary school teachers is likely to occur with self-report measures. Out of the total sample of 850 teachers, 200 more effective and 200 less effective teachers were identified. This number was further categorized into gender and type of school.

It is clearly noted that 200 secondary school teachers fall in the less effective category (*see*, table 3.2, p. 122). Out of these male teachers are 52 per cent as compared to 48 per cent female teachers. As far as their classification in terms of the type of school is concerned evidence of an almost same percentage of less effective teachers was seen in government (47%) and private school teachers. Whereas 47 per cent less effective teachers were found in government schools, 53 per cent were found in private schools. In terms of rural/urban division, 55.81 per cent teachers are rural and 44.8 per cent teachers are urban. The distribution also reveals that 50 per cent (200) teachers fall in the more effective category among the total of 850 secondary school teachers. However, in the more effective category the percentage of male teachers at 55.50 per cent is greater as compared to female teachers at 44.50 per cent. On the other hand in this category the number of government teachers at 60 per cent is greater than private school teachers 40 per cent.

Descriptive Analysis of General Intelligence, Emotional Intelligence, Social Intelligence and Creativity of More and Less Effective Secondary School Teachers

In the third part of this section these identified more and less effective secondary school teachers have been studied in relation to the different variables of general intelligence, emotional intelligence, social intelligence and creativity with descriptive measures (*see*, table 3.3). Descriptive measures such as mean, median, mode, SD, skewness, kurtosis have been applied to describe characteristics of identified teachers.

General Intelligence among More and Less Effective

It is observed that the mean value of general intelligence of less effective secondary school teachers is 44.05 with SD 7.59 (*see*, Table 3.3, p. 122). The median and mode values are 45.89 and 49.69 respectively. The scores range from 27 to 59 and value of skewness is -0.727. Table 3.3 also shows mean general intelligence score of more effective secondary school teachers is 44.55 with SD 7.21. The median and mode values are 44.89

and 45.58 respectively. The score ranges from 30 to 60 and value of skewness and kurtosis are -0.141 and 0.236 respectively. From the above results, it is clear that both the more effective and less effective groups have above average general intelligence. It is relevant to note that Service (2003) has elaborated that IQ is a factor of success in life, especially within educational organizational systems; but it is by no means the only factor, or even the key one. A high IQ can help an engrossed person learn more about a situation allowing them to become more effective or successful.

Emotional Intelligence among More and Less Effective Teachers

Table 3.3 shows that mean emotional intelligence score of less effective secondary school teachers is 132.80 with SD 15.25. The median and mode values are 133.76 and 135.68 respectively. The range of score is 80 to 167. The value of skewness and kurtosis are -0.188 and 0.270 respectively. Table 3.3 further shows that mean emotional intelligence scores among more effective secondary school teachers is 150.55 along with SD 14.40. The values of median and mode are 153.00 and 157.91 respectively. The range of score is 80 to 170. The value of skewness and kurtosis are -0.510 and 0.253 respectively.

Social Intelligence among More and Less Effective Teachers

Table 3.3 also shows that mean social intelligence score among less effective secondary school teachers is 107.10 with SD 10.21. The median and mode values are 108.98 and 112.74 respectively. The range of score is 73-138. The value of skewness and kurtosis are -0.552 and 0.270 respectively. Further table 3.3 also shows mean social intelligence score among more effective secondary school teachers is 109.60 along with SD 9.59. The median and mode values are 111.20 and 114.40 respectively. The range of score is 80-123. The value of skewness and kurtosis are -0.500 and 0.260 respectively. Based on the figures, it can be inferred that more and less effective secondary school teachers have above average level of social intelligence.

Creativity among More and Less Effective Teachers

Table 3.3 shows that the mean creativity score for less ef7fective secondary school teachers is 384.75 with SD 53.10. The median and mode values for creativity scores for less effective secondary school teachers are 376.42 and 359.76 respectively. The range of score in creativity for less effective secondary school teachers is 301.85-550.77. The value of skewness is 0.470 and value of mean is greater than median. The table 3.3 further shows that mean creativity score for more effective secondary school teachers is 416.25 with SD 59.50. The median and mode values for creativity scores for more effective secondary school teachers are 399.50 and 366.00 respectively. The range of score in creativity scores for more effective secondary school teachers is 306.58 to 574. The value of skewness and kurtosis are 0.281 and 0.250 respectively.

SECTION (B)
Teacher Effectiveness and its Psychological Dimensionality: Multivariate Analysis

Behavioural research is being revolutionized by multivariate thinking and analysis. Multivariate analysis is a general term used to describe a group of mathematical and statistical methods whose purpose is to analyze multiple measures related to a number of individuals. These methods may be listed as multiple regression analysis, multivariate analysis of variance (MANOVA), canonical correlation, discriminant analysis and factor analysis. Much of behavioural research, today, is multivariate in nature. The phenomena that the present study wishes to explain and predict are complex, subtle and difficult to calibrate. A number of variables related to such phenomena and multivariate methods are ways of studying multiple influences of several independent variables on one or more dependable variables. It can be said that multivariate methods mirror the actual complexity of behavioural "reality". They make it possible for the behavioural scientist to probe more deeply and realistically into the psycho-social phenomena. Hence in this study to analyze multivariate nature of different variables such as general, emotional, social intelligence and creativity on teacher effectiveness. multivariate analysis of variance (MANOVA), multiple regression, discriminant analysis and path analysis has been applied.

Comparison of General, Emotional, Social Intelligence and Creativity of Secondary School Teachers in relation to Gender, Type of School and Teacher Effectiveness (2×2×2) N = 240

The first part of this section deals with comparison of general intelligence, emotional intelligence, social intelligence and creativity of secondary school teachers across teacher effectiveness, gender and type of school on the basis of three way analysis of variance.

Method and Formation of Factorial Design

In order to achieve the theoretical objective of the study, different types of factorial designs have been used for appropriate application of analysis of variance.

The ex-post facto research design has been used to study the main and interaction effects of independent variables namely, teacher effectiveness, gender and type of school on general, emotional, social intelligence and creativity among secondary school teachers. The AxBxC (2x2x2) factorial design was formed as shown below:

1. Teacher effectiveness (A): Less effective (A_1) and More effective (A_2)
2. Gender (B): Male (B_1) and Female (B_2)
3. Type of school (c): Private (C_1) and Government (C_2)

The less and more effective groups were formed on the basis of P_{25}(200) and P_{75}(200) cut points on teacher effectiveness scores. The secondary school teachers scoring above 331 (i.e. > 331) were treated as more effective and those scoring below 290 (i.e. < 290) were treated as less effective secondary school teachers. The school teachers having teacher effectiveness score in the range of P_{25} and P_{75} i.e. 290 to 330 falling in average group were not considered in the design.

The distribution of sample in terms of AxBxC factorial design is shown in the table 3.4 (*see*, page 123).

It may be seen from the table 3.4 that 400 out of 850 secondary school teachers (47.05%) could be classified in less and more effective groups. A considerable percentage of cases did not fall in groups by virtue of being on cut points. Also it may be observed that only 32 female secondary school teachers were classified as low scorers in less effective group. This happens to be the minimum number in any category. Thus keeping in view the requirements of analysis of variance to have equal number of cases, 30 subjects were randomly assigned to each cell in 2x2x2 factorial design for computational purposes. It may also be stated that 240 subjects included in teacher effectiveness x gender x type of school (2x2x2) factorial design constituted more than one fourth but nearly less than one third of sample (28.23%), under study.

It may be mentioned here that the assumption of normalcy was not tested in the light of Norton's and Box's findings that F is rather insensitive to variations in shape of population distributions—may be leptokurtic, rectangular, markedly skewed, and even J-shaped (Guilford and Fruchter, 1981).

The mean general, emotional, social intelligence and creativity scores of secondary school teachers along with their standard deviations in teacher effectiveness x gender x type of school factorial design are given in the table 3.5 (*see*, page 123).

It is noted that more effective female secondary school teachers from government schools have the highest mean general intelligence score of 47.83 as compared to the lowest mean score of 39.67 in the case of their male counterparts in the more effective group from private secondary school teachers (*see*, table 3.5). The mean general intelligence score of other groups of secondary school teachers in terms of gender, type of school and teacher effectiveness factorial design fall between these two mean scores.

It is noted that female less effective group of secondary school teachers from private schools have lowest mean emotional intelligence score of 130.17 as compared to the highest mean emotional intelligence score of 154.16 in the case of their male counterparts forming more effective group of secondary school teachers from government schools. The mean emotional intelligence scores of other groups of secondary school teachers in terms of teacher effectiveness, gender and type of school factorial design lie between of these two mean scores.

It is evident from table 3.5 that mean scores of social intelligence among female secondary school teachers from more effective group in private schools turned out to be the highest score i.e. 110.50. In comparison to them female teachers from government secondary school teachers in more effective group had the lowest scores i.e. 104.50. The mean social intelligence scores of other groups of secondary school teachers in terms of teacher effectiveness, gender and type of school factorial design are between of these two mean scores.

It is observed that male more effective secondary school teachers from private schools have the highest mean creativity score of 432.64 as compared to the lowest mean score of 368.45 in the case of their counterparts in the category of male less effective secondary school teachers from government schools. The mean creativity scores of other groups of secondary school teachers in terms of teacher effectiveness x gender x type of school factorial design are between these two mean scores.

The mean performance on general, emotional, social intelligence and creativity among secondary school teachers in a combination of these three independent variables namely teacher effectiveness, gender, and type of school groups for double order interactions are given in the table 3.6 (*see*, p. 124).

In order to find out the significance of main and interactive effects of teacher effectiveness, gender and type of school on general, emotional, social intelligence and creativity—three way analysis of variance was worked out. The summary of ANOVA is given in the table 3.7 (*see*, p. 125).

1. Comparison of General Intelligence in relation to Gender, Type of School and Teacher Effectiveness

Main Effects

(*i*) *Teacher Effectiveness:* It can be observed from table 3.7 that F-value for the main effect of teacher effectiveness on general intelligence turned out to be 1.23 which is not significant at 0.05 level. Though the difference mean scores favouring more effective secondary school teachers but this differences is not significant. This implies that more and less effective secondary school teachers do not differ significantly in their intelligence (44.91vs 43.95) (Table 3.6).

(*ii*) *Gender:* The F-value for the main effect of gender on general intelligence came out to be 4.30 which is significant at 0.05 level. This shows that male and female secondary school teachers differ significantly in their general intelligence (43.54 vs 45.33) (Table 3.6). This proves that female secondary school teachers are significantly more intelligent than male secondary school teachers. The reasons for this difference could be that female teachers are more involved in mental ability tasks, sincere and task oriented as compared to male teachers. On the other hand teaching is usually considered a feminine job, as generally speaking a larger number of females take up teaching as profession as compared to males. This is evident from the fact that the number of girls in training colleges is more than boys. At the time of selection also girls hold meritorious positions in large numbers as compared to boys.

(*iii*) *Type of school:* It may also be observed from table 3.7 that F-value for the main effect of type of school came out to be 7.57 which is significant at 0.01 level. It may be concluded that government secondary school teachers have significantly higher level of general intelligence as compared to private secondary school teachers (45.62 vs 43.25) (Table 3.6). This implies that government and private secondary school teachers differ significantly in their general intelligence. Therefore it can be concluded that government secondary school teachers are significantly more generally intelligent than private secondary school teachers.

Interactive Effect

(*i*) *Teacher Effectiveness x Gender:* The F-value for the interactive effect of teacher effectiveness and gender turned out to be 5.15, which is significant at 0.05 level (Table 3.7). This shows that main effects of teacher effectiveness and gender are dependent upon each other to explain general intelligence among secondary school teachers.

It may be observed from table 3.8 (*see*, page 126) that significant mean difference in more and less effective group of secondary school teachers, is in favour of less effective secondary school teachers. It is much marked in case of male secondary school teachers (45.00 vs 42.08; $t = 2.01$; $p<0.05$). However in the case of female group, the more effective secondary school teachers tend to be more intelligent than their less effective secondary school teachers (44.83 vs 45.83; $t = 0.79$; $p>0.05$).

This is indicative of the fact less effective secondary school teachers are more intelligent than more effective teachers secondary school teachers in male group. In female group more effective and less effective secondary school teachers do not differ significantly in intelligence as is clearly observed in table 3.8 and figure 3.1(a).

On the basis of the figures above, it can be concluded that less effective secondary school teachers show higher level of intelligence than more effective secondary school teachers in the male group of secondary school teachers (45.00 vs 42.08).

It may also be observed from table 3.8 that significant mean difference in male and female secondary school teachers is in favour of female secondary school teachers and is much marked in case of more effective secondary school teachers (45.83 vs 42.08; $t = 2.06$; $p<0.05$). However, less effective group of secondary school teachers do not differ significantly in their intelligence. In the case of less effective group of secondary school teachers, male secondary school teachers tend to be more intelligent than female secondary school teachers (45.00 vs 44.83; $t = 1.86$), though this difference is not significant (Figure 3.1(b)). The reversal of mean difference in intelligence of male and female teachers across teacher effectiveness groups makes the overall mean difference negligible and non-significant.

(*ii*) *Gender x Type of School:* The F-value for the interactive effect of gender and type of school turned out to be 0.01 which is not significant at 0.05 level. This is indicative of the fact that significant main effect of gender and are type of school are independent to explain general intelligence among secondary school teachers.

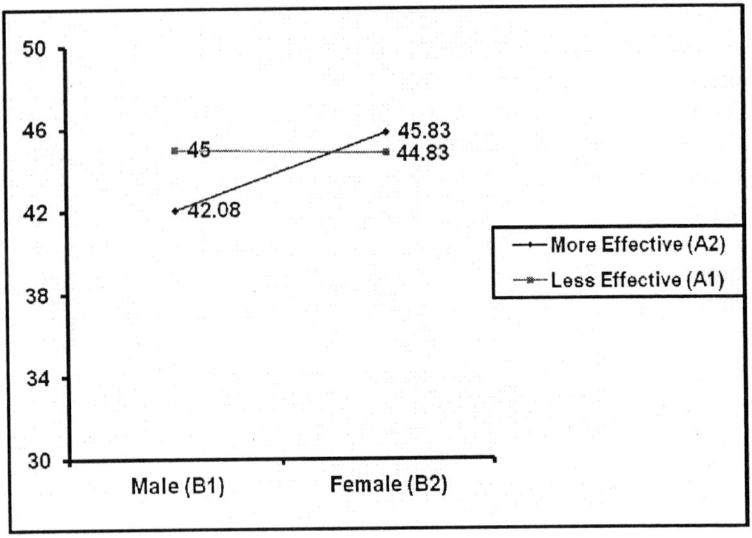

Fig. 3.1 (a): Teacher Effectiveness × Gender (A × B)

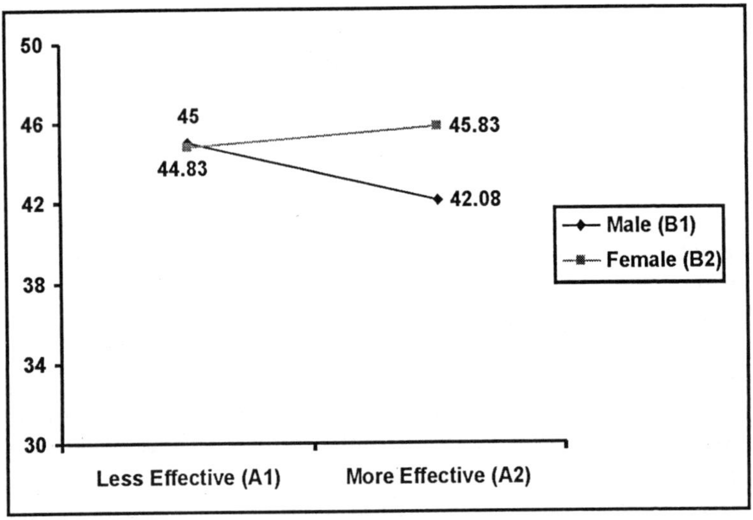

Figure 3.1(b): Teacher Effectiveness × Gender (A × B)

(*iii*) *Type of School x Teacher Effectiveness:* It is noted from table 3.7 that F-value for interactive effect of type of school and teacher effectiveness came out to be 5.61, which is significant at 0.05 level. This indicates that type of school and teacher effectiveness are dependent upon each other to explain general intelligence among secondary school teachers. The main effects of type of school and teacher effectiveness dependent upon each other to explain general intelligence among secondary school teachers. In order to find out significance of mean differences, t-value was applied in the table 3.9.

It may be seen from table 3.9 (*see*, p. 126) that in more effective group of teachers, private and government secondary school teachers differ significantly (46.16 vs 41.75; t-value = 2.43; $p<0.05$) (figure 3.2(a)). It can be concluded that government secondary school teachers are more intelligent than private secondary school teachers in more effective group of secondary school teachers. In other words, it may be stated that type of school plays a significant role in determining general intelligence of secondary school teachers only in case of more effective teachers, whereas such difference is not significant in less effective group of secondary school teachers (44.75 vs 45.08; t-value = 0.184; $p>0.05$) figure 3.2(a).

More effective secondary school teachers show high level of intelligence than the less effective secondary school teacher in government schools (46.16 vs 45.08; t-value = 0.91) but this difference is not significant. Less effective secondary school teachers show high level of general in difference than more effective secondary school teachers in private schools (44.75 vs; t-value = 1.64), this difference is not significant can be seen in figure 3.2(b).

(*iv*) *Teacher Effectiveness × Gender × Type of School:* The triple interaction AxBxC was found to be non-significant as F-value 0.18, which is not significant even at 0.05 level (Table 3.7). This means that significant main effect of type of school (Government > Private) is restricted to more effective secondary school teachers. The significant main effect of type of school dependent upon teacher effectiveness to explain general intelligence of secondary school teachers. The non-significant main effect of teacher effectiveness is dependent upon gender. It is seen that whereas more effective secondary school teachers have higher level of intelligence than less effective secondary school teachers in female group; in a reverse trend more effective secondary school teachers have lower level of intelligence than less effective secondary school teachers in the male group of secondary school teachers. The non-significant main effect of gender is dependent upon teacher effectiveness, female secondary school teachers have higher level of intelligence than male secondary school teachers only in case of more effective secondary school teachers.

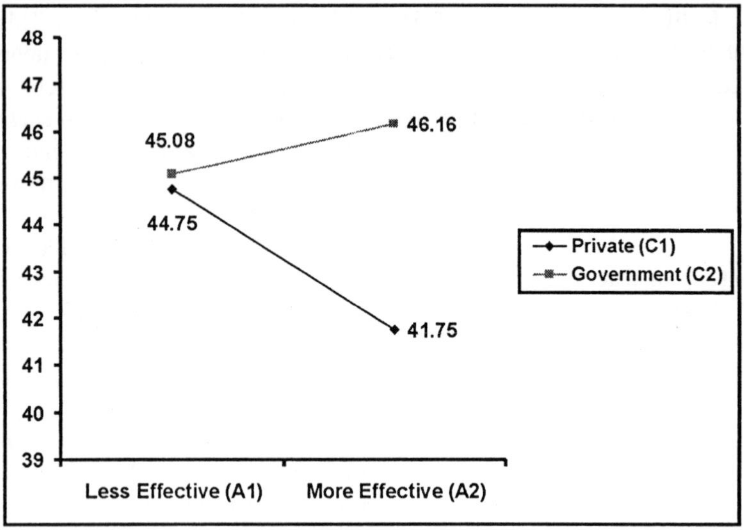

Fig. 3.2(a): Teacher Effectiveness × Type of School (A × C)

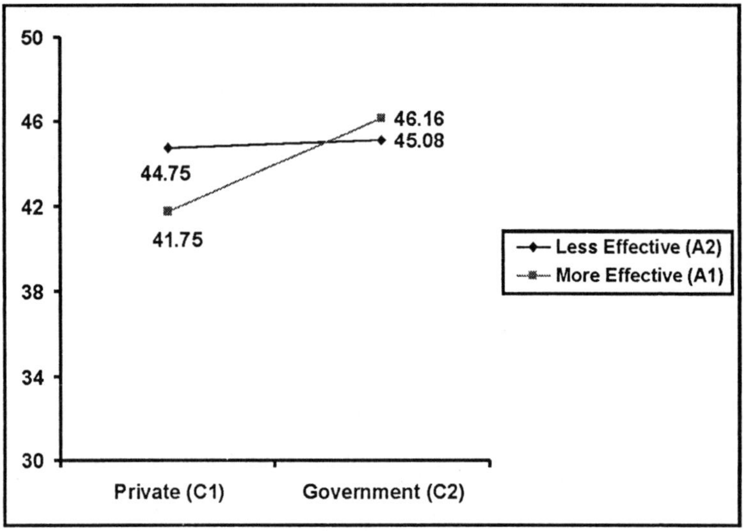

Fig. 3.2(b): Teacher Effectiveness × Type of School (A × C)

2. Comparison of Emotional Intelligence in relation to Gender, Type of School and Teacher Effectiveness

Main Effects

(*i*) *Teacher Effectiveness:* It is observed from the table 3.7 that F-value for the main effect of teacher effectiveness turned out to be 95.46 ($p<0.01$), thereby meaning that emotional intelligence of secondary school teachers of more effective group is significantly higher as compared to their counterparts from less effective group of secondary school teachers (133.25 vs 150.89) (Table 3.6).

(*ii*) *Gender:* The F-value for the main effect of gender came out to be 3.23 which is not significant. This indicates that male secondary school teachers have significantly higher emotional intelligence as compared to female secondary school teachers (143.70 vs 140.75) but this difference is not significant.

(*iii*) *Type of School:* F-value for the main effect of type of school on emotional intelligence came out to be 1.79, which is not significant at 0.05 level. This means that private and government secondary school teachers do not differ significantly in emotional intelligence. (140.86 vs 143.28) (Table 3.6)

Interactive Effects

(*i*) *Teacher Effectiveness x Gender:* The F-value for the interactive effect of teacher effectiveness and gender turned out to be 0.02 which is not significant at 0.05 level. This is indicative of the fact that significant main effects of teacher effectiveness is independent to explain emotional intelligence among secondary school teachers. It does not depend upon gender to explain emotional intelligence of secondary school teachers.

(*ii*) *Gender x Type of School:* Further the F-value for the interactive effect of gender and type of school came out to be 0.01, which is also not significant at 0.05 level. This shows that the result of non-significant main effect gender and type of school are independent to explain emotional intelligence among secondary school teachers.

(*iii*) *Type of School x Teacher Effectiveness:* It may also be noted from table 3.7 that the F-value for interactive effect of type of school and teacher effectiveness came out to be 0.012 which is not significant at 0.05 level. This implies that significant main effect of teacher effectiveness is independent to explain emotional intelligence among secondary school teachers. Significant main effect of teacher effectiveness does not depend upon type of school to explain emotional intelligence among secondary school teachers.

(*iv*) *Teacher Effectiveness x Gender x Type of School:* The triple interaction AxBxC was also found to be non-significant even at 0.05 level. This means that secondary school teachers do not differ in emotional intelligence across teacher effectiveness, gender and type of school when taken cojointly.

3. Comparison of Social Intelligence of Secondary School Teachers in relation to Gender, Type of School and Teacher Effectiveness

Main Effects

(i) *Teacher Effectiveness*: It is observed from table 3.7 that F-value for the main effect of teacher effectiveness turned out to be 0.64, which is not significant. This means that more and less effective secondary school teachers do not differ significantly in social intelligence (107.62 vs. 108.58) when taken independently.

(ii) *Gender:* The F-value for the main effect of gender on social intelligence came out to be 0.65 which is not significant at.05 level. This indicates that male and female secondary school teachers do not differ significantly in social intelligence (108.58 vs 107.62). Social intelligence of secondary school teachers do not effect by their gender.

(iii) *Type of School:* It is also be noted from table 3.7 that F-value for the main effect of type of school on social intelligence came out to be 1.26 which is not significant at 0.05 level. This indicates that secondary school teachers do not differ significantly in social intelligence across type of school when considered independently (108.83 vs 108.10).

Interaction Effect

(i) *Teacher Effectiveness x Gender:* The F-value for the interactive effect of teacher effectiveness x gender turned out to be 0.56 which is not significant at 0.05 level. This is indicative of the fact that non-significant main effects of teacher effectiveness and gender are independent of each other to explain social intelligence among secondary school teachers.

(ii) *Gender x Type of School:* It may also be noted from table 3.7 that the F-value for interactive effect of gender x type of school came out to be 3.31, which is not significant. This indicates that non-significant main effects of gender and type of school are independent to explain social intelligence among secondary school teachers.

(iii) *Type of School x Teacher Effectiveness:* The F-value for the interactive effect of type of school and teacher effectiveness turned out to be 1.29, which is not significant. This is indicative of the fact that type of school and teacher effectiveness are independent of each other to explain social intelligence among secondary school teachers. The results of non-significant main effects type of school and teachers differences are independent in their way.

(iv) *Teacher Effectiveness x Gender x Type of School:* The triple order interaction of teacher effectiveness x gender x type of school on social intelligence turned out to be 0.19, which is not significant. These results are suggestive of the fact that secondary school teachers do not differ significantly in their social intelligence in relation to teacher effectiveness, gender and type of school either independently or conjointly.

4. Comparison of Creativity in relation to Gender, Type of School and Teacher Effectiveness

Main Effects

(*i*) *Teacher Effectiveness:* It can be observed from table 3.7 that F-value for the main effect of teacher effectiveness turned out to be 20.08 ($p<0.01$), thereby meaning that creativity of secondary school teachers of more effective group is significantly higher as compared to their counterparts from less effective group of secondary school teachers (382.88 vs 415.43) (Table 3.6).

(*ii*) *Gender:* The F-value for the main effect of gender came out to be 0.26, which is not significant at 0.05 level. This indicates that male and female secondary school teachers do not differ significantly in creativity (401.00 vs 397.31) when taken independently.

(*iii*) *Type of School:* Further F-value for the main effect of type of school came out to be 0.11, which is not significant at 0.05 level. This indicates that private and government secondary school teachers do not differ significantly in their creativity (400.33 vs 397.99) when taken independently.

Interactive Effect

(*i*) *Teacher Effectiveness x Gender:* The F-value for the interactive effect of teacher effectiveness and gender turned out to be 7.69 which is significant at 0.01 level. The results of significant main effect of teacher effectiveness dependent upon gender to explain creativity among secondary school teachers. It was concluded that teacher effectiveness and gender are dependent upon each other to explain creativity among secondary school teachers. This shows that more and less effective teachers differ significantly from each other variedly across male and female secondary school teachers (table 3.6). In order to find out mean difference, t-ratio was applied, *see* table 3.10, p. 127.

It is observed from table 3.10 and figure 3.3 (a) that more effective secondary school teachers are more creative than less effective secondary school teachers in both groups but difference is significant only in male group (427.35 vs 374.66; t-value = 7.20; p<0.01), whereas in female group, more effective group of secondary school teachers do not differ significantly than less effective group of secondary school teachers. (403.52 vs 391.11; t-value = 1.80; p>0.05).

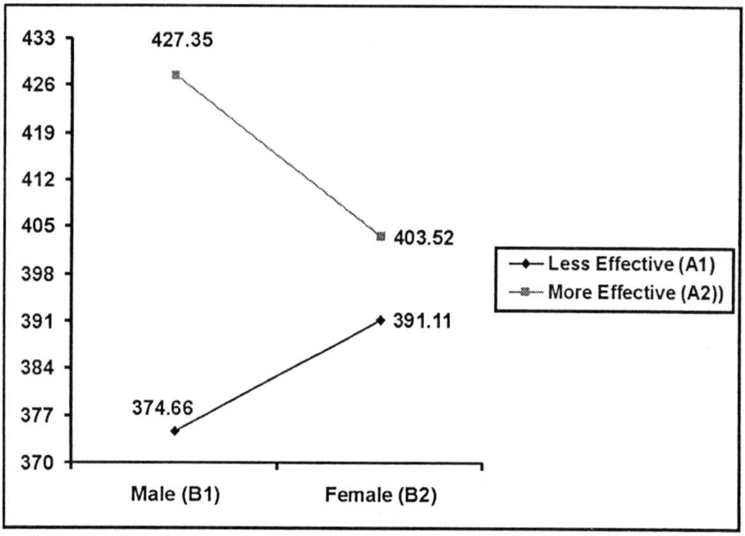

Fig. 3.3(a): Teacher Effectiveness X Gender (A x B)

It may also be observed from table 3.10 and figure 3.3(b) that male and female secondary school teachers differ significantly in terms of creativity in more effective group of secondary school teachers 427.35 vs 403.52; t-value = 3.28; p<0.01). Male and female secondary school teachers also differ significantly in creativity in less effective group of secondary school teachers 374.66 vs 391.11; t-value = 2.37; p<0.05). Reversal of results make the main effect of gender non-significant. Male secondary school teachers are more creative in more effective group of secondary school teachers and female secondary school teachers are more creative in less effective secondary school teachers.

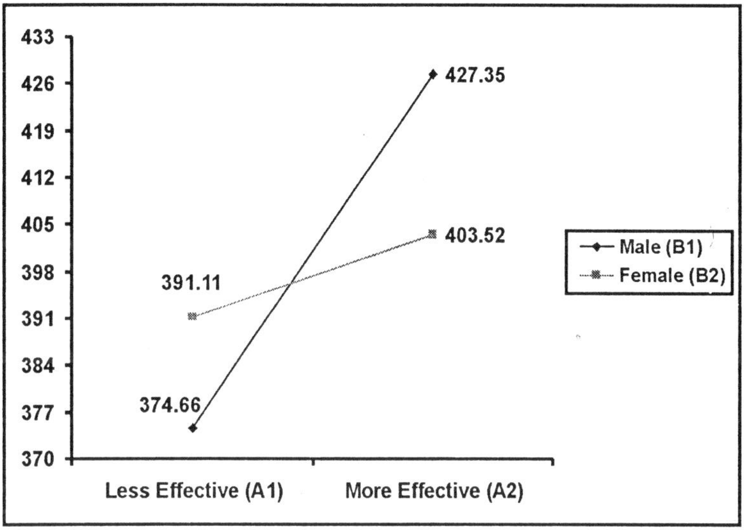

Fig. 3.3(b): Teacher Effectiveness X Gender (A × B)

(*ii*) *Gender x Type of School:* The F-value for the interactive effect of gender and type of school turned out to be 1.37 which is not significant at 0.05 level (Table 3.7). It can be concluded that non-significant main effect of gender and type of school are independent to explain creativity among secondary school teachers.

(*iii*) *Type of School x Teacher Effectiveness:* Further the F-value for the interactive effect of type of school and teacher effectiveness came out to be 1.58, which is also not significant at 0.05 level. This shows that result of significant main effect of teacher effectiveness is independent to explain creativity among secondary school teachers. Teacher effectiveness do not depend upon type of school to explain creativity among secondary school teachers.

(*iv*) *Teacher Effectiveness x Gender x Type of School:* The triple interaction AxBxC was also found to be non-significant as the F-value is 1.68, which is not significant even at 0.05 level. This means that significant teacher effectiveness and gender interaction results are true across government and private schools. But when teacher effectiveness, gender and type of school taken conjointly do not effect creativity of secondary school teachers.

Correlational Analysis

The second part of this section focuses on tracing correlation of teacher effectiveness with general intelligence, emotional intelligence, social intelligence and creativity in a total sample of secondary school teachers (N = 850) and across sub groups i.e. male, female, private, government, more effective and less effective secondary school teachers. For this purpose product moment coefficients of correlation were computed. Further, inter-correlations among general intelligence, emotional intelligence, social intelligence and creativity have been worked out for the total group of secondary school teachers.

(A) Correlation of Teacher Effectiveness with General, Emotional, Social Intelligence and Creativity Among Secondary School Teachers

The values of coefficients of correlation of teacher effectiveness with different independent variables namely general intelligence, emotional intelligence, social intelligence and creativity for male, female, private, government, more effective, less effective and total group of secondary school teachers are discussed hereunder.

(i) Correlation of teacher effectiveness with general intelligence

The table 3.11 (*see*, p. 127) indicates that coefficient of correlation between teacher effectiveness and general intelligence in the total group is positive and significant ($r = 0.072$, $p<0.05$). The table further shows general intelligence is positively and significantly correlated with teacher effectiveness in female group ($r = 0.146$, $p<0.01$) but this relationship for male group is not significant ($r = 0.016$, $p>0.05$). There is positive and significant correlation in the case of government and secondary school group ($r = 0.154$, $p<0.01$). Correlation of coefficient in case of private group of secondary school teachers is positive but not significant ($r = 0.022$, $p>0.05$). Further general intelligence is positively related with teacher effectiveness ($r = 0.080$) in more effective teachers but this relationship is not significant in more effective group of secondary school teachers. In less effective group correlation between teacher effectiveness and general intelligence is 0.076 which is positive and not significant. It is inferred that teacher effectiveness is neither in less effective group nor in more effective group significantly related with general intelligence but this relationship is significant among total, female and government groups.

(ii) Correlation of teacher effectiveness with emotional intelligence

The coefficients of correlation of teacher effectiveness with emotional intelligence among secondary school teachers for different groups are given in the table 3.11. Table 3.11 indicates that the coefficient of correlation between teacher effectiveness and emotional intelligence of the total group of secondary school teachers is 0.394, which is positive and significant at 0.01 level. It may be seen that in the male group of secondary school teachers value of correlation (0.413, $p<0.01$) is positive and significant. This is true in case of female group of secondary school teachers (0.374, $p<0.01$). The coefficient of correlation between teacher effectiveness and emotional intelligence in private and government secondary school teachers is positive and significant at 0.01 level ($r =$ 0.422, 0.394). Emotional intelligence is positively and significantly related with teacher effectiveness in the case of more effective group of secondary school teachers ($r = 0.184$, $p<0.01$). Though it is positively related in less effective group of secondary school teachers but this relationship is not significant ($r = 0.101$, $p>0.05$).

(*iii*) *Correlation of teacher effectiveness with social intelligence*

It is (Table 3.11) revealed that coefficient of correlation of teacher effectiveness with social intelligence is positive and significant in the total group of secondary school teachers ($r = 0.130$, $p<0.01$). This relationship is positive and significant in male group ($r = 0.169$, $p<0.01$) and this is also true in case of female group of secondary school teachers ($r = 0.080$). But this correlation is not significant.

The relationship of teacher effectiveness with social intelligence is positive and significant in private secondary school teachers ($r = 0.201$, $p<0.01$). However, it is not true in case of government secondary school teachers, because this correlation is positive but not significant ($r = 0.081$, $p>0.05$).

The coefficient of correlation of teacher effectiveness with social intelligence is positive and significant in more effective group of secondary school teachers ($r = 0.149$, $p<0.05$) and positive but not significantly related in less effective group of secondary school teachers ($r = 0.066$, $p> 0.05$).

(*iv*) *Correlation of teacher effectiveness with creativity and its dimensions: Fluency, flexibility, originality and elaboration*

The coefficients of correlation of teacher effectiveness with creativity among secondary school teachers for different groups are given in the table 3.11.

(a) Fluency: Table 3.11 indicates that correlation coefficient of teacher effectiveness with fluency in case of the total group of secondary school teachers came out to be 0.201, which is positive and significant at 0.01 level. Further relationship between teacher effectiveness with fluency in female group is positive and significant at 0.05 level ($r = 0.124$) and for male group this relationship is also positive and significant ($r = 0.259$, $p<0.01$). This relationship is positive and significant in case of government and private group of secondary school teachers ($r = 0.157, 0.201, p<0.01$). The coefficient of correlation between teacher effectiveness and fluency for more effective group is ($r = 0.078, p>0.05$) and for less effective group it is also significant and positive ($r = 0.174, p<0.05$).

(b) Flexibility: The correlation coefficient between teacher effectiveness with flexibility for the total group is positive and significant ($r = 0.149, p<0.01$). Further table 3.11 shows that correlation values between flexibility and teacher effectiveness for male and female secondary school teachers lie at 0.176 ($p<0.01$) and 0.115 ($p<0.05$). The value of coefficient of correlation between flexibility and teacher effectiveness is positive and significant ($r = 0.149, p<0.01$) for private school teachers and this value is positive and significant for government secondary school teachers ($r = 0.101, p<0.05$). This correlation is positive but not significant in case of more effective and less effective group of secondary school teachers ($r = 0.102, 0.132\ p>0.05$).

(c) Originality: Table 3.11 also reveals that coefficient of correlation between teacher effectiveness and originality for total group is 0.111 which is positive and significant at 0.01 level. For male group of secondary school teachers coefficient of correlation between originality and teacher effectiveness is positive and significant (0.184, $p<0.01$). However in the case of female group of secondary school teachers coefficient of correlation is positive but not significant (0.013, $p>0.05$).

The correlation coefficient between originality and teacher effectiveness for private group of secondary school teachers is 0.196 which is positive and significant at 0.01 level. For the group of government secondary school teachers this relationship is positive but not significant ($r = 0.019$, $p>0.05$). The values of correlations between teacher effectiveness and originality dimension of creativity in more effective and less effective groups of secondary school teachers are 0.104 and 0.162 ($p<0.05$) respectively.

(d) Elaboration: Further table 3.11 shows that the coefficient of correlation between teacher effectiveness and elaboration for the total group is positive and significant (0.180, $p<0.01$). The value of correlation between teacher effectiveness and elaboration in female secondary school teacher group (r = 0.142) and in male group is (r = 0.212). The values correlation for private secondary school teachers came out to be (r = 0.142), which is significant at 0.01 level. In the case of government secondary school teachers group the value of correlation is positive and significant (r = 0.198), p<0.01. Table 3.11 further shows that correlation coefficients between teacher effectiveness and elaboration are 0.066 for more effective group and 0.126 for less effective group of teachers which are not significant.

(e) Creativity: The coefficient of correlation between teacher effectiveness and creativity is positive and significant among all groups of secondary school teachers. The values of correlation between teacher effectiveness and creativity lie at 0.210 (p<0.01), 0.188 (p<0.05) for the total group and less effective group of secondary school teachers respectively and for more effective group the correlation between teacher effectiveness and creativity is positive (0.102) but not significant. Further correlation between teacher effectiveness and creativity among male and female group of teachers came out to be 0.261 and 0.138 (p<0.01). The coefficient of correlation between teacher effectiveness and creativity among private and government group of secondary school teachers came out to be 0.249 and 0.159 (p<0.01).

(B) Inter-Correlation of General Intelligence, Social Intelligence, Emotional Intelligence and Creativity Among Secondary School Teachers

In order to study inter correlation of general intelligence, emotional intelligence, social intelligence and creativity, coefficients of correlation was traced out between variables. Table 3.12 (*see*, p. 127) shows inter-correlation of general intelligence, emotional intelligence, social intelligence and creativity among secondary school teachers.

Table 3.12 shows that there is positive and significant relationship of general intelligence with social intelligence (r = 0.085, p<0.05) and emotional intelligence (r = 0.042, p>0.05) among secondary school teachers.

It is observed that general intelligence is positively and significantly related with fluency (r = 0.105, p<0.01), flexibility (0.064, p<0.05) originality (0.027) and elaboration (0.029). These correlations are positive but not significant in case of originality and elaboration. Further inter-correlation between general intelligence and creativity is positive and significant (r = 0.087, p<0.05).

Further table 3.12 also shows coefficients of correlation between social intelligence and emotional intelligence 0.051 to be positive but not significant at 0.05 level.

The co-efficient of correlation of social intelligence and fluency, flexibility, originality and elaboration are 0.269, 0.257, 0.124 and 0.130 respectively. All values of correlations are positive and significant at 0.01 level. Further it can be seen from table 3.12 that creativity and social intelligence are related with each other ($r = 0.274$, $p<0.01$).

From the correlation analysis it is revealed that coefficients of correlation of emotional intelligence and dimensions of creativity are positive and significant. The coefficients of correlation of emotional intelligence with fluency, flexibility, originality and elaboration came out to be 0.073, 0.087, 0.082, 0.141 respectively. All correlations are positive and significant at 0.01 level. There is positive and significant relationship between creativity and emotional intelligence ($r = 108$, $p<0.05$).

Table 3.12 also depicts that inter-correlation between creativity and its dimensions are positive and significant. All the dimensions fluency, flexibility, originality and elaboration and creativity share marked relationship amongst each other and are significant at 0.01 level.

Regression Analysis

Multiple regression analysis is an efficient and powerful hypothesis testing and influence making technique, since it helps the scientist study with relative precision, complex interrelations between independent variables and a dependent variable and thus helps to "explain the presumed phenomenon represented by the dependent variables" (Kerlinger, 2001, 631). In the fourth part, the statistical technique of multiple the statistical technique of multiple regression analysis was employed with teacher effectiveness as dependent variable, whereas factors, namely general intelligence, emotional intelligence, social intelligence and creativity are taken as independent variables. This has been done with the purpose of identifying the predictors of teacher effectiveness among secondary school teachers.

In order to find out the contribution of general intelligence, emotional intelligence, social intelligence and creativity (fluency, flexibility, originality and elaboration) to teacher effectiveness among secondary school teachers, step-wise multiple regression analysis were carried out for different groups such as total group of teachers 'more and less effective', 'male and female' and 'private and government' secondary school teachers. Since the purpose of the study was to determine the predictors of teacher effectiveness, only the values of coefficients of correlation(r) and multiple correlation (R^2) determining the total effect of contributory factors, adjusted R^2 and R^2 change along with percentage variance in the set of predictors are reported in table 3.13 (*see*, page 128).

The results of step-wise multiple regression reveal in table 3.13 that emotional intelligence, fluency and social intelligence emerged as significant predictors of teacher effectiveness among secondary school teachers (N = 850) while explaining only 17.60 per cent variance (R^2 = 0.179) in the equation. As per this equation, out of 17.60 per cent total variance, 14.43 per cent variance was explained by emotional intelligence, followed by fluency 2.90 per cent and social intelligence 0.60 per cent.

The results of step-wise multiple regression for male group of secondary school teachers reveals that emotional intelligence, creativity, flexibility, social intelligence emerged as significant predictors of teacher effectiveness while explaining 21.3 per cent variance. Teacher effectiveness among male secondary school teachers has been explained by emotional intelligence (14.90% variance), creativity (4.50% variance) whereas flexibility (1.20%) and social intelligence too contributed (0.70%).

Table 3.13 reveals that teacher effectiveness among female secondary school teachers has been explained by emotional intelligence with 13.6 per cent variance. General intelligence also emerged as a significant predictor explaining 1.90 per cent variance (R = 0.391). In total emotional intelligence and general intelligence explained 15.50 per cent in determining predictors of teacher effectiveness in female secondary school teachers.

Table 3.13 reveals that teacher effectiveness among government secondary school teachers has been explained by general intelligence with 15.8 per cent variance. Elaboration emerged as another significant predictor explaining 2 per cent variance (R = 0.426) and general intelligence is too an important and significant predictor of teacher effectiveness explaining only 1.30 per cent variance (R = 0.444). In total emotional intelligence, elaboration and general intelligence explained 19.1 per cent variance.

From table 3.13 it is observed that teacher effectiveness among private secondary school teachers has been explained by emotional intelligence with 11.50 per cent variance (R = 0.343), followed by fluency with 4.90 per cent variance (R = 0.410) and social intelligence with 1.40 per cent variance (R = 0.429). In total, emotional intelligence, fluency, social intelligence contributed to 17.8 per cent variance in teacher effectiveness among private secondary school teachers. Hence it is concluded that emotional intelligence, fluency, social intelligence contributed to teacher effectiveness among private secondary school teachers.

The table 3.13 depicts that teacher effectiveness among more effective secondary school teachers has been explained by emotional intelligence with 2.30 per cent variance. Creativity also emerged as a significant predictor explaining 2.10 per cent variance. While emotional intelligence and creativity compositely explained 4.90 per cent variance.

Table 3.13 reveals that teacher effectiveness among less effective secondary school teachers has been explained only by creativity with 2.40 per cent variance. So it is concluded that creativity plays a significant role in determining teacher effectiveness among less effective secondary school teachers.

Path Analysis

A path analytic approach was used to examine the direct and indirect effects of general intelligence, social intelligence, emotional intelligence and creativity on teacher effectiveness among secondary school teachers. A research based path model was developed in which general intelligence, social intelligence, emotional intelligence and creativity are independent variables and teacher effectiveness is dependent variable of the model (*see* table 3.14, page 128 and figure 3.4). The model summarized the research assumption that general intelligence, social intelligence, emotional intelligence, creativity and teacher effectiveness are interrelated.

In the fifth part path analysis has been carried out to examine the effects of general intelligence, social intelligence, emotional intelligence and creativity as independent variables on teacher effectiveness as dependent variables. This phase of study was designed to explain relationships between these factors by developing path model.

For each independent variable, the magnitude, direction and percentage of direct and indirect effect were calculated. The standardized regression coefficient (Beta) and coefficient of determination (R^2) for equation of independent variables are given in the table below:

The four independent variables hypothesized to impact teacher effectiveness in the model explained 18 per cent of the variance of teacher effectiveness of secondary school teachers. All variables are hypothesized to have a direct effect on teacher effectiveness among secondary school teachers. Teachers' emotional intelligence, social intelligence, creativity and general intelligence indicated direct effect on teacher effectiveness of secondary school teachers but their magnitude of effects values from each other.

This finding suggests that higher the values of these variables, higher the teacher effectiveness of the teachers. Emotional intelligence of teachers (Beta = 0.361) had the strongest effect among the variables having a significant direct effects. The direct effects of teacher's creativity (Beta = 0.140), social intelligence (Beta = 0 .078) and general intelligence (Beta = 0.051) can also be considered as strong, medium and low respectively.

In regard to direct effects, on teacher effectiveness emotional intelligence had strongest direct effect (95%), followed by general intelligence (75.85%), creativity (67.30%) and social intelligence (61.41%). Emotional intelligence had the highest effect on teacher effectiveness, which is a result of significant direct influence on teacher effectiveness. General intelligence, creativity and social intelligence had the second, third and fourth strongest direct effects on teacher effectiveness, which is mainly the result of their indirect effects of intervening variables.

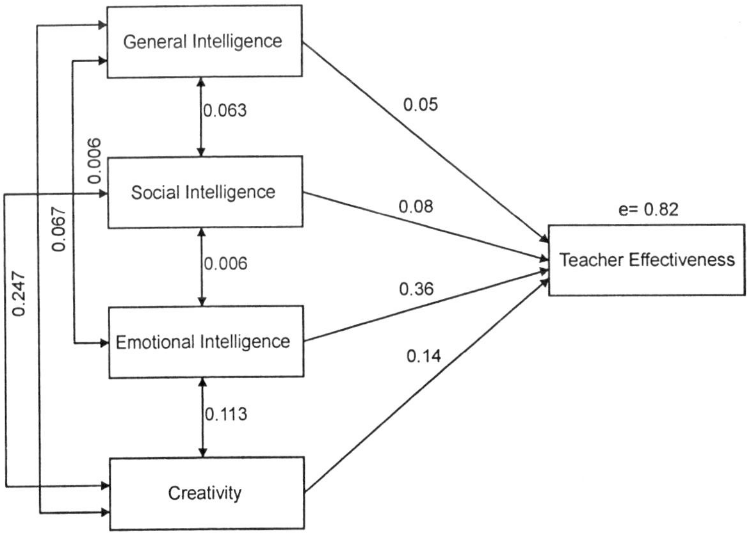

Fig. 3.4: Path Model Showing Effects of General Intelligence, Social Intelligence, Emotional Intelligence, Creativity on Teacher Effectiveness

Discriminant Analysis

Discriminant analysis is a parametric technique to determine which weightings of quantitative variables or predictors best discriminate between 2 or more than 2 groups of cases and do so better than chance.

The technique of discriminant analysis, developed by R.A. Fisher (1936), is one method for multivariate study of group differences. It is appropriate statistical technique when the dependent variable is categorical and independent variables are quantitative. In many cases, the dependent variables consist of two groups or classifications. The most frequent applications of discriminant analysis are for predictive purposes, that is, for situations in which it is necessary or desirable to classify subjects into groups or categories. The results of a discriminant analysis allow the prediction of group membership based on the best linear composite or combination of predictor scores. Discriminant analysis is analogous to multiple regressions in that both involve prediction from a set of continuous predictor variables (sometimes designated independent variables) to a criterion. The major difference between them is that multiple regression predicts a continuous criterion variable (sometimes designated the dependent variable), whereas discriminant analysis predicts a categorical criterion, that is, group membership. Thus, given multiple predictor variables, multiple regression would be the appropriate method of analysis if the dependent variables were continuous, and discriminant analysis would be appropriate if the dependent variables were categorical, with two or more levels. Multiple regression analysis is a method of studying the effect and the magnitude of the effects of more than one independence variable on one dependable variable using principles of correlation and regression.

In the present study discriminant analysis was carried out with teacher effectiveness as categorical dependent variable (more effective and less effective) with general intelligence, emotional intelligence, social intelligence and creativity as independent variables.

In the sixth phase, discriminant analysis carried out with teacher effectiveness as categorical dependent variable (more effective vs. less effective) with general intelligence, emotional intelligence, social intelligence and creativity as quantitative independent variables.

Mean difference between emotional intelligence and creativity may be good discriminators as their separations are large. The difference between mean scores of more effective and less effective teachers is large in case of emotional intelligence and creativity (150.55>132.80; 416.25>384.75) as in table 3.3.

The table 3.15 (*see*, page 128) provides strong statistical evidence of significant differences between means of more and less effective groups for all independent variables with emotional intelligence and creativity are producing high 'F' values.

The canonical function is the multiple correlations between the predictors and the discriminant function. With only one function it provides an index of overall model fit which is interpreted as being the proportion of variance explained (R^2). The value of canonical correlation of .545 suggests the model explains 29.70 per cent of the variation in the grouping variable i.e. neither the teacher effective.

The value of Wilks' Lambda (.703) indicates the significance of the discriminant function. A highly significant function and provides the proportion of total variability not explained i.e. it is the converse of the squared canonical correlation. So we have 70.33 per cent unexplained.

The interpretation of the discriminant coefficients (or weights) is like that in multiple regression. Table 3.16 (*see*, page 129) provides an index of the importance of each predictor like the standardized regression coefficients (beta's) did in multiple. The sign indicates the direction of the relationship. Emotional intelligence was the strongest predictor while creativity was next in importance as a predictor. These two variables, with large coefficients, stand out as those that strongly predict allocation to the more effective or less effective. General intelligence and social intelligence were less successful as predictors.

Table 3.17 (*see*, page 129) provides another way of indicating the relative importance of the predictors. It can be seen below that the same pattern holds. The structure matrix correlations are used because they are considered more accurate than standardized canonical discriminant function coefficients. The structure matrix table (Table 3.17) shows the correlation of each variable with discriminate function. These Pearson coefficients are structure coefficients or discriminant loadings. They serve like factor loading in factor analysis. By identifying the largest loadings for each discriminate function the researcher gains insight into how to name each function. Here it can be seen that emotional intelligence and creativity which suggests a label of personal confidence and effectiveness as the function that discriminate between more and less effective teachers.

The Canonical Discriminant Function Coefficient: Just as a multiple regression equation can be used to calculate a predicted score on the criterion for each subject, a discriminant function can be used to calculate an individual's discriminant score. Again, on the basis of the general formula for a linear equation ($Y = bX + a$), the individual's scores on each variable are multiplied by the corresponding discriminate weight. Multiplication of raw scores by unstandardized weights would result in a discriminant score in the same units as the original variables. Multiplication of standard scores by standardized weights would yield discriminant scores in standard score units. Application of Equation 2 to the calculation of the standardized discriminant score for the tth individual would result in the following:

$$D_i = b_1X_{1i} + b_2X_{2i} + b_3X_{3i} + \ldots\ bpX_{pi}$$

(Note that in the calculation of standardized scores the constant dropouts. Subsequent formulas assume that standardized discriminant scores and centroids rather than their unstandardized equivalents, are being calculated).

There unstandardized coefficients (b) are used to create discriminant function (equation). It operates just like a regression equation. In this case we have (Table 3.18, p. 129).

The discriminant function indicates the partial contribution of each variable to the discriminate function controlling for all other variables in the equation. They can be used to assess each independent variables unique contribution to the discriminate function and therefore provide information on the relative importance of each variable.

Group Centroids

In order to understand the concept of a centroid, consider the fact that the distribution of discriminant scores of members of a group, like any set of continuous scores, would have a certain distribution with a mean and standard deviation. The mean of discriminant scores within a group is known as the group centroid. The group centroid is calculated by applying the discriminant weights to the group means on each variable. Equation would be the formula for calculating the centroid of Group A.

As mentioned previously, the discriminant function yielded is that which maximizes the difference between group centroids and which therefore also minimizes overlap between the distributions of scores for the groups. The most important use of discriminant scores and centroids is in the prediction of group of membership for individuals, in other words, for classification.

A further way of interpreting discriminant results is to describe each group in terms of its profile, using the group means of the predictor variables. These group means are called centroids. These are displayed in the group centroids table. In this study, more effective have a mean of .648 while less effective produce a mean of -.648. Cases with scores near to a centroid are predicted as belonging to that group.

The classification results (Table 3.19, p. 129) reveal that 75.8 per cent respondents were classified correctly into more effective or less effective group. The overall predictive accuracy of the discriminant function is called the 'hit-ratio'. More effective were classified with slightly better accuracy (78.0%) than less effective (73.5%).

Discriminant analysis was conducted to predict whether teacher was effective or not. Predictor variables were general intelligence, social intelligence, emotional intelligence and creativity. Significant mean differences were observed for all the predictors on the depended variable. The discriminate function revealed a significant association between groups and all predictors, accounting for 29.70 per cent of between group variability, although closer analysis of the structure matrix revealed only two significant predictors, namely emotional intelligence (.951) and creativity (.344) with general intelligence and social intelligence poor predictors (Table 3.17). The cross validated classification showed that overall 75.8 per cent were correctly classified.

Discussion of Results

Results of the study show that teacher effectiveness does not relate significantly with general intelligence of secondary school teachers, yet its dependence on type of school and gender explains varied role of intelligence in explaining teacher effectiveness, i.e. more effective secondary school teachers being more intelligence than less effective secondary school teachers only in case of (i) female group of secondary school teachers and (ii) government secondary school teachers. The results of the present investigation are substantiated by the results of the studies conducted by Sharma (1977) that there is significant difference in intelligence level of government and private secondary school teachers. According to Singh (1987) the differences in the mean intelligence score in male and female teachers was also not significant. The present results further amplify previous findings by Chan (2007) which indicated that gender had a significant effect on successful intelligence that is analytical, synthetic and practical abilities.

The results of comparison of emotional intelligence in terms of teacher effectiveness, gender and type of school are suggestive of the fact that significant main effects of teacher effectiveness to explain emotional intelligence of secondary school teachers are independent each other. Hence it may be concluded that more effective secondary school teachers are emotionally more intelligent as compared to less effective secondary school teachers. These findings are in line with findings of Indu (2009) Gowdhaman and Murugan (2010), and Singaravelu (2007) who have revealed that emotional intelligence of student teachers is above average. Further Patil and Kumar (2006) and Khatoon and Sultana (2012) have stated that there is no significant difference between emotional intelligence of male and female student teachers. Recently, in a study by Kauts and Chechi (2014) it has been concluded that teachers with low emotional intelligence are less effective in teaching as compared to teachers with high emotional intelligence.

The non-significant gender difference in emotional intelligence is in line with the research findings of Petrides and Furnham (2000) who have contended that overall self-motivation estimates of emotional intelligence of males were significantly higher than the estimates of females. A recent study by Srinivason (2005) also shows that male teachers exhibit more emotional intelligence than female teachers. Males score higher on self-awareness, empathy and social skills (Jarmali *et al.*, 2008). Indu (2009) has also concluded that emotional intelligence is not affected by type of institution and gender. Schuttle *et al.* (1998) and Van Rooy and Viswas (2005), Varshney (2007) and Anari (2012) have theorized that females report significantly higher emotional intelligence than males.

In the present study emotional intelligence of secondary school teachers is not affected by type of school i.e. Government and private. Such a finding does not find corroboration in research findings of (Amirtha and Kadhirawan, 2006; Gowdhaman and Murugan, 2010; Begum, 2014) who hold that type of institution influences emotional intelligence of school teachers. Findings of present study can be more meaningfully seen and understood in the light of findings of Mandell and Phawani, 2003; Chouhan and Bhatnagar, 2003; Punia, 2005; Penrose, Perry and Ball, 2007; Neelkandan, 2007; Sameer, 2008; Basu and Saxena, 2010 and more recently those of Kauts and Chechi, 2011 and 2014. These research findings show that women are likely to score high on emotional intelligence as compared to men and government and private school teachers do not differ in their emotional intelligence.

More effective teachers are significantly more emotionally intelligent than less effective teachers. The possible explanation for this may be that the more effective teachers are more secure in their ability to perceive and respond to their own emotional needs. They are in a better emotional state to handle different situations in life effectively. They are able to strike a balance between emotions and reasons and are empathetic and compassionate towards others. Emotional intelligence skills are important to work more effectively and to impart knowledge to students as well as in maintaining a cordial relationship with colleagues and others. Brophy and Good (1986) have also emphasized the role of emotional skills in effective teaching. In their study they have concluded that students prefer teachers who listen to their arguments and assist them in working out their problems. They want teachers who believe in mutual respect and are willing to talk about their own personal lives and experiences. According to them, through appropriate self-disclosure teachers become ordinary human beings in the eyes of students. Being available to students and showing deep understanding of students legitimizes the teacher as a person when he or she demonstrates genuine concern and empathy towards students. Effective teachers care for students first as individuals and secondly as students. They respect each student as an individual. Effective and successful teachers consistently emphasize their love for children as one key element of their success. Glaser-Zikuda and Fu (2008) confirm the assumption that perceived teacher competencies have an impact on students' emotions. Emotional climate, care about students, interaction with students, learning activities, discussion have been reported for effective teachers than ineffective teachers (Walls *et al.* 2002). Other personality characteristics of effective teachers are accepting and posing challenges, sense of humour, enthusiasm, creativity, caring demeanour, ability to explain complicated material well, and possessing flexible instructional style (Mailkow, 2005).

Effective teachers know how to manage a classroom effectively and maintain a productive learning environment. They make use of humour and expression of positive emotions rather than of predominance of negative emotions (Turner *et al.* 2003). Teachers' mastery over social and emotional challenges makes teaching more enjoyable and a teacher feels more efficacious (Goddard *et al.*, 2004). In a the realm of education where success is dependent upon team work, collaboration and good interpersonal relationships, the importance of emotional intelligence, which reflects one's ability to interact with others in an effective manner may be emphasized.

Further, Tiddlie and Lieu (2008) have forwarded the thesis that teachers in more effective schools exhibit more effective teaching practices than those in less effective schools. Effective teachers have friendly, mature relationships with their students, and demonstrate caring, humour and commitment (Ayres *et al.* 2004). All teachers who demonstrate effective and constructive social skills are perceived as effective teachers (Juchniewicz, 2010). Effective teachers give feedback in a manner that is supportive and encouraging to students (Peart and Campbell, 1999). As a matter of fact, social skills are fundamental to any profession that requires interaction among people and within an organization. Teaching is no exception, because clear communication of expectations, encouragement and caring are fundamental to the very idea of teaching. Effective teachers respond to questions and comments in a way that promote positive relationships and foster an atmosphere of high expectations within the classroom. In the eyes of students, the teachers' affective characteristics are often of primary concern. An effective teacher must constantly build a climate of support and encouragement to ensure that students participate actively in the two way teaching and learning process. Effective teachers have a good sense of humour and are willing to share jokes (NASSP, 1997 and Peart and Campbell, 1999).

The non-significant main effect of teacher effectiveness is not dependent upon gender and type of school to explain social intelligence among secondary school teachers. In a nutshell, teacher effectiveness does not relate significantly with social intelligence of secondary school teachers. Teacher effectiveness, gender and type of school do not effect significantly social intelligence of secondary school teachers. The findings of this investigation are in conformity with the findings of Lovejoy (2008) and Suresh and Rao (2009) which show that female and male teachers did not show significant difference on the overall level of social intelligence. The findings of the present study are contradictory to the findings of the studies by Jain (1998), Babu (2007), Agrawal (2003) and Kaur (2012) that proved that gender based comparison of social intelligence is proved significant. Female subjects have high social awareness and social skills (Vasilova and Baumgaither, 2004). Male student teachers have high social intelligence than female student teachers (Nikose, 2010).

More effective secondary school teachers have higher level of creativity than less effective secondary school teachers. This finding is true only in the case of male teachers and not significantly true in the case of female teachers. On the other hand male secondary school teachers are more creative than female secondary school teachers in more effective group of secondary school teachers and this finding is reverse in less effective secondary school teachers whereas female secondary school teachers are more creative than male secondary school teachers. The male and female secondary school teachers differ significantly across teacher effectiveness in creativity. These findings can be seen and understood in accordance to the findings of Chadha and Sen (1981) who have stated that boys and girls differ significantly on fluency factor but no significant difference exists in other creativity measures i.e. flexibility, originality and elaboration. On the composite creativity scores also there is no significant difference between the groups. These results are substantiated by a number of studies conducted earlier, such as (Jarial, 1981; Raina, 1982; Chaudhary, 1983; Desai, 1987; John, 1988; Gautam, 1990; Santhana, 1990 and Mary, 1992) where boys and girls were found to be identical on creativity scores. Aggarwal and Aggarwal (1999) also contended that boys have been found to be more creative than girls whereas Goyal and Singh (2010) has stated that girls have been found to be superior to boys in language creativity.

These findings are not consistent with the findings of Kaur (1998); Reddy and Geethanath (1999); Pal (2001) which hold that male and female teacher do not differ in their creativity. Further these findings are in contradiction with the findings of Kaur (2001) that private institutions teacher educators are more creative than those in government institutions.

The reason for this may be that less effective teacher's creative ability is not being identified by themselves, because many teachers do not understand and are not prepared to cope with scholarly discussion of convergent and divergent thinking. Chakraborthy (1992) has argued that no attempt is made by the teachers in Indian schools to encourage divergent thinking abilities of children. Such absence of effort to promote thinking abilities of pupils may be attributable to the scanty knowledge of teachers about the nature of talent and strategies for its development.

The reason for this may be that less effective teachers are under the impression that valuable time will be wasted and prescribed syllabus may not be completed for introduction of new teaching strategies. The society likewise expects the teacher to teach only those components which are prescribed and are useful to students for the examination. As a result even if there is a teacher who discourages rote learning and makes serious efforts to encourage creative learning by pupils his/her efforts may not endure. Consequently valuable creative potential of both teachers and students are lost. Further, creative teaching requires extra effort, flexibility and more time. However, when a teacher introduces creativity in teaching learning process, it follows the psychological process of learning, at the same time, providing stimulation, enjoyment and motivation to self-learning. There is evidence to prove that learning through creative expression leads to better retention and recall of material learnt. There is better all-round learning, confidence, a perception of success, joy and satisfaction. If children are learning through creative ways, they tend to become more involved in their work, more tolerant to ideas of others, free in expression, better motivated and curious. That is indeed the biggest reward for the teachers to get motivated and continue their efforts towards teaching for creativity (Pachaury, 2000). This in turn, can provide a more solid basis for the planning of professional training experiences that will increase teachers' effectiveness in facilitating creativity.

The argument that creative skills are necessary to make teaching more effective stimulating and fulfilling is gaining favour (Singh, 1996). Fryer (1989) suggests that if a teacher is creative it helps children to develop their creativity. When teachers are aware of and interested in creativity, children's scores for creative thinking rise sharply (Torrance 1965). Kottler *et al.* (2005) also has also discussed the importance of creativity, emotional stability as one of the element among the important human dimensions of effective teaching.

On the basis of the results pertaining to correlational analysis of teacher effectiveness with general intelligence it is concluded that teacher effectiveness is positively and significantly related with general intelligence. This finding is true in case of female and government teachers as well as the total group of secondary school teachers.

Emotional intelligence is positively and significantly related with teacher effectiveness in all groups of secondary school teachers except less effective group of secondary school teachers, thereby indicating that higher emotional intelligence means greater teacher effectiveness in the total group of school teachers as well as all sub-groups. Emotional intelligence has a stronger relationship with teacher effectiveness as compared to general and social intelligence. The reason for this could be that emotions appear to be involved in all aspects of human life. Our emotions are something that we are familiar with in our daily life, as well as something that we recognize readily in everyday situations as we read peoples' faces or body language. Ciariochi *et al.* (2001) have stated that an individual's perception, expression, understanding and management of emotions are directly related to the major life events that they have experienced. Thus, a in the overall success of a teacher, emotions can play a major role. It can be said that educators with high EI competencies are optimistic, adaptable, collaborative, confident, authoritative, open, approachable and enthusiastic (Mortiboys, 2005). They have better communication skills, better abilities for conflict resolution (Ming, 2003) and problem solving, better impulse and self-control and higher self-esteem. With higher level of motivation they are more assertive and more responsible and cope better with stress (Salami, 2010). Emotional

Intelligence provides a foundation for emotional competencies which are strong predictors of job performance as different jobs require different competencies. Haskett (2003) found a significant link between specific emotional intelligence competencies, and behaviors of effective teaching in higher education. Caruso *et al.* (2002) have expressed the opinion that when an individual works in an administrative or work environment that requires cooperation and collaboration, skills of emotional intelligence become even more essential. Emotional intelligence competencies are critical for success in most of the jobs (Cherniss, 2000). Emotional intelligence and teacher effectiveness are positively and significantly related with each other (Singh and Jha, 2012; Tajudin *et al.*, 2014; Hassan *et al.*, 2015).

Contradictory of the above discussion Witty (2004) has shown that emotional intelligence may not be predictive as IQ in career success. Unlike, traditional IQ which is thought to be a fixed characteristic, emotional intelligence is considered a learnable intelligence (Goleman, Boyatzis and Mckee, 2002).

Social intelligence is positively and significantly related to teacher effectiveness as a whole however it is applicable in case of male, private more effective teachers and total group of secondary school teachers which means social intelligence facilitates teacher effectiveness among secondary school teachers.

Social intelligence is required to facilitate teacher effectiveness because socially competent teachers have high level of social awareness. They are able to build strong and supportive relationships through mutual understanding and cooperation and can effectively negotiate solutions to conflict situations. Socially competent teachers are sensitive. They can appreciate and understand that others may have different perspectives than they do, and adopt this perspective in relationships with students, parents and colleagues. Socially competent teachers exhibit pro-social values and make responsible decisions based on an assessment of factors including how their decisions may affect themselves and others (Jennings and Greenberg, 2009).

Bagely and Keith (1924) have enumerated social intelligence behaviour such as tact, sympathy and leadership as qualities of effective teachers. Rushton *et al.* (1983) have also concluded that an effective teacher is best described as liberal, sociable, showing leadership, extroverted, non-anxious, objective, supporting, non-authoritarion, inoffensive, intelligent and aesthetically sensitive. Further Chickering and Gamson (1991) have identified traits like enthusiasm, clarity, interpersonal skills as marks of effective teachers along with knowledge of subject matter and organizational skills. Social intelligence is positively and significantly related with academic and professional dimensions of teacher effectiveness (Agrawal, 2003).

Teacher effectiveness is positively and significantly related with fluency, flexibility, originality and elaboration. Hence to increase the effectiveness of the teachers, their fluency, flexibility, originality and elaboration of ideas must be enhanced. Creativity is positively and significantly related with teacher effectiveness among secondary school teachers among all groups except more effective group of secondary school teachers. Rao (1995) in his work has come out with the same results. He has arrived at the opinion that teacher effectiveness, creativity and interpersonal relationship are related with each other. On the other hand Goyal (1973) has opined that creativity and success in teaching are positively correlated with each other. Flexibility, verbal creative thinking and elaboration in figural creative thinking have been identified to be best predictors of teaching success. Davidoritch and Milgram (2006), Kumar and Awati (2012) in their studies have also confirmed that creative thinking and teacher effectiveness are positively related with each other.

Majority of earlier studies in the area of teacher effectiveness have linked teacher effectiveness with outgoing extroverted tendencies, confidence (Soloman, 1965; Srivastava and Bhargava, 1984) emotional stability, emotional maturity, calmness, low anxiety, warm and empathetic personality (Gage, 1965); problem-solving ability (Gage, 1965; Matieson, 1974); less inhibition, control, less impulsive personality, sense of humour and flexibility.

On the basis of the above results pertaining to correlational analysis among general intelligence, social intelligence, emotional intelligence and creativity it can be concluded that general intelligence and social intelligence are positively and significantly related with each other. General intelligence and emotional intelligence are positively related, though not significantly so. General intelligence is positively related with fluency, flexibility, originality and elaboration and creativity but this relationship is not significant in case of originality and elaboration. Social intelligence and emotional intelligence are related with each other but this relationship is not significant. Social intelligence and fluency, flexibility, originality and elaboration are related with each other. Social intelligence and creativity are positively and significantly related with each other. Emotional intelligence and all dimensions of creativity fluency, flexibility, originality and elaboration are related with each other. There is significant and positive relationship between emotional intelligence and creativity.

The findings of the present study show that there is positive relationship between emotional intelligence and general intelligence but this relationship is not significant. The reason for this could be that general intelligence is a cognitive ability which focuses on facts, knowledge, mental capabilities, ability to reason and ability to solve problems. On the other hand emotional intelligence represents a collaboration of personal and social competencies that include the ability to recognize personal feelings and emotions of others and to use that information to resolve conflict and improve interactions with others. Goleman (1995) has described IQ as playing a sorting function, determining the types of jobs that individuals are capable of holding. He theorizes that IQ is a strong predictor of what job an individual can enter as well as a strong predictor of success among the general population as a whole. Emotional intelligence, on the other hand, is described by Goleman as a stronger predictor of who will excel in a particular job.

Campbell (1990) has also explored the relationship between general mental ability and emotional intelligence. He has found general mental ability to be closely related to the cognition domain of the human mind and it is primarily related to declarative knowledge (Knowledge about fact, principle, self-knowledge, goals) and parts of procedural knowledge and skills (cognitive skills, psychoticism skills, physical skills, self-management and interpersonal skills). Further Bar-On *et al.* (2003) has also elaborated the concept by saying that emotional and social intelligence are different from cognitive intelligence. Cognitive intelligence is more dependent on cortical structures that support logical reasoning, whereas emotional and social intelligence are more dependent on limbic and related neural systems that support the processing of emotions and feelings.

These findings can be seen in the light of findings of Jadhav and Patil (2010) who hold that emotional intelligence and general intelligence are not related with each other. On the other hand the study conducted by Bansal and Kaur (2011) has revealed that emotional stability and intelligence are positively related with each other.

Psychological research demonstrates that IQ is a reliable measure of cognitive capacity and is stable over time. But EQ is non-cognitive and dynamic and it can be learned or increased (Bradberry and Greaves, 2005). Goleman (1995) also believes that emotional intelligence is learnable and one can learn to control emotions to a certain degree. Bar-On (2000) defines emotional intelligence as non-cognitive intelligence that is defined as an array of emotional, personal and social abilities and skills that influence an individual's abilities to cope effectively with environmental demand and pressure. It has been reported that intelligent persons are emotionally stable (Arora, 1992; Murthy, 1966) socially mature (Mulia, 1991; Rao, 1978).

From the results it was found that general intelligence and social intelligence are related with each other. These findings are in line with the findings that social intelligence is related with general intelligence but that they have low correlation (Dodge, 1937). These results are supported by David Wechsler's study carried out in 1950s on social intelligence which sees it merely as "general intelligence applied to social situation".

The results also show that there is a positive and significant relationship between creativity and intelligence. This finding is in agreement with the findings of Chadha and Sen (1981) Aggarwal and Aggarwal (1999) and Gupta (1984) that both creativity and intelligence are considered to be cognitive aspects, they are also related on the basis of scores and a positive significant correlation is expected between the two. It is also held that persons with higher IQ are more curious, keen and observant. Therefore they show more creativity. It is often observed that there is moderate correlation between creativity and intelligence below the threshold of 120 measured IQ beyond which creativity and intelligence are seen to be apart (Sternberg and O-Hala, 2000).

From the results it can be concluded that emotional intelligence and creativity are related with each other. The reason for this could be that emotional intelligence can assist in facilitating work in helping to generate new and creative ideas as well as solutions to problems. Further emotional intelligence can help the individual to think creatively in many ways such as viewing the problem from multiple perspectives, brainstorming or generating new, original creative ideas, being innovative and finding solutions to problems, and defining and recognizing new solutions. It was also found that curiosity is a predictor of emotional intelligence (Leonard and Harvey, 2007).

Social intelligence and creativity are positively and significantly related. Singh (2007) in his study has revealed no significant difference in social intelligence between low creative and high creative adolescents and between high creative boys and high creative girls. Further it has been found that significant difference exists between low creative boys and girls in social intelligence (Gakhar *et al.* 2008). Social intelligence and creativity are related with each other. The reason may be that social ability and social responsibility, leadership, unconventional personality, orientation and task persistence such as relational, social and interpersonal behaviour are perceived as part of creative behaviour (Panda and Yadva, 2005).

Emotional intelligence and social intelligence are positively and significantly related with each other. High emotionally intelligent students are more socially competent than low emotionally intelligent students (Srivastava and Mallick, 2009). Vora (1980) found that there was a close and effective relationship between social maturity and emotional stability. Research on emotional intelligence has revealed that people who are high on emotional intelligence are happier, healthier and more successful in their relationships. They strike a balance between emotions and reasons and are aware of their own feelings. Besides they are empathetic and compassionate towards others (Raghuvansh, 2008).

From the results it was found that social and emotional intelligence are related with each other. The reason for this could be that emotional intelligence has its roots in the concept of social intelligence, first coined by E.L. Thorndike in 1920. Thorndike defined it as an ability to act wisely in human relations. Social intelligence is the ability to understand people whereas emotional intelligence is correlative ability turned inward.

The single best predictor of teacher effectiveness was emotional intelligence in total group of secondary school teachers. The second and third factors in order of importance were fluency and social intelligence. In male group of senior secondary school teachers emotional intelligence was also worked out to be single best predictor. The second and third factors worked out to be creativity, flexibility and social intelligence respectively. In female group of secondary school teachers' emotional intelligence worked out to be the best predictor followed by general intelligence. From these results it is concluded that emotional intelligence and general intelligence plays a significant role in determining teacher effectiveness among female secondary school teachers. From these results it is concluded that emotional intelligence, elaboration and general intelligence play a significant role in determining teacher effectiveness among government secondary school teachers. Emotional intelligence, fluency, social intelligence contribute to teacher effectiveness among private secondary school teaches. From above discussion it can be concluded that emotional intelligence and creativity play a significant role in determining teacher effectiveness among more effective secondary school teachers. Creativity plays a significant role in determining teacher effectiveness among less effective secondary school teachers.

The findings of present study are supported by Feist and Barron

(1996) who found that social and emotional abilities were four times more important than IQ in determining professional success and prestige. Rosenthal (1977) has found that people who were best in identifying other's emotions were more successful on their work as well as in their social lives. Emotional intelligence is significantly related to the ability to exercise personal judgement in decision-making which helps to explain why this concept is highly connected with human performance (Bar On *et al.* 2003). Emotional intelligence is a predictor of significant outcomes across different samples in a number of real world domains. It predicts social relations, workplace performance and mental and physical well-being. The relation between emotional intelligence and life outcomes suggests that emotional intelligence may valuably inform the practitioners' understanding of and interventions in human behaviour (Mayer *et al.* 2001).

In fact, in adulthood, practical intelligence appears to be more predictive of everyday competence than intelligence as assessed by traditional psychometric measures of aptitude or IQ (Willis and Schair, 1986). Indeed, social skills that promote adaptations and integration into social settings are critical throughout the life span (Sternberg and Wagner, 1986).

The reason for this could be that teachers are expected to have emotional qualities such as pro-social values, social sensitivity, action tendencies and affective states (Sibia and Mishra, 2004). Moreover teaching is a helping profession, teacher are oriented to work with teachers, students, parents and are usually capable of managing human relationships. For Rushton *et al.* (2005) an effective teacher is best described as liberal, sociable, showing leadership, extroverted, non-anxious, objective, supporting, non-authoritarian, non-defensive, intelligent and aesthetically sensitive. In the case of Sherry (1964) intelligence, emotional quality, attitude towards children and professional skills were found important predictors of teaching efficiency. Whereas Donga (1989) has expressed the opinion that attitude towards children, general ability and professional knowledge were the effective predictors for teaching efficiency of student teachers.

These findings can find support in Sutton and Wheatley (2003) who suggest that the substantial variation in teacher efficacy may result in part from variance in teachers' emotions. The extent to which teachers are able to deal effectively with their own and others' emotions can be considered as reflection of their own emotional intelligence (Atkins and Stough, 2005). Penrose *et al.* (2007) hold that emotional intelligence and status together explained 20 per cent of the variance in personal teaching efficacy and of the two, emotional intelligence makes the greater contribution to the predicted model. Emotional intelligence was able to contribute 23.5 per cent of variance in explaining teacher effectiveness (Tajudin *et al.*, 2014). Singh and Jha (2012) and Ghosh (2015) have also concluded that emotional stability, self-motivation, managing relations, self-awareness and integrity emerged as best predictors of teacher effectiveness.

From the results it was found that general intelligence is not a predictor of teacher effectiveness among all groups except female secondary school teachers. These findings are supportive of the findings of Nair (1974) who found that intelligence cannot be considered as a predictive criterion for teaching ability.

The amount of contribution of the predictors which have been proved effective for predicting teaching efficiency was not remarkable in total variance of criterion variable of teaching effectiveness. It was emotional intelligence (14.43%), fluency (2.90%), social intelligence (0.6%) for total sample of secondary school teachers. It shows that the set of predictors selected in the present study were not sufficient. It means that no single teacher attribute or characteristic is adequate to explain effective teacher. The reason may be that all other variables general intelligence, emotional intelligence, social intelligence and creativity have positive inter-correlation with each other. Generally, the findings do not indicate any particular behaviour which would lead to higher levels of teacher effectiveness. Rather, a combination of significant but modest or weak relationships emerged. There must be some other variables also which can predict teacher effectiveness efficiently.

It can be concluded that emotional intelligence positively and directly influences teacher effectiveness of the teachers. General intelligence, creativity and social intelligence mediated the indirect effects of teacher effectiveness of the secondary school teachers. Emotional intelligence, general intelligence, creativity and social intelligence directly and indirectly increases teacher effectiveness. Despite the lack of direct influence of social intelligence and creativity on teacher effectiveness has considerably high influence on all intervening variables, so its effects were indirect in nature. Teachers' interpersonal skills at identifying and supporting students' emotions as well as their intrapersonal understanding and expression of their own emotions are integral to effective teaching (Goleman, 1995; Hargreaves, 2001). Rosenthal and his colleagues at Harvard discovered over two decades ago that people who were best at identifying others' emotions were more successful in their work as well as in their social lives (Rosenthal, 1977). Significant relationships were found between emotional intelligence and job performance by Dulewicz and Higs (2003). D'Costa and Deshmukh (2010) found that existential and interpersonal intelligence have a marked effect on teacher effectiveness. Walter and Marcel (2013) used path analysis and concluded that emotional intelligence had a significant indirect effect on the success of the student teachers in their practical work, a positive effect in the regulation and utilization of emotions and a negative effect in expression of emotions. The ability to utilize emotions is important for teachers who need to develop abilities to control their inner world on the one hand (emotions, thoughts and beliefs) and to be capable of instructing, teaching and advising their students within educational frameworks on the other hand. These abilities help improve their teaching abilities and also add a value of content knowledge and correct teaching methods (Gibbs, 2003). Teaching requires recruiting emotional capabilities (Hochschild, 1983): the conscious ability to separate the teachers' personal emotions and the intelligent emotional response, the ability to avoid expressing emotions of freedom and liberty, and being able to utilize and regulate emotions in his educational position.

Testing of Hypotheses

It may be concluded on the basis of these results that the type of school has an effect on general intelligence of secondary school teachers. Government secondary school teachers exhibit significant higher level of intelligence than private secondary school teachers but only in case of more effective teachers. More effective secondary school teachers exhibit significantly higher level of general intelligence than less effective secondary school teachers only in case of female group and results are reverse though not significant in case of male secondary school teachers. Female secondary school teachers exhibit significantly higher level of general intelligence than male secondary school teachers only in case of more effective secondary school teachers and results are reverse though not significant in case of less effective secondary school teachers.

> Hence, first hypothesis, *"There is significant mean difference in general intelligence of more and less effective secondary school teachers across gender and type of school"*, is accepted in female and government secondary school teachers but rejected in case of male and private secondary school teachers.

Emotional intelligence of secondary school teachers do not differ significantly in terms of gender and type of school. Hence it may be concluded that more effective secondary school teachers are emotionally more intelligent as compared to less effective secondary school teachers.

> Hence second hypothesis, *"There is significant mean difference in emotional intelligence of more and less effective secondary school teachers across gender and type of school"*, is accepted in more effective group of secondary school teachers but rejected in its applicability across gender and type of school.

The non-significant main effect of teacher effectiveness is not dependent upon gender and type of school to explain social intelligence among secondary school teachers. In a nutshell, teacher effectiveness does not relate significantly with social intelligence of secondary school teachers.

> Hence third hypothesis, *"There is significant mean difference in social intelligence of more and less effective secondary school teachers across gender and type of school"* is rejected.

More effective secondary school teachers have higher level of creativity than less effective secondary school teachers. This finding is true only in the case of male teachers and not significantly true in the case of female teachers. On the other hand male secondary school teachers are more creative than female secondary school teachers in more effective group of secondary school teachers and this finding is reverse in less effective secondary school teachers whereas female secondary school teachers are more creative than male secondary school teachers.

> Hence, fourth hypothesis, *"There is significant mean difference in creativity of more and less effective secondary school teachers across gender and type of school"*, is accepted in case of male and more effective group of secondary school teachers but rejected across type of school.

On the basis of the results pertaining to correlational analysis of teacher effectiveness with general intelligence it is concluded that teacher effectiveness is positively and significantly related with general intelligence. This finding is true in case of female and government teachers as well as the total group of secondary school teachers. Emotional intelligence is positively and significantly related with teacher effectiveness in all groups of secondary school teachers except less effective group of secondary school teachers. Social intelligence is positively and significantly related to teacher effectiveness as a whole however it is applicable in case of male, private more effective teachers and total group of secondary school teachers. Creativity is positively and significantly related with teacher effectiveness among secondary school teachers among all groups except more effective group of secondary school teachers

> Hence fourth hypothesis "*There is significant relationship between general intelligence, emotional intelligence, social intelligence and creativity with teacher effectiveness of secondary school teachers*" is accepted in total group but not in all sub groups.

On the basis of the above results pertaining to correlational analysis among general intelligence, social intelligence, emotional intelligence and creativity it can be concluded that general intelligence and social intelligence are positively and significantly related with each other. General intelligence and emotional intelligence are positively related, though not significantly so. General intelligence is positively related with fluency, flexibility, originality and elaboration and creativity but this relationship is not significant in case of originality and elaboration. Social intelligence and emotional intelligence are related with each other but this relationship is not significant. Social intelligence and fluency, flexibility, originality and elaboration are related with each other. Social intelligence and creativity are positively and significantly related with each other. Emotional intelligence and all dimensions of creativity fluency, flexibility, originality and elaboration are related with each other. There is significant and positive relationship between emotional intelligence and creativity.

> Hence fifth hypothesis "*There is significant inter correlation between general intelligence, emotional intelligence, social intelligence and creativity among secondary school teachers*" is accepted in case of general intelligence and social intelligence, general intelligence and creativity with all its dimensions except originality and elaboration, social intelligence and emotional intelligence with creativity and its dimensions. However, this hypothesis is rejected in the case of inter-correlation between general and emotional intelligence; general intelligence and originality, elaboration; social and emotional intelligence because all these correlations are positive but not significant.

From results it is clear that emotional intelligence is a predictor of teacher effectiveness in all sub groups such as total groups of teachers, male, female, private, government and more effective group of secondary school teachers but it did not emerge as significant predictor only in less effective group of secondary school teachers.

From the results of present study pertaining to psychological predictors, it is evident that emotional intelligence, social intelligence, general intelligence, fluency, flexibility, elaboration and creativity play a significant role in determining teacher effectiveness among all groups.

> Hence sixth hypothesis "*General intelligence, emotional intelligence, social intelligence and creativity will be significant predictors of teacher effectiveness of secondary school teachers*" is accepted.

It has been concluded that emotional intelligence positively and directly influences teacher effectiveness of the teachers. General intelligence, creativity and social intelligence mediated the indirect effects of teacher effectiveness of the secondary school teachers. Emotional intelligence, general intelligence, creativity and social intelligence directly and indirectly increases teacher effectiveness. Despite the lack of direct influence of social intelligence and creativity on teacher effectiveness has considerably high influence on all intervening variables, so its effects were indirect in nature.

> Hence seventh hypothesis "*General intelligence, emotional intelligence, social intelligence and creativity will directly or indirectly affect teacher effectiveness of secondary school teachers*" is accepted.

The discriminate function revealed a significant association between groups and all predictors, accounting for 27.32 per cent of between group variability, although closer analysis of the structure matrix revealed only two significant predictors, namely emotional intelligence and creativity with general intelligence and social intelligence poor predictors.

> Hence seventh hypothesis "*General intelligence, emotional intelligence, social intelligence and creativity will significantly discriminate more and less effective secondary school teachers*" accepted in case of emotional intelligence and creativity but rejected in case of general and social intelligence.

TABLES

Table 3.1: Descriptive Analysis of Teacher Effectiveness, General, Emotional, Social Intelligence and Creativity of Secondary School Teachers (N = 850)

Descriptive Statistics	*Teacher Effectiveness*	*General Intelligence*	*Emotional Intelligence*	*Social Intelligence*	*Creativity*
Mean	308.78	44.95	140.70	108.65	398.50
Median	312.86	45.50	142.82	110.30	391.76
Mode	320.98	46.60	148.06	113.60	378.28
SD	27.07	7.30	16.12	8.43	52.86
Skewness	–0.450	–0.226	–0.390	–0.587	0.383
Kurtosis	0.280	0.250	0.250	0.270	0.260
Minimum	220	27	80	73	301.85
Maximum	345	60	170	138	574

Table 3.2: Distribution of More and Less Effective Secondary School Teachers (Gender and Type of School)

Groups		*Sub-Groups*	*N*	*%*
Teacher Effectiveness		More Effective	200	50.00
		Less Effective	200	50.00
Less Effective	Gender	Male	104	52.00
		Female	96	48.00
	Type of School	Private	106	53.00
		Government	94	47.00
More Effective	Gender	Male	111	55.50
		Female	89	44.50
	Type of School	Private	80	40.00
		Government	120	60.00

Table 3.3: Descriptive Analysis of General, Emotional, Social Intelligence and Creativity among More and Less Effective Secondary School Teachers

Descriptive Statistics	*General Intelligence*		*Emotional Intelligence*		*Social Intelligence*		*Creativity*	
	More Effective	*Less Effective*	*More Effective*	*Less Effective*	*More Effective*	*Less Effective*	*More Effective*	*Less Effective*
Mean	44.55	44.05	150.55	132.80	109.60	107.10	416.25	384.75
Median	44.89	45.89	153.00	133.76	111.20	108.98	399.50	376.42
Mode	45.58	49.69	157.91	135.68	114.40	112.74	366.00	359.76
SD	7.21	7.59	14.40	15.25	9.59	10.21	59.50	53.10
Skewness	–0.141	–0.727	–0.510	–0.188	–0.500	–0.552	0.281	0.470
Kurtosis	0.236	0.239	0.253	0.270	0.260	0.270	0.250	0.260
Minimum	30	27	80	80	80	73	306.58	301.85
Maximum	60	59	170	167	123	138	574	550.77

Table 3.4: Distribution of Sample in Terms A×B×C Factorial Design

	Teacher Effectiveness (A)			
	Less Effective (A1)		*More Effective (A2)*	
	Male (B1)	*Female (B2)*	*Male (B1)*	*Female (B2)*
Private (C1)	56	50	48	32
Government(C2)	48	46	63	57
Total	**104**	**96**	**111**	**89**
Total	**200**		**200**	

Table 3.5: Means and SDs of General, Emotional, Social Intelligence and Creativity of Secondary School Teachers in Terms of Gender X Type of School X Teacher Effectiveness (N = 240)

Type of School	*Gender*	*Teacher Effective-ness*		*General Intelligence*	*Emotional Intelligence*	*Social Intelligence*	*Creativity*
Govt.	Male	Less	Mean	45.00	135.64	108.84	368.45
		Effective	S.D	6.89	17.68	10.54	43.22
		More	Mean	44.50	154.16	109.50	422.07
		Effective	S.D	8.23	13.07	9.53	61.37
	Female	Less	Mean	45.16	132.84	106.67	403.48
		Effective	S.D	6.14	15.68	10.59	50.90
		More	Mean	47.83	150.30	104.50	397.96
		Effective	S.D	6.03	11.73	10.00	48.22
Private	Male	Less	Mean	45.00	134.17	106.17	380.87
		Effective	S.D	6.78	11.64	12.67	68.21
		More	Mean	39.67	150.63	109.84	432.64
		Effective	S.D	7.00	10.84	11.78	65.22
	Female	Less	Mean	44.50	130.17	108.84	378.75
		Effective	S.D	7.76	15.41	7.61	62.83
		More	Mean	43.83	148.50	110.50	409.09
		Effective	S.D	6.95	12.95	12.00	58.42

Table 3.6: Mean Performance of General, Emotional, Social Intelligence and Creativity among Secondary School Teachers In terms Of Gender x Type of School X Teacher Effectiveness

	Groups	*General Intelligence*	*Emotional Intelligence*	*Social Intelli-gence*	*Creati-vity*
AXB					
Male (B1)	Total	43.54	143.69	108.58	401.00
	Less Effective	45.00	135.00	107.50	374.66
	More Effective	42.08	152.39	109.67	427.35
Female (B2)	Total	45.33	143.28	107.62	397.31
	Less Effective	44.83	131.50	107.75	391.11
	More Effective	45.83	149.40	107.50	403.52
AXC					
Less Effective (A1)	Total	44.91	133.25	107.62	382.88
	Male	45.00	135.00	107.50	374.66
	Female	44.83	131.50	107.75	391.11
More Effective (A2)	Total	43.95	150.89	108.58	415.43
	Male	42.08	152.39	109.67	427.35
	Female	45.83	149.40	107.50	403.52
BXC					
Male (B1)	Total	43.54	143.70	108.58	401.00
	Govt.	44.75	145.00	109.17	395.26
	Private	42.33	142.40	108.00	406.75
Female (B2)	Total	45.33	140.75	107.62	397.31
	Govt.	46.44	141.75	104.56	400.72
	Private	44.16	139.33	109.67	393.92

Table 3.7: Summary of Analysis of Variance (Gender X Type of School X Teacher Effectiveness) on General, Emotional, Social Intelligence and Creativity of Secondary School Teachers

Source of Variance	*General Intelligence*				*Emotional Intelligence*				*Social Intelligence*				*Creativity*			
	SS	***df***	***MS***	***F-ratio***	***SS***	***df***	***MS***	***F-ratio***	***SS***	***df***	***MS***	***F-ratio***	***SS***	***df***	***MS***	***F-ratio***
Teacher Effectiveness	55.01	1	55.01	1.23	118675.47	1	118675.47	95.46**	76.34	1	76.34	0.64	63573.08	1	63573.08	20.08**
Gender	191.71	1	191.71	4.30*	632.78	1	632.78	3.23	76.91	1	76.91	0.65	814.64	1	814.64	0.26
Type of School	337.73	1	337.73	7.57**	350.66	1	350.66	1.79	149.51	1	149.51	1.26	331.42	1	331.42	0.11
Teacher Effectiveness x Gender	229.91	1	229.91	5.15*	3.89	1	3.89	0.02	66.83	1	66.83	0.564	24347.45	1	24347.45	7.69*
Gender x Type of School	0.36	1	0.36	0.01	1.99	1	1.99	0.01	392.65	1	392.65	3.31	5017.59	1	5017.59	1.58
Teacher Effectiveness x Type of School	250.30	1	250.30	5.61*	4.26	1	4.26	0.02	153.83	1	153.83	1.29	4335.76	1	4335.76	1.37
Teacher Effectiveness x Gender x Type of School	8.07	1	8.07	0.181	27.30	1	27.30	0.14	22.73	1	22.73	0.192	5330.69	1	5330.69	1.68
Within	10341.41	232	44.57		45384.76	232	195.62		27457.95	232	118.49		734224.43	232	3164.76	
Total	**11415.31**	**239**			**65081.11**	**239**			**28395.95**	**239**			**837975.06**	**239**		

* Significant at 0.05 level.

** Significant at 0.01 level.

Table 3.8: The t-values of Testing Significance of Mean Difference on General Intelligence in Teacher Effectiveness × Gender (A×B) Interaction

Group Comparison	*Mean*	*MD*	*t-value*
Male Secondary School Teachers			
More Effective	42.08	2.92	2.01*
Less Effective	45.00		
Female Secondary School Teachers			
More Effective	45.83	1.00	0.79
Less Effective	44.83		
More Effective Secondary School Teachers			
Male	42.08	3.75	2.06*
Female	45.83		
Less Effective Secondary School Teachers			
Male	45.00	1.83	0.096
Female	44.83		

* Significant at 0.05 level.

Table 3.9: The t-values of Testing Significance of Mean Difference on General Intelligence in Teacher Effectiveness × Type of School (A × C) Interaction

Group Comparison	*Mean*	*MD*	*t-value*
Less Effective Secondary School Teachers			
Private	44.75	0.33	0.184
Government	45.08		
More Effective Secondary School Teachers			
Private	41.75	4.41	2.43*
Government	46.16		
Private Secondary School Teachers			
More Effective	41.75	3.00	1.64
Less Effective	44.75		
Government Secondary School Teachers			
More Effective	46.16	1.08	0.91
Less Effective	45.08		

*Significant at 0.05 level.

Table 3.10: The t-value Testing Significance of Mean Difference on Creativity in Teacher Effectiveness × Gender (A×B) Interaction

Group Comparison	*Mean*	*MD*	*t-value*
Male Secondary School Teachers			
More Effective	427.35	52.69	7.20**
Less Effective	374.66		
Female Secondary School Teachers			
More Effective	403.52	12.41	1.80
Less Effective	391.11		
More Effective Secondary School Teachers			
Male	427.35	23.83	3.28**
Female	403.52		
Less Effective Secondary School Teachers			
Male	374.66	16.45	2.37*
Female	391.11		

* Significant at 0.05 level, ** Significant at 0.01 level.

Table 3.11: Coefficients of Correlation of Teacher Effectiveness with General, Emotional, Social Intelligence and Creativity among Secondary School Teachers

Groups	*G.I.*	*E.I.*	*S.I.*	*F*	*Fli*	*Ori*	*E*	*C*
Total	0.072*	0.394**	0.130**	0.201**	0.149**	0.111**	0.180**	0.210**
Male	0.016	0.413**	0.169**	0.259**	0.176**	0.184**	0.212**	0.261**
Female	0.146**	0.374**	0.080	0.124*	0.115*	0.013	0.142**	0.138**
Government	0.154**	0.422**	0.081	0.157**	0.101*	0.019	0.198**	0.159**
Private	0.022	0.349**	0.201**	0.201**	0.149**	0.196**	0.149**	0.249**
More Effective	0.080	0.184*	0.149**	0.078	0.102	0.104	0.066	0.102
Less Effective	0.076	0.101	0.066	0.174*	0.132	0.162*	0.126	0.188*

* Significant at 0.05 Level, ** Significant at 0.01 Level

Note: G.I. = General Intelligence, E.I. = Emotional Intelligence, S.I. = Social Intelligence, F = Fluency, Fli = Flexibility, Ori = Originality, E = Elaboration, C = Creativity.

Table 3.12: Inter-correlation of General Intelligence, Social Intelligence, Emotional Intelligence and Creativity among Total Group of Secondary School Teachers (N = 850)

	G.I.	*S.I.*	*E.I.*	*Fluency*	*Flexibility*	*Originality*	*Elaboration*	*Creativity*
G.I.	–	0.085**	0.042	0.105**	0.064*	0.027	0.029	0.087**
S.I.	–	–	0.051	0.269**	0.257**	0.124**	0.130**	0.274**
E.I.	–	–	–	0.073*	0.087**	0.082**	0.141**	0.108**
Fluency	–	–	–	–	0.695**	0.355**	0.412**	0.901**
Flexibility	–	–	–	–	–	0.648**	0.462**	0.893**
Originality	–	–	–	–	–	–	0.375**	0.638**
Elaboration	–	–	–	–	–	–	–	0.625**

* Significant at 0.05 level, ** Significant at 0.01 level.

Note: G.I. = General Intelligence, S.I. = Social Intelligence, E.I. = Emotional Intelligence

Table 3.13: Contribution of General Intelligence, Emotional Intelligence, Social Intelligence and Creativity to Teacher Effectiveness among Secondary School Teachers

Groups	*Variables*	*R*	*R2*	*Adjusted R2*	*R2 Change*	*Variance*
Total (850)	Emotional Intelligence	0.380	0.144	0.143	-	14.43%
	Fluency	0.416	0.173	0.171	0.029	2.90%
	Social Intelligence	0.423	0.179	0.176	0.006	0.60%
Male (450)	Emotional Intelligence	0.389	0.151	0.149	-	14.90%
	Creativity	0.442	0.196	0.192	0.045	4.50%
	Flexibility	0.456	0.208	0.202	0.012	1.20%
	Social Intelligence	0.464	0.215	0.208	0.007	0.70%
Female (400)	Emotional Intelligence	0.372	0.138	0.136	-	13.6%
	General Intelligence	0.391	0.153	0.149	0.019	1.90%
Government (450)	Emotional Intelligence	0.399	0.160	0.158	-	15.08%
	Elaboration	0.426	0.182	0.178	0.02	2.00%
	General Intelligence	0.444	0.197	0.191	0.013	1.30%
Private (400)	Emotional Intelligence	0.343	0.118	0.115	-	11.50%
	Fluency	0.410	0.168	0.164	0.049	4.90%
	Social Intelligence	0.429	0.184	0.178	0.014	1.40%
More Effective(200)	Emotional Intelligence	0.167	0.28	0.023	-	2.30%
	Creativity	0.222	0.049	0.040	0.021	2.10%
Less Effective(200)	Creativity	0.170	0.029	0.024	-	2.40%

Table 3.14: Direct, Indirect and B Values on Teacher Effectiveness among Secondary School Teachers

	r	*β Values*	*Direct Effect (%)*	*Indirect Effect (%)*	*Importance*
General Intelligence vs Teacher Effectiveness	0.07	0.051	72.85	27.14	4
Social Intelligence vs Teacher Effectiveness	0.127	0.078	61.41	38.58	3
Emotional Intelligence	0.380	0.361	95	5	1
Creativity vs. TE	0.208	0.140	67.30	32.69	2

Multiple Correlation (R2)= r x β values

= 0.07 x 0.051 + 0.127 x 0.078 + 0.380 x 0.361 + 0.208 x 0.140 = 0.18

e = 1 – R_2 = 1 – 0.18 = 0.82

Table 3.15: Tests of Equality of Group Means

	Wilks' Lambda	*F*	*df1*	*df2*	*Sig.*
General Intelligence	.998	.697	1	398	.404
Social Intelligence	.981	7.750	1	398	.006
Emotional Intelligence	.723	152.108	1	398	.000
Creativity	.952	19.885	1	398	.000

Table 3.16: Standardized Canonical Discriminant Function Coefficients of Teacher Effectiveness

Independent Variables	*Discriminant Function Coefficients*
General Intelligence	.052
Social Intelligence	.061
Emotional Intelligence	.931
Creativity	.285

Table 3.17: Structure Matrix Correlations with Teacher Effectiveness

Independent Variables	*Correlation*
Emotional Intelligence	.951
Creativity	.344
Social Intelligence	.215
General Intelligence	.064

Table 3.18: Canonical Discriminant Function Coefficients of Teacher Effectiveness

Independent Variables	*Coefficients*
General Intelligence	.007
Social Intelligence	.006
Emotional Intelligence	.063
Creativity	.005
(Constant)	–11.953
Un-standard Coefficients	

Table 3.19: Classification Results

		TE	*Predicted Group Membership*		*Total*
			1	2	
Original	Count	More Effective	156	44	200
		Less Effective	53	147	200
	%	More Effective	78.0	22.0	100.0
		Less Effective	26.5	73.5	100.0
Cross-validateda	Count	More Effective	155	45	200
		Less Effective	55	145	200
	%	More Effective	77.5	22.5	100.0
		Less Effective	27.5	72.5	100.0

a. Cross validation is done only for those cases in the analysis. In cross validation, each case is classified by the functions derived from all cases other than that case.

b. 75.8% of original grouped cases correctly classified.

c. 75.0% of cross-validated grouped cases correctly classified.

4

The Way Forward

Recommendations and Suggestions

The whole educational process revolves round the teacher. Teacher plays an indispensable role not as a mere transmitter of knowledge and culture but also as an agent of social change. It is the responsibility of the teacher to guide and inspire students, to inculcate values in consonance with our cultural heritage and our social objectives in the ever changing socio-economic order.

Thus an effective teacher must be a good human being as s/he must have elements of human dimension along with other professional characteristics. A teacher applies what s/he knows and understands and can act for the betterment of the society not only when s/he stands in front of the classroom but also as s/he walks through life. The teacher education system through its initial and continuing professional development programmes is expected to ensure an adequate supply of professionally competent teachers to run the nation's schools. Initial teacher education especially, has a major part to play in the making of a teacher. It marks the initiation of novice entrant to the calling and as such has tremendous potential to imbue the would-be teacher with the aspirations, knowledge-base, repertoire of pedagogic capacities and humane attitudes (NCFTE, 2009). Teachers need to be prepared to care for children, enjoy to be with them, seek knowledge, own responsibility towards the society and work to build a better world. They must also develop sensitivity to the problems of the learners and demonstrate commitment to justice and zeal for social reconstruction. The programme should engage teachers with children in real contexts rather than teach them about children through theories alone. It should help them understand the psycho-social attributes and needs of learners, their special abilities and characteristics, their preferred methods as part of the training of teacher educators.

In order to achieve high goals and expectations of education in the present era, the interventions for inclusion and development of social-emotional intelligence skills in teacher preparation programmes are needed. Further, development of the creative thinking abilities is the heart and soul of the achievements of even the most fundamental educational objectives. Hence series of recommendations are made on the basis of results of the study:

1. For increasing teacher effectiveness of private school teachers, there should be change in managerial ideology, a healthy presence of personal relationships and democratic school environment. Government should take appropriate steps for securing, nurturing and retraining professional teachers, with the ultimate goal of utilizing their position in the education to deliver goods in effective manner.
2. It is true that intelligence is inherited but still some part of it can be acquired also. In the schools, teachers should be engaged in higher order mental exercises, so that their intellect is further polished and enhanced.
3. Less effective secondary school teachers should be given training for improving emotional intelligence which includes management training, communication and empathy training, conflict resolution and stress management training as well as self-management training. Emotional intelligence is a factor which is developed and nourished depending upon environmental experiences provided by parents, teachers and society. The teacher can play a pivotal role in improving the emotional intelligence among the students by providing a suitable environment in which they can master their emotions. So it may be suggested that emotional intelligence should be incorporated into teacher education programmes and school education curriculum. It should also be used as a tool for the selection and recruitment of teachers. It is also suggested that seminars, workshops and refresher courses should be organized to enhance the emotional intelligence of in-service teachers and teacher educators.
4. It is necessary to educate school teachers about the relevance of social intelligence in the workplace. Education policy should provide a framework to develop and enhance their ability to interact with others. There should be teacher exchange programmes for government school teachers. There should be

more community involvement in the form of parent teacher association. There should be regular meetings between faculty members, teachers, principals, educational administrators for implementing all the desirable new aspects being introduced in educational policy in schools.

5. For nurturing creative ability among school teachers, there should be no imposition of any authority on them. They should be free to express their views in all decision making activities in schools. The school teachers should be encouraged to use the discovery method or problem-solving method their teaching.
6. From the results it was found that most of the teachers have been perceived as more effective. In the light of this finding it may be suggested that NCERT, SCERT and DIETs and teachers themselves should provide the guiding principles in assessing teacher effectiveness through well-designed and professionally conducted appraisals. Teachers need to be convinced as to the desirability of accepting such assessment, since it provides an opportunity for remedial inputs for both themselves and their institutions.
7. Teacher effectiveness and emotional intelligence are integral factors that improve the quality of teaching. Teachers having high level of emotional intelligence and teacher efficiency are active in their orientation to students' work and life. Hence, it is time to incorporate a set of programmes in teacher education programmes for developing emotional skills and knowledge simultaneously, enhancing efficacy of teachers. Creativity and social intelligence are positively related. So teachers must be provided freedom to respond, think and act which in turn will help in the development of their creative potential. Being creative, they will be in better positions to deal with complex social situations.
8. There is need to redraft teacher education courses dealing with totally specialized knowledge, specialized skills and inherent code of ethics. It can be done by having good theoretical base of philosophy, psychology or such other subjects that they should create a body of knowledge so that the future teachers start philosophizing or thinking psychologically with the aim of developing their effectiveness.
9. There should be proper synchronization between the activities of the teacher education institutions and those of schools,

resulting in adequate practical experiences at the training stage. The teacher education system needs to give practical shape to the critical role of teacher education in the context of providing a good quality school education for all.

10. In a workplace dealing with dissemination of education where success is dependent upon team work, collaboration and good interpersonal relationships, the importance of emotional intelligence, which reflects one's ability to interact with others in an effective manner, may be emphasized. National Curriculum Framework for Teacher Education-2009 also recommended that there is need to prepare professional and humane teachers. Students want teachers who listen to their arguments and assist them in working out their problems. They want teachers who hold mutual respect and are willing to talk about their experiences. Through appropriate self-disclosure teachers becomes humane in the eyes of students. Being available to student and showing deep understanding of students' needs legitimizes the teacher as a person as he/she demonstrates genuine concern and empathy toward students. Classroom behaviour should be intelligence friendly where teaching learning process is governed by what is known about developing the intellectual potential of human beings. It is friendly to growth patterns of human intellect and friendly to the learner in fostering intelligent behaviour for problem solving, decision making and creative thinking. The intelligence friendly classroom serves as a caring companion and useful guide to the intellect of each person in it.
11. The present analysis suggests that emotional intelligence has the potential to contribute to effective teaching. He/she should have adequate realization of the importance of being able to express feelings, being able to induce feelings in others and even having the fact of knowledge of how and why emotions are tied up with cultural forms.
12. Above all the attitude of teachers is the most important characteristic for fostering creativity. To a large extent, creativity is not just a matter of thinking in a certain way, but rather it is an attitude towards life (Sternberg and Lubart, 1995, 1996). As we know that schools need and are looking for creative ideas with creative persons to help young generations to grow as creative individuals with innovative ideas. So an attempt should be made

to inculcate such traits in the teacher training. Developing positive thinking, opening lines of communication, self-esteem, discipline, personality development, developing positive perception level, thinking reasoning, independence in assigning certain work and above all, timely appreciation for better work go a long way in developing creativity in person, both the teacher and the being taught.

In nut shell, it may be recommended that socio-psychological environment of a school needs to be honed for enhancing teacher effectiveness and all other positively related factors, such as general, social and emotional intelligence as well as creative aspect of human intellect. It is also recommended that teacher education programmes need to address all these issues related with teacher effectiveness, to provide a continuous and effective academic support to school education.

Suggestions

On the basis of the major findings and the gaps found during the process of research, following are some of the potential areas which need attention and further study.

1. Similar studies can be done on elementary school teachers, teacher educators and teacher trainees.
2. Teaching methods and techniques play an important role in the development of creativity. In this context it will be worthwhile to undertake some studies for developing instructional strategies on the basis of findings reported here in the volume.
3. Another area that needs attention of future researches is that of inner experience, motivation, teacher success teaching style, organization climate as related to creativity.
4. More research is needed to determine the exact connection of emotional intelligence, personal constructs and if certain models or measures of emotional intelligence are accounting for additional variance in performance or behaviour of school teachers over and above that of personality factors.
5. Considering the debate regarding the validity and applicability of I.Q. tests, additional research is required to establish if emotional intelligence is best modeled after standard intelligence other than self-report measures, other ratio or information measures, performance measure can be used. More research is required on the reliability and validity of the measures of

emotional intelligence.

6. The extent to which emotional intelligence can be taught can be further explored. As evidence exists both for and against ability for emotional intelligence competencies to be developed. It is important that future research should determine the extent to which such learning may occur before an organization invests considerable funds into a development programme.
7. Additionally, qualitative mixed method research designs might be employed to examine the interaction effect of effectiveness on interpersonal relationships.
8. Teacher effectiveness can be studied with some learning factors, learning strategies, intellectual stimulation, self-efficacy, moral development, cognitive styles, self-concept, curriculum factors, evaluation factors, classroom environment, school management factors and teacher quality.
9. A comparative study of school effectiveness may be undertaken in which the factors that make a school effective can be studied. There should be in ultra variate, longitudinal research designed for inferences about causation of effective school in terms of school, teacher and student related factors.
10. Teacher's sense of personal effectiveness can be studied that how teachers see their own capacities with regard to the process and outcomes of schooling.
11. The teachers in present study were generally positive about themselves as effective teachers. The self-ratings of effectiveness, pedagogic and student performance could be identified. The studies should be done on students' achievement and teacher effectiveness because students' achievement can be an important source of feedback on the effectiveness of school, administration and teachers.
12. Studies may be taken up taking the state and nation as units to identify the level of teacher effectiveness, social intelligence, emotional intelligence, general intelligence and creativity.

Glossary

Adaptability E.Q: The ability to adapt to change and to solve problems of a personal or a social nature.

Box's Test of Equality of Covariance Matrices: The equality of group co-variance matrices can be tested by using Box's M test, which test the null hypothesis. In ANOVA, an assumption is that the variances were equivalent for each group but in Discriminant Analysis the basic assumption is that the variance-co-variance matrices are equivalent. Box's M tests the null hypothesis that the covariance matrices do not differ between groups formed by the dependent. The researcher wants this test not to be significant so that the null hypothesis that the groups do not differ can be retained.

The Canonical Discriminant Function Coefficient: Just as a multiple regression equation can be used to calculate a predicted score on the criterion for each subject, a discriminant function can be used to calculate an individual's discriminant score. Again, on the basis of the general formula for a linear equation ($Y = bX + a$), the individual's scores on each variable are multiplied by the corresponding discriminate weight.

Canonical Discriminant Function: This provides information on each of the discriminate functions (Equation) produced. The maximum number of discriminate function is the number of group—1(g-1). We are using only two groups here namely more effective and less effective so only one function is displayed. The canonical function is the multiple correlations between the predictors and the discriminant function.

Canonical Correlation: It is a logical extension of multiple regression. Indeed, it is a multiple regression method. It adds more than one dependent variable to the multiple regression model. In other words, it handles the relations between sets of independent variables and sets of dependent variables.

Classification Table: In discriminant analysis, also called a confusion table, is simply a table in which the rows are the observed categories of the dependent and the columns are the predicted categories. When prediction is perfect all cases will lie on the diagonal. The percentage of cases on the diagonal is the percentage of correct classifications. The cross validated set of data is a more honest presentation of the power of the discriminant function than that provided by the original classifications and often produces a poorer outcome. The cross validation is often termed a 'jack-knife' classification, in that it successively classifies all cases but one to develop a discriminant function and then categorizes the case that was left out. This process is repeated with each case left out in turn. This cross validation produces a more reliable function. The argument behind it is that one should not use the case you are trying to predict as part of the categorization process.

Classroom Climate: Mcber's (2000) Model of Teacher Effectiveness defined classroom climate as measured through interviews with pupils that included pupils perceptions of the clarity of each lesson, an orderly climate, clear behaviour standards, a perception of teacher fairness, the opportunity for pupils to participate feeling emotionally supported in class, the perception that classroom is a safe, comfortable, interesting and exciting place, surrounded well organized and attractive physical environment.

Correlational Analysis: Correlation and regression analysis are related in the sense that both deal with relationships among variables. The correlation coefficient is a measure of linear association between two variables. Values of the correlation coefficient are always between -1 and +1. Neither regression nor correlation analysis can be interpreted as establishing cause-and-effect relationships. They can indicate only how or to what extent variables are associated with each other. The correlation coefficient measures only the degree of linear association between two variables.

Creativity: Creativity is complex in nature. It is difficult to understand it by adopting one single definition. Creativity is multifaceted These strands were the creative person (clustered around personality-related traits and the mental ability to the person to create something new), the *creativity process* (the function of the mind in creating ideas in the creative person like searching, combining and synthesizing), creative product (the outcome or product being original, unique, valuable and novel), and the creative press (or environment) which influence the ecological press on the person and upon his mental processes and outcomes.

Descriptive Analysis: Descriptive statistical measures are used to describe the characteristics of the sample of population in totality. They limit generalization to the particular group of individuals observed or studied.

Differentiated Teacher Effectiveness: The differentiated effectiveness of the teacher is combination of teacher knowledge and teacher behaviour which are related to students' achievement. A model of differentiated teacher effectiveness investigates that a teacher might be differentially effective (subjects, differential pupil characteristics, different roles and different contexts). A teacher have to teach pupils with different intelligences, pupils with special educational needs, developing leadership for school improvement, becoming effective pastoral careers, developing the teaching for problem solving.

Direct Effect: A direct effect indicates the relationship between two variables with no mediating (Intervening) variables. The direct causal effects are represented by standardized regression coefficients (beta).

Discipline Knowledge: Discipline knowledge encompasses an understanding of the salient concepts, relating concepts, ideas and skills of the subject.

Content knowledge or discipline knowledge is first prerequisite of ability to effectively teach a particular discipline.

Discriminant Analysis: The technique of discriminant analysis, developed by R.A. Fisher (1936), is one method for multivariate study of group differences. Before the method and results of discriminant analysis are described it may be useful to compare the discriminant analysis with other approaches to similar research problems. Discriminant analysis is related to a whole class of methods, including regression and MANOVA that are based on the general multivariate linear model. It is appropriate statistical technique when the dependent variable is categorical and independent variables are quantitative.

E.Q. Competencies: Includes intentionally, creativity, resilience, inter-personal connections and constructive discontent.

Emotional Intelligence: The concept of emotional intelligence derives partly from earlier ideas about social intelligence which was first determined by Thorndike in 1920's as one of the many different types of intelligence individuals possess. It is concerned with processing and utilization of emotional information. It is different from cognitive intelligence. Emotional intelligence as the ability to know and manage one's own emotions, recognize them in others and to handle relationships.

Elaboration: Elaboration is the process of enhancing ideas by providing more detail, Additional detail and clarity improves interest in, and understanding of, the topic.

Emotional Literacy: includes emotional self-awareness, emotional expressions and emotional awareness of others.

E.Q. Outcomes: includes general health, quality of life, relationship quotient and optimal performance.

Intra-personal E.Q.: The ability to be aware of, to understand, and to express oneself;

E.Q. Values and Attitudes: includes outlook, compassion, intuition, trust, personal power and integrated self.

Emotional Self-awareness: includes accurate self-assessment and self-confidence.

Emotional Self-management: includes self-control, trust worthiness, conscientiousness, adaptability, achievement, orientation and initiative.

Factor Analysis: Factor analysis attempts to analyze the inter-correlations among the variables so as to reduce them to a smaller number of psychological dimensions which will account for the wide diversity of individual performance. This technique, therefore, is helpful in factorial purification of psychological tests and a consequent reduction in the degree of overlapping among them.

Factorial Design: A factorial design, or statistical model of a process with two or more inputs, that explores the output values for all possible combinations of input values to a business or manufacturing process. A full factorial experiment design takes longer to execute than a partial or fractional factorial design, but provides process output measurements for all possible input values rather than a subset of those values.

Fluency: Fluency refers to the production of a great number of ideas or alternate solutions to a problem. Fluency implies understanding, not just remembering information that is learned.

Flexibility: Flexibility refers to the production of ideas that show a variety of possibilities or realms of thought. It involves the ability to see things from different points of view, to use many different approaches or strategies.

General Intelligence: Intelligence is a type of mental ability that concerns the handling of and reasoning about—information of various sorts. The ability to carry on abstract thinking. The capacity to inhibit an instinctive adjustment, the capacity to redefine the inhibited instinctive adjustment in the light of imaginarily experienced trial and error, and the capacity to realize the modified instinctive adjustment in overt behaviour to the advantage of the individual as a social animal. The capacity to learn or to profit by experience, sensation, perception, association, memory, imagination, discrimination, judgment, and reasoning.

General Mood E.Q.: the ability to look at the brighter side of life and to enjoy oneself and others.

Group Centroids: In order to understand the concept of a centroid, consider the fact that the distribution of discriminant scores of members of a group, like any set of continuous scores, would have a certain distribution with a mean and standard deviation. The mean of discriminant scores within a group is known as the group centroids.

Indirect Effect: An indirect effect indicates the effect of an independent variables on a dependent variable through one or more mediating variables. The indirect effects are calculated by the sums of the products of direct effects through intervening variables in the model.

Inter-personal Intelligence: The inter-personal intelligence consists of the ability to understand others. Ability to sense and respond to the moods, temperaments, motivations and desire of others.

Interpersonal E.Q.: the ability to be aware of, to understand, and to relate to others;

Intra-personal Intelligence: Intra-personal intelligence is the ability to develop an accurate model of the self and use it effectively to operate throughout life. Ability to understand personal feelings that guide behaviour, knowledge of personal strengths, weaknesses and desires.

Knowledge of Context: Context includes the knowledge of classroom, school, culture, community, educational system and students.

Multivariate Analysis: Behavioural research is being revolutionized by multivariate thinking and analysis. Multivariate analysis is a general term used to describe a group of mathematical and statistical methods whose purpose is to analyze multiple measures of number of individuals: Multiple regression analysis, multivariate analysis of variance (MANOVA), canonical correlation, discriminant analysis and factor analysis. Much behavioural research is multivariate in nature. The phenomenon we wish to explain and predict are complex: achievement, learning, aggression, intelligence, creativity, organizational productivity, and many others. Many variables such phenomena and multivariate methods are ways of studying multiple influences of several independent variables on one or more dependable variables. Multivariate methods, then mirror the actual complexity of behavioural "reality". They make it possible for the behavioural scientist to probe more deeply and realistically into phenomena.

Multiple Regression Analysis: Multiple regression analysis is a method of studying the effect and the magnitude of the effects of more than one independence variable on one dependable variable using principles of correlation and regression.

Originality: Originality involves the production of ideas that are unique or unusual. It involves synthesis or putting information about a topic back together in a new way.

Path Analysis: It is an advanced statistical technique for examination of dependent and independent variables to reveal the relative effects of each variance on the other variables in the model. Path analysis starts with a theory bound approach revealed with the construction of an explicitly formulated structural model (Path diagram) that provides a pictorial representation of relationships among variables.

Pedagogical Knowledge: The art and science of teaching is pedagogy. It includes the knowledge about classroom management, organization of classroom activities, methods for motivation of students, personal knowledge about particular student and his family and social interactional skills.

Personal Knowledge: Components of personal knowledge are moral code of behaviour such as honesty, integrity, teacher's personal philosophy and self belief.

Professional Characteristics: Mcber's (2000) Model of Teacher Effectiveness defined professional characteristics as included teacher leadership qualities, their ability to relate to others, their analytic and conceptual thinking skills, their professionalism and expecting setting abilities.

Relationship Management: includes developing others, leadership, influence, communication, change catalyst, conflict management, building bonds, team work and collaborations.

Social Awareness: refers to a spectrum that runs from instantaneously knowing another's inner state, to understand his feelings and thoughts to know complicated social situations. It includes primal empathy, attunement, empathic accuracy and social cognition.

Social Communication: referential communication and social problem solving.

Social Competence: Social competence has been defined as "the possession and use of the ability to integrate thinking, feeling and behaviour to achieve social tasks and outcomes valued in host context and culture.

Social Facility: Social facility builds on social awareness to allow smooth and effective interactions. The spectrum of social facility includes synchrony, self presentation and concerns.

Social Intelligence: "Social intelligence" is frequently defined as "ability to deal with people". The term social intelligence, "social adaptability" and "sociability" are sometimes used inter changeably. Gilliland and Burke (1926) expands this simple definition as follows: The sociable individual may be defined as having ability to get on agreeably, adapted or society, friendly, fond of mixing with others. In short, he is the type of individual usually called a "good mixer".

Social Insight: including social comprehension, psychological insight, moral judgment.

Stress Management E.Q.: The ability to deal with strong emotions and control one's impulses;

Social Sensitivity: Reflected in role making and social inference.

Student Development: Wimberly 1978 discussed one of the dimensions of effectiveness of teacher is student development. Enhancing intellectual skills, better interpretive powers and new viewpoints combine with greater learning stimulation and understanding in to student development dimension.

Teacher Capability: Wimberly 1978 discussed one of the dimensions of effectiveness of teachers is teacher capability. Teachers command of the subject, interest in subject, command of material and not being threatened by questions and enjoyment of teaching.

Teacher Competence: (i.e. the set of knowledge, abilities and beliefs that is in teacher training program).

Teacher Effectiveness/Effective Teacher: The term 'teacher effectiveness' and 'effective teacher' can be used interchangeably. Teacher effectiveness includes multitude of skills and different combination in different contexts. Effectiveness of teacher stems from a combination of knowledge, skills and personal characteristics. An effective teacher helps the students in the development of basic skills, understanding, proper work habits and desirable attitude, value judgement and adequate personal adjustment.

Teacher Performance: (i.e. the behaviour of a teacher at teaching that may change differently when the teaching environment is changed);

Teaching Skills: Mcber's (2000) Model of Teacher Effectiveness defined teaching skills such as time on task, high expectations, effective planning, varied teaching, classroom and behavioural management and effective use of assessment and homework.

Teacher Task Responsiveness: Wimberly 1978 discussed one of the dimensions of effectiveness of teachers is teacher task responsiveness. It includes clear grading procedures, fair grading, informing students where they stand and expedient return of examination and assignments, defining expectations of students.

Total Teacher Effectiveness: It provides a holistic picture of the nature of teacher effectiveness by taking multi-domains of competence and performance of teachers and students at the multi-levels into consideration. This framework assumes that teacher effectiveness is inevitably related to teacher's teaching process and student's learning process.

Triangulation: Triangulation may be defined as the use of two or more methods of data collection in the study of some aspect of human behaviour. The use of triangular techniques, it is argued, will help to overcome the problem of 'method boundedness', as it has been termed; indeed Gorard and Taylor (2004) demonstrated the value of combining qualitative and quantitative methods.

Validating Findings: means that the researcher determines the accuracy or credibility of the findings through strategies such as member checking or triangulation.

Wilks' Lambda: Wilks Lambda indicates the significance of the discriminant function coefficients.

Bibliography

Abler, D.A. (2002) Relationship of Teacher Organizational Commitment and Teacher Efficacy to School Academic Standing and Teaching Experience. *Dissertation Abstracts International,* May 2003, 63(11), 3795-A.

Abraham, R. (2000) The Role of Job Control as a Moderator of Emotional Dissonance and Emotional Intelligence—Outcome Relationships. *The Journal of Psychology,* 134(2), 169-184.

Ackerman, P.L., and Heggested, E.D. (1997) Intelligence, Personality and Interests: Evidence for Overlapping Traits. *Psychological Bulletin,* 121(2), 219-245.

Adaval, S.B. (1979) *Qualities of Teachers.* Allahabad: Amitabh Parkashan.

Adler, A. (1927) *The Practice and Theory of Individual Psychology.* New York: Harcourt Bruce.

Agarwal, A., Prakash, P. Singh, B.G., and Alam, S. (2007) Lay People's Understanding and Use of Intelligence. In Srivastava, A.K. and Misra, G. (2007) *Rethinking Intelligence Conceptualizing Human Competence in Cultural Context.* New Delhi: Concept Publishing Company, 158-210.

Agarwal, S., and Agarwal, S. (1999) Creativity and Intelligence: Exploration with Sex Differences. *Psycho-Lingua,* 29(2), 127-132.

Aggrawal, S. (1998) Emotional Intelligence: Mays to Include Affective Domain in Teacher Education for Optimum HRD. *The Progress of Education.* LXXII (9), 213-216.

Agrawal, R. (2013) Social Intelligence and Teacher Effectiveness. *Ph.D Thesis in Education*, Bundelkhand University Jhansi.

Agresh, A. (1996) *An Introduction to Categorical Data Analysis.* John Wiley and Sons.

Agresh, A. (1996) *An Introduction to Categorical Data Analysis.* John Wiley and Sons.

Akiri, A., and Ugborugbo, N. (2009) Teacher Effectiveness and Student's Academic Performance in Public Secondary Schools in Delta State, Nigeria. *Studies on Home and Community Science,* 3(2), 107-113.

Allington, R.L., and Johnston, P.H. (2000) What do We Know about Effective Fourth Grade Teachers and Their Classrooms? *Research Report, National Research Center on English Learning and Achievement.* University at Albany, Albany, New York.

Amabile, T.M. (1987) The Motivation to be Creative Quoted from S.G. Isaksen. (Eds.) *Frontiers of Creativity Research: Beyond the Basics.* Buffallo, New York: Bearly Limited, 223-254.

Amandeep and Gurpreet (2005) A Study of Some Factors Effecting Teacher Effectiveness. *The Progress of Education,* 71(6), 137-140.

Amritha, M., and Kadhiravan, S. (2006) Influence of Personality on the Emotional Intelligence of Teachers. *Edutracks,* 5(12), 25-29.

Anari, N.N. (2012) Teachers: Emotional Intelligence, Job Satisfaction and Organizational Commitment. *Journal of Work Place Learning,* 24(4), 256-269.

Anderson, L.W. (1991) *Increasing Teacher Effectiveness.* Paris: International Institute for Educational Planning. UNESCO.

Annm, W. (2008) The Relationship of the Emotional Intelligence of Elementary School Principals and Collective Efficacy of their Staff as Perceived by Teachers. *DAI,* 68(12), 4944-A.

Anyalewechi, P.O. (1994) A Comparative Study of Teachers and Principal's Perception of Characteristics of Effective Teachers and Factors that are Influential in Teacher Effectiveness. *DAI*, October, 55(4), 806-A.

Aregbeyen, O. (2010) Students Perceptions of Effective Teaching and Effective Lecturer Characteristics at the University of Ibadan, Nigeria. *Pakistan Journal of Social Sciences,* 7(2), 62-69.

Arokiadoss, S.A. (2005) Teacher Effectiveness of College Teachers. *Perspectives in Education*, 21(2), 106-116.

Arora, G.K. (1976) A Study of Relationship between Anxiety and Creative Thinking Ability. *Indian Educational Review,* 2(3), 91-96.

Arora, K. (1978) *Difference between Effective and Ineffective Teachers*. New Delhi: S. Chand & Co. Ltd.

Arora, R.K. (1992) Interactional Effect of Creativity and Intelligence on Emotional Stability, Personality Adjustment and Academic Achievement. *Indian Educational Review,* 27, 86-94.

Askew, M., Rhodes, V., Brown, M., William, D., and Johnson, D. (1997) *Effective Teachers of Numeracy: Report of a Study Carried out for the Teacher Training Agency*. London: King's College, University of London.

Atkins, P., and Stough, C. (2005) Does Emotional Intelligence Change with Age? *Paper Presented at the Society for Research in Adult Development. Annual Conference*, Atlanta, Georgia.

Ayres, P., Sawyer, W., and Dinham, S. (2004) Effective Teaching in the Context of a Grade 12 High Stakes External Examination in New South Wales, Australia. *British Educational Research Journal,* 30(1), 141-165.

Baacke, A. (1985) Teacher's Personality Correlates and Scholastic Competence Related to Teacher Effectiveness. *Indian Educational Review,* 21(III), 78-81.

Babu, M.S. (2007) Social Intelligence and Aggression among Senior Secondary School Students: A Comparative Sketch. *Project Done as a Part and PGDHE of IGNOU, New Delhi.*

Bagali, M.M. (2000) Creativity in Organization Psychological: Trait Analysis. *Indian Psychological Review,* 54(1 and 2), 49-54.

Bagley W.C., and Keith J.A.H. (1924) *An Introduction on to Teaching*. New York: MacMillian.

Bain, H.P., and Jacobs, R. (1990) The Case for Smaller Classes and Better Teachers. *Streamlined Seminar—National Association of Elementary School Principals,* 9(1), 1-9, www.eric.ed.gov.

Bansal, S., and Kaur, K. (2011) Emotional Stability of Adolescents in Relation to their Intelligence. *Research's Tandem*, 2(5) 14-21.

Bansibihari, P., and Surwade, L. (2006) The Effect of Emotional Maturity on Teacher Effectiveness. *Indian Educational Abstracts,* January and July 2007, 7(1 and 2), 38-39.

Baral, B.D., and Das, J.P. (2004) Intelligence: What is Indigenous to India and What is Shared? In R.J. Sternberg (Eds.) *International Handbook of Intelligence*. Cambridge: Cambridge University Press. 270-301.

Bardoch, R.H. (2008) Leading School with Emotional Intelligence: A Study of the Degree of Association between Middle School Principal Emotional Intelligence and School Success. *Ph.D. Thesis in Social Sciences,* Capella University, Minneapolis.

Bar-On Fund, S., and Handery, R. (2003) The Impact of Emotional Intelligence on Performance. In: Druskat V., Sala F., Mount. G. (Eds.) Emotional Intelligence and Performance at Work. San Francisco: Jossey-Bass.

Bar-On, R. (1997) *Bar-on Emotional Quotient Inventory: A Measure of Emotional Intelligence*. Toronto: Multi-Health systems.

Bar-On, R., and Parker, J. (2000) *The Handbook of Emotional Intelligence*. San Francisco. CA: Jossey-Bass.

Bar-On, R., Tranel, D., Denburg, N.L., and Bechara, A., (2003) Exploring the Neurological Subtrate of Emotional and Social intelligence. *Brain: A Journal of Neurology,* 126(8), 1790-1800.

Barron, E. (1988) Putting Creativity to Work in R.J. Sternberg (Eds.). *The Nature of Creativity: Contemporary Psychologist Perspectives* New York: Cambridge University Press.

Barron, F. (1963) *Creativity and Psychological Health.* Princeton, NJ: Van Nostrand.

Barron, F. (1963) The Psychology of Creativity. In *Encyclopaedia Britannica.* New York: Encyclopaedia Britannica, Inc., 6, 711-712.

Barron, F. (1969) *Creative Person and Creative Process*. New York: Holt, Rinhert and Winston Inc.

Barron, F. (1988). Putting Creativity to Work. In R.J. Sternberg (Ed.), *The Nature of Creativity.* Cambridge: Cambridge University Press, 76-98.

Basu, S. and Saxena, P. (2010) Emotional Intelligence of B.Ed. Trainees. *Indian Journal of Psychometry and Education.* 41(1), 80-83.

Bedi, R.K. (1974) Experimental Attitude and Creativity. *Unpublished M.Ed. dissertation*, Indore University, Indore.

Begum, Dhilsath (2014) A Study of Emotional Intelligence among Teachers with Special Reference to Erode District. *Research Journal of Social Science and Management*, 4(8) www.internationaljournals.org.

Bennett, A., Bridglall, B., Cauce, A., Everson, H.T., Gordon, E., Lee, C., Mendoza-Denton, R., Renzulli, J., and Steward, J. (2004) *All Students Reaching the Top: Strategies for Closing Academic Achievement Gaps: A Report of the National Study Group for the Affirmative Development of Academic Ability.* Naperville: Learning Point Associates.

Bennett, N. (1988) The Effective Primary School Teacher: The Search for a Theory of Pedagogy. *Teacher and Teacher Education*, 4(1), 19-30.

Berendt, P.R., and Koski, B. (1999) No Shortcut to Success. *Educational Leadership.* 56(6), 45-47.

Best, J.W. (1978) *Research in Education*. New Delhi: Prentice Hall of India Pvt. Ltd.

Bhagirathi, S. (2007) *New Educational Philosophy*. New Delhi: Sarup & Sons.

Bhatnagar, A., and Mittal, A. (2010) Emotional Intelligence as a Function of Some Personal Variables. *Indian Journal of Psychometry and Education,* 41(2), 153-156.

Binet, A., and Simon, T. (1911) *A Method of Measuring the Development of Intelligence of Young Children*. London: IL; Courier.

Birknerova, Z. (2011) Social and Emotional Intelligence in School Environment. *Asian Social Science.* 7(10), 241-248.

Biswas, Chandra, P., and Tinku (1995) A Survey on Effectiveness of Secondary School Teachers in Tripura. *Indian Journal of Psychometry and Education,* 26(1), 17-24.

Bock, R.D. (1975) *Multivariate Statistical Methods in Behavioural Research.* New York: McGraw Hill.

Bock, R.D. (1975) *Multivariate Statistical Methods in Behavioural Research.* New York: McGraw Hill.

Boden, M.A. (1994) (Eds.) *Dimensions of Creativity.* London: A Bradford Book, The MIT Press, 76-77.

Borgen, F.H. and Seling, M.J. (1978) Uses of Discriminant Analysis Following MANOVA: Multivariate Statistics for Multivariate Purposes. *Journal of Applied Psychology,* 63, 689-697.

Borgen, F.H., and Seling, M.J. (1978) Uses of Discriminant Analysis Following MANOVA: Multivariate Statistics for Multivariate Purposes. *Journal of Applied Psychology,* 63, 689-697.

Boynd Mary, Ann. (2005) The Emotional Intelligences of Teachers and Student's Perception of their Teacher's Behaviour in the Classroom, *DAI.* September, 66(3), 898-A.

Bradberey, I., and Greaves, J. (2005) *The Emotional Intelligence Quick Look: How to put your E.Q to Work.* New York: Simon and Schuster.

Brookhart, S.M., and Loadman, W.E. (1992) Teacher Assessment and Validity: What Do We Want to Know? *Journal of Personnel Evaluation in Education,* 5(4), 347-357.

Brophy, J., and Good, T.L. (1986) Teacher Behaviour and Student Achievement in M.C. Wittrock (Eds.) (3/e) *Handbook of Research in Teaching,* New York: Macmillan, 328-371.

Brown, L.T., and Antnony, R.G. (1990) Continuing the Search for Social Intelligence. *Personality and individual differences.* 11(5), 463-470.

Brown, S., and McIntyre, D. (1993) *Making Sense of Teaching,* Buckingham: Open University Press.

Bruce, W. Tuckman (1972) *Conducting Educational Research.* New York: Harcourt, Bruce Jovanovich Inc., 288.

Bruner, J.S., Shapiro, D.J., and Tagiuri, R. (1958) The Meaning of Traits in Isolation and in Combination. In R. Tagiuri and L. Petrollo (Eds.) *Person Perception and Interpersonal Behaviour,* Standford, CA: Stanford University Press.

Campbell, J., Kyroakides, L., Muijs, D., and Robinson, W. (2004) *Assessing Teacher Effectiveness: Developing a Differentiated Model.* New York: Routledge Falmer Press.

Campbell, J.P. (1990) Modeling the Performance Prediction Problem in Industrial and Organizational Psychology. In Law, K., Wong, C., Huang. G, and Li, X. (2008) The Effects of Emotional intelligence on Job Performance and Life Satisfaction for the Research and Development Scientists in China. *Asia Pacific,* 25, 51-69.

Cantor, N. (1978) Prototypicality and Personality Judgements. *Doctoral Dissertation in Psychology,* Stanford University, Stanford.

Cantor, N., and Harlow, R. (1994) Social Intelligence and Personality: Flexible Life-task Pursuit. In R.J. Sternberg and P. Ruzgis (Eds.) *Personality and Intelligence,* Cambridge: Cambridge University Press.

Cantor, N., and Kihlstrom, J.F. (1987) *Personality and Social Intelligence,* New Jersey: Prentice-Hall, Englewood Cliffs.

Carr, A. (2007) *Positive Psychology: The Science of* Happiness *and Human Strengths. London*: Routledge Taylor and Francis Group.

Carroll, J.B. (1993) *Human Cognitive Abilities: A Survey of Factor-Analytic.* New York: Cambridge University Press.

Carroll, J.B. (1997) The Three-stratum Theory of Cognitive Abilities. In D.B. Flangan, J.L. Genshaft and P.L. Harrison (1996) *Contemporary Intellectual Assessment: Theories, Tests and Issues.* New York: Guilford Publications.

Caruso, D.R., Mayer, J.D., and Salovey, P. (2002) Emotional Intelligence and Emotional Leadership. In R.E. Riggo, S.E., Murphy, F.J., Pilozzolo (Eds.) Multiple Intelligence and Leadership. New Jersey: Lawrence Erebaum Associates. 55-74.

Cattell, R.B. (1971) *Abilities: Their Structure, Growth and Action.* Boston: Hughton Mifflin.

Ceci, S.J. (1991) How Much Does Schooling Influence General Intelligence and Its Cognitive Components? A Reassessment of the Evidence. *Development Psychology,* 27(5), 703-723.

Ceci, S.J., and Williams, W.M. (1997) Schooling, Intelligence and Income. *American Psychologist,* 52(10), 1051-1058.

Chadha, N.K. (2005) *Human Resource Management Issues: Case Studies and Experimental Exercises.* Delhi: Shri Sai Printographers.

Chadha, N.K., and Ganesan, U. (2004) *Social Intelligence Scale.* Agra: Natinal Psychological Corporation.

Chadha, N.K., and Sen, A.K. (1981) Creativity as Function of Intelligence, Socio-Economic Status and Sex among 12th Grade School Students. *Journal of Education and psychology,* XXXIX (1), 52-56.

Chadha, N.K., and Sen, A.K. (1984). Creativity as a Function of Intelligence, Socio-economic Status and Sex among the 12th Grade School Students. *Journal of Educational Psychology,* 39, (1), 52-56.

Chakraborty, B.D. (1992) *Education of the Creative Children.* Delhi: Konarak Publishers, Pvt. Ltd.

Chan, D.W. (2007) Burnout, Self-Efficacy and Successful Intelligence among Chinese Perspective and In-Service School Teachers in Hong Kong. *Educational Psychology,* 27(1), 33-49.

Chaudhary, G.G. (1983) *An Investigation Into the Trends of Creative Thinking Ability of Pupils of Age Group 11+ to 13+ in relation to Some Psycho-Socio Correlates.* Ph.D. Thesis in Education, Sardar Patel University, Vallabh Vidyanagar, Anand District.

Chaudhary, S. (1989) Relationship between Creative Thinking Abilities of Student Teachers and Intellectual Climate Index of the Classroom. *Ph.D. Thesis in Education,* Delhi University, Delhi.

Chen, M.J. (1994) Chinese and Australian Concept of Intelligence. *Psychology and Developing societies,* 6(2), 103-117.

Chen, M.J. and Chen, H.C. (1988) Concepts of Intelligence: A Comparison of Chinese Graduates from Chinese and English schools in Hong Kong. *International Journal of Psychology,* 23(1-6), 471-487.

Cheng, Y.C., and TSUI, K.T. (1983) A Framework of Total Teacher Effectiveness, Quoted from Cheng, Y.C., Mok, M.M.C. and TSUI, K.T. (2001) (Eds.). *Teaching Effectiveness and Teacher Development: Towards a New Knowledge Base,* The Hong Kong Institute of Education: Kluwar Academic Publishers.

Cheng, Y.C., Mok, M.M.C., and Tsui, K.T. (2001) (Eds.) *Teaching Effectiveness and Teacher Development: Towards a New Knowledge Base.* Hong Kong: Kluwar Academic Publishers.

Chennabatham, R. (2006) Case Study of a Creative Teacher. *DAI,* September, 68(3), 873-A.

Cherniss, C. (2000) Social and Emotional Competence in the Workplace In R. Bar-On and J. Parker (Eds.) The *Handbook of Emotional Intelligence.* San Francisco: Jossey-Bass.

Cheung, H.Y. (2006) The Measurement of Teacher Efficacy: Hong Kong Primary In-Service Teachers. *Journal of Education for Teaching,* 32(4), 435-451.

Chikering, A.W., and Gamson, Z.F. (Eds.) (1991) *Applying Seven Principles for Good Practice in Undergraduate Education* (47/e). San Francisco: Jossy-Bass.

Chouhan, V.L., and Bhatanagar, T. (2003) Assessing Emotional Maturity Emotional Expression and Emotional Quotient of Adolescent Male and Female Adolescents. *Journal of Community Guidance and Research,* 20(2), 157-167.

Christine, C., Basham, K.M., and Elliott, J.O. (2005) Examining Gender with General Creativity and Preferences for Creative Persons in the Science and Arts College Students. *Journal of Creative Behaviour,* 42(3), 216-222.

Ciarrochi, J.P., Chan, A.Y., Caputi, P., and Roberts, R. (2001) Cited in Candace M. Wannamaker (2005). *A Study of the Need for Emotional Intelligence in University Judicial Officers.* Ph.D. Thesis in Faculty of Public Safety, Drexel University, Philadelphia.

Ciarrochi, J.V., Chan, A.Y., and Caputi, P. (2000) A Critical Evaluation of the Emotional Intelligence Construct. *Personality and Individual Differences*, 28(3), 539-561.

Clark, K.C., and Walsh, J.C. (2002) Elements of a Model of Effective Teachers. www.aare.edu.cu.

Clarkson, A. (2005) Educating the Creative Imagination. A Course Design and Its Consequences. *Jung: The E-Journal*, 1(2). www.thejungian_society.org.

Cohen, L., Manion, L., and Morrison, K. (2007) *Research Methods in Education* (*6/e*). London and New York: Routledge Taylor and Francis Group, 141.

Colker, L.J. (2008) Twelve Characteristics of Effective Early Childhood Teachers. *Journal of National Association for the Education of Young Children*, www.journal.naeyc.org.

Cooper, R. (1996/1997) *E.Q. Map.* San Francisco, CA: AIT and Essi Systems.

Cotton, K. (2000) *The Schooling Practices that Matter Most.* Portland, OR: Northwest Regional Educational Laboratory and Alexandria, VA: Association for Supervision and Curriculum Development.

Creswell, J.W. (2014) *Educational Research: Planning, Conducting and Evaluating Quantitative and Qualitative Research.* Delhi: PHI learning Private Limited.

Cropley, A.J. (1966) Creativity and Intelligence. *British Journal of Educational Psychology*, 36, 259-266.

Csikszentmithalyi, M. (1988) Society, Culture and Person. A System View of Creativity. In R.J. Sternberg (Eds.) *The Nature of Creativity*, U.S.A: Cambridge University Press, 325-399.

Cunningham, T.D. Jr. (1997) Components of Greenspan's 1979 model of Social Intelligence with 18 to 24 Year Old Adults with Learning Abilities. *DAI*, July, 58(1), 95-A.

D.A., Adeyemo and Chukwudi, A.R. (2014) Emotional intelligence and Teacher Efficacy as Predictors of Teacher Effectiveness among Pre-Service Teachers in Some Nigerian Universities. International Journal of Evaluation and Research in Education, 3(2), 85-90.

Dacey, J.S. (1989) *Fundamentals of Creative Thinking.* Toronto: D.C. Health and Company, 42-53.

Dalal, A.K., Singh, A.K., and Mishra, G. (1988) Reconceptualization of Achievement Behaviour: A Cognitive Approach. In A.J. Dalal, (Eds.), *Attribution Theory and Research*, New Delhi: Sage Publications.

Dalton, S.S. (2008) *Five Standards for Effective Teaching: How to Succeed with Learners.* San Francisco, CA: John Wiley and Sons.

Damasio, A. (1994) *Decrates' Error, Emotion, Reason and the Human Brain.* New York: Avon Books.

Daniel, R.K. (1978) A Search for Social Intelligence. *Journal of Educational Psychology,* 70(2), 218-223.

Das, M. (1986) *Attitude of Teachers towards Creative Learning and Teaching.* Ph.D. Thesis in Education, Agra University, Agra.

Dass, J.P. (1994) Eastern Views on Intelligence in R.J. Sternberg (Eds.) *Encyclopedia of Intelligence*, New York: Macmillan, 387-391.

Dass, P. (1995) *A Study of Teacher Effectiveness In Relation to Intelligence, Emotional Maturity, Self-Concept and Attitude towards Teaching Profession.* Ph.D. Thesis in Education, Panjab University, Chandigarh.

Davidovitch, N., and Milgram, R.M. (2006) Creative Thinking as a Predictor of Teacher Effectiveness in Higher Education. *Creative Research Journal,* 18(3), 385-390.

Davies, M., Stankov, L., and Robert, R.D. (1998) Emotional Intelligence: In Search of an Elusive Construct. *Journal of Personality and Social Psychology,* 75(4), 989-1015.

Day, C.G.S., Sammons, P., Kington, A., G.U.Q., Smees, R., and Mujtaka, T. (2007) Variations in Teachers Work, Lives and Effectiveness. *Research Report No. 743.* London: Department for Education and Skills, University of Nottingham. www.dcsf.gov.uk.

Day, S.L. (2002) Read kids, Real Risks: Effective Instruction of Students at Risk of Failure. *National Association of Secondary School Principals Bulletin,* 86(682), 19-32.

D'Costa, C., and Deshmukh, V. (2010) A Study of the Relationship between Teacher Effectiveness and Multiple Intelligence of Secondary School Teachers. www.wikieducator.org.

De Bono, E. (1992) *Serious Creativity.* London: Harper Collins Publishers, 55-56, 69-73.

Deary, J.J. (2000) *Looking Down on Human Intelligence.* Oxford: Oxford University Press.

DeHaan, R.F., and Havighurst, R.J. (1957) *Educating Gifted Children.* Chicago: Chicago University Press.

Demmon-Berger, D. (1986) *Effective Teaching: Observations from Research.* Arlington, VA: American Association of School Administrators.

Demos, G.D., Gowan, J.C., and Torrance, E.P. (1967) (Eds.) *Creativity: Its Educational Implications.* New York: John Willey and Sons Inc.

Desai, N.N. (1987) *An Investigation Into the Creative Thinking Ability of Students of Higher Secondary of Gujarat State in the Context of Some Psycho-Socio Factors.* Ph.D. Thesis in Education, Sardar Patel University, Vallabh Vidyanagar, Anand District.

Deshmukh, N.H., and Sawalakhe, S.P. (2010) Self Concept, Emotional Intelligence and Adjustment of Adults. *Indian Journal of Pschometry and Education,* 41(2), 181-185.

DFEE (2000) A Model of Teacher Effectiveness. *Report by Hay Mcber to the Department for Education and Employment. www.teachernet.gov.uk.*

Dhaliwal, A.S., and Saini, B.S. (1976) Relationship of Creativity with Over and Under Academic Achievement. *Psychological Studies,* 21(2), 30-40.

Dhawan, R.B. (1996) *Relationship of Mental Health of Prospective Secondary School Teachers with Creativity, Achievement Motivation and Attitude towards Teaching Profession.* Ph.D. Thesis in Education, Panjab University, Chandigarh.

Diakidoy, I.A., and Kanari, E. (1999) Student Teachers' Beliefs about Creativity. *British Educational Research,* 25(2), 225-243.

Dodge, A.F. (1937) Relation of Social Dominance to General Intelligence. *Journal of Educational Psychology,* 28(5), 387-390.

Donga, N.S. (1989) Effectiveness of Certain Predictors for Teaching Efficiency of Student Teachers. *Journal of Educational Research and Extension,* 26(2), 83-93.

Drevdahl, J.E. (1956) Factors of Importance for Creativity. *Journal of Clinical Psychology,* 12(22), 23-26.

Duckworth, A.L., Quinn, P.D., and Seligman, M.E.P. (2009) Positive Predictors of Teacher Effectiveness. *The Journal of Positive Psychology,* 4(6), 540-547.

Dulewicz, V., and Higgs, M. (2003) Measuring Emotional Intelligence: Content, Construct and Criterion related Validity. *Journal of Management Psychology,* 18(5), 405-420.

Dutt, N.K., and Lal, G. (1977) *The Creative Potential and Education.* Ambala: Indian Books Agency, 40-52.

Dutt, N.K., Bountra, P. and Sabhrawal, V.K. (1977) A Study of Creativity in Relation to Intelligence, Extraversion and Neuroticism. *Indian Educational Review*, 8(2), 81-85.

Eva Justina Ramoold, E.J. (2006) Enhancing Emotional Intelligence of Student Teachers through Ennegram Educational Programme. *Educational Tracks.* 6(3), 25-31.

Eysenk, H.J. (1993) Creativity and Personality: Suggestions for a Theory. *Psychological Inquiry,* 4(3), 147-178.

Feldman (1988) Creative: Dreams, Insights and Transformations. In R.J. Sternberg (Eds.), *The Nature of Creativity*. Cambridge: Cambridge University Press, 271-297.

Fiest, G.J., and Barron, F. (1996) Emotional Intelligent and Academic Intelligent in Career and Life Success. *Paper Presented at Annual Convention at American Psychological Society*. San Francisco. CA: Jossey-Bass.

Firestein, R.L. (1993) The Power of Product in Scott, G. Isaksen. Mary C. Murdock (Eds.) *Understanding and Recognizing Creativity: The Emergence of Discipline.* New Jersey: Ablex Publishing Corporation, 261-277.

Flanders, N.A., and Simon A. (1969) Teaching effectiveness in R.L. Ebet (Eds.) *Encyclopedia of Educational Research.* New York: Free Press, 1423-1437.

Flangan, D.P., Genshaft J. and Harrison P.L. (Eds.) (1996) *Contemporary Intellectual Assessmani: Theories, Tests and Issues.* New York: Guilford Publishers.

Flescher, I. (1963) Anxiety and Achievement of Intellectually Gifted and Creatively Gifted Children. *Journal of Psychology: Interdisciplinary and Applied,* 56(2), 251-268.

Floistad, G. (1993). Creativity, Past, Present and Future: A Philosophical Perspective. In Scott G. Isaken, Mary C. Murdock, Roger L. Firestein and Donald J. Treffinger (Eds.) *Understanding and Recognizing Creativity: The Emergence of a Discipline.* New Jersey: Albex Publishing Corporation. 203-206, 261-262.

Ford, M.E. (1982) Social Cognition and Social Competence in Adolescence. *Development Psychology*, 18(3), 323-340.

Ford, M.E. and Tisak, M.S. (1983) A Further Search for Social Intelligence. *Journal of Educational Psychology*, 75(2), 196-206.

Ford, M.E., and Miura (1983) Children's and Adult's Conception of Social Competence. Quoted in Sternberg, R.J. (1985) *Beyond I.Q. A Triachic Theory of Human Intelligence.* New York: Cambridge University Press.

Fox, S., and Spector, P.E. (2000) Relation of Emotional Intelligence, practical Intelligence, General Intelligence Affectivity with Interview Outcomes, its Not All Just 'G'. *Journal of Organizational Behaviour,* 21(2), 203-220.

Freud, S. (1958) *On Creativity and Unconscious.* New York: Harper.

Frigda, N.H. (1988) The Laws of Emotions. *American Psychologist*, 43, 349-58.

Fructsler, R., and Nishida, T., Rosenberg, D. (2005) Understanding Mediate Communication: The Social Intelligence Design (SID) Approach. AI and Society, 19(1), 1-7.

Fryer, M. (1989) *Teachers' Views on Creativity.* Ph.D. Thesis in Education, Leeds Metropolitan University, Leeds.

Fryer, M. (1993) Facilitators of Creativity. *Paper Given at the 39th Creative Problem Solving Institute of the Creative Education Foundation*, Buffalo: New York.

Fryer, M. (1995) *Creative Teaching and Learning.* London, UK: Paul Chapman Publishing Ltd.

Fryer, M., and Collings, J.A., (1991) Teachers' views about Creativity. *British Journal of*

Educational Psychology, 61(2), 207-219.

Fuchs-Beauchamp, K.D., and Karnes, M.B., and Johnson, L.T. (1993) Creativity and Intelligence in Pre-scholars. *Gifted Child Quarterly*. 37(3), 113-117.

Fund, S. (2000) Examining the Contribution of Emotional Intelligence in Occupational Performance, *Unpublished Manuscript*. In Bar-On and J.D.A. Parker (Eds.) The Handbook of Emotional Intelligence. San Francisco: Jossy-Bass.

Gage, M.L. (1965) Desirable Behaviour of Teacher. *Urban Education*, 1(2), 85-95.

Gagne, R.M. (1970) *The Conditions of Learning*. 2/e, New York: Holt, Rinehart and Winston.

Gakhar, S., and Kaur, N. (1976-77) Creativity Intelligence: A study of Structural Relationship and Threshold Hypothesis. *Creativity Newsletter*, 1 and 2 (5 and 6), 27-37.

Gakhar, S.C., and Bains, G. (2010) A Study of Social Intelligence and Achievements Motivation of Arts and Science Stream. *Journal of Educational Studies*. 1(7), 56-59.

Gakhar, S.C., and Brar, P.K. (2009) A Study of Emotional and Social Intelligence of General and Scheduled Caste Students. *Researcher's Tandom*, 1(1), 31-35.

Gakhar, S.C., Chopra, S., and Singh, S. (2008) Social Intelligence Adolescents with High and Low Creativity. *Journal of Teacher Education and Research*, 3(2), 48-53.

Ganeswara, R.K. (1995) *A Study of Teacher Effectiveness in Relation to Creativity and Interpersonal Relationships*. Ph.D. Theiss in Education, Andhra University, *Sixth Survey of Educational Research*, NCERT, New Delhi, II, 509.

Gardner, H. (1983) *Frames of Mind: The Theory of Multiple Intelligence*. New York: Basic.

Gardner, H. (1983/1993) *Frames of Mind*. NY: Basic Books Inc.

Gardner, H. (1988) *Creativity: An Interdisciplinary Perspective, Creativity Research Journal*, 1(1), 8-26.

Gardner, H. (1993) *Creating Minds*. New York: Basic.

Gardner, H. (1995) *Leading Minds*. New York: Basic.

Gautam, R. (1990) *A Study of Creativity, Values, Educational Achievement and Attitude Towards Education among Scheduled Caste and other Caste Students*. Ph.D. Thesis in Education, Agra University, Agra.

George Wishington Social Intelligence Test (GWSIT) (1949) Quoted from Ruth Strang (1930) Measures of Social Intelligence. *American Journal of Sociology*, 36(2), 263-269.

George, J.M., and Brief, A.P. (1996) Motivational Agendas in the Workplace: The Effects of Feelings on Focus of Attention and Work Motivation. In B.M. Staw and L.L. Cumming (Eds.) *Research in Organizational Behaviour*, Greenwich: CT: JAI Press, 18, 75-109.

George, K.S. (2002) *Identification of Certain Factors Influencing the Optimum Utilization of Teacher Effectiveness in the Primary Schools of Kerala*. PhD Thesis in Education, M.G University Kottayam, Kerala.

Getzels, J.W., and Jackson, P.W. (1962) *Creativity and Intelligence: Explorations with Gifted Students*. New York: John Wiley & Sons, Inc., 20, 56-64

Ghiselin, B. (1963). Ultimate Criteria for Two Levels of Creativity. In C.W. Taylor and F. Barron (Eds). *Scientific Creativity: Its Recognition and Development*, New York: Robert E. Krieger Publishing Company, 30-43.

Ghiselin, B. (Eds.) (1955) *The Creative Process*. New York: A Mentor Books.

Ghoniem, A., Elkhouly, S., Mohsen, G., and Ibrahim, M. (2011) Impact of Emotional Intelligence and Gender on Job Satisfaction Among Egyptian Government Sector Employees. *Current Research Journal of Social Sciences*, 3(1), 22-27.

Ghosh, N.B. (2015) Impact of Emotional Intelligence on the Relative Competiveness of Educationists: A Requisite for Quality Education in India. *International Journal of Humanities and Social Sciences Invention*, 4(1) 7-16.

Gibbs, C. (2003) Explaining Effective Teaching: Self-efficacy and Thought Control of Action.*Journal of Educational Enquiry*, *4*(2), 1-14.

Gilliland, A.R., and Burke, R.S. (1926) A Measurement of Sociability. *Journal of Applied Psychology*, X(3), 315-326.

Glaser-Zikuda, M., and Fu. S. (2008) Impact of Teacher Competencies on Student Emotions: A Multi-Method Approach. *International Journal of Educational Research*, 47(12), 136-147.

Gnanadevan, R. (2011) Social Intelligence of Higher Secondary Students in Relation to their Socio-Economic Status. *MIER Journal of Educational Studies Trends and Practices*, 1(1), 60-66.

Goddard and R.D., Hoy, W.K., and Woolfork, H.A. (2004) Collective Efficacy Beliefs: Theoretical Developments, Empirical Evidence, and Future Directions. *Educational Research*, 33(3), 3-13.

Goleman, D. (1990) *Emotional Intelligence*. New York: Bantam Books.

Goleman, D. (1998) *Working with Emotional Intelligence*. New York: Bantam.

Goleman, D. (2006) Social Intelligence: *The New Science of Human Relationships*. London: Arrow books.

Goleman, D., Boyatzis, R., and Mckee A. (2002) *Primal Leadership*. Boston: Harvard Business School Publishing.

Goleman, D. (1995) *Emotional Intelligence. Why it can Matter more than IQ*. New York: Bantam.

Gomez, J.S. (2007) What Do We Know About Creativity? *The Journal of Effective Teaching*, 7(1), 31-43.

Good C.V. (1959) *Dictionary of Education*, 2/e. New York: McGraw Hill Company.

Good, T.L., and Brophy, J.E. (1997) *Looking in Classrooms*, 7/e. New York: Addison-Wesley.

Gorard, S., and Taylor, C. (2004) *Combining Methods in Educational and Social Research*. London: Open University Press.

Government of India, Ministry of Human Resource Development (1990) Report of the Committee of Review of National Policy of Education 1986. New Delhi: Government of India Press.

Government of India, Statistical Abstract of India (2007) 43/e, New Delhi, 565-580.

Government of Punjab, Statistical Abstract of Punjab (2008) *Department wise Number of Teachers of Punjab by District on 30th December*, Chandigarh. 536.

Government of Punjab, Statistical Abstract of Punjab (2008) *District wise Number of Recognized Institution in Punjab*, Chandigarh. 508.

Government of Punjab, Statistical Abstract of Punjab (2008) *District wise Rural and Urban Literates and Literacy Rate by Sex*, Chandigarh. 70.

Government of Punjab, Statistical Abstract of Punjab (2013) Chandigarh, 406-419.

Gowan, J.C., Demos, G.D., and Tarrance, E.P. (1967) *Creativity: Its Educational Implications*. New York: John Wiley and Sons. Inc.

Gowdhaman, K., and Murugan, M.B. (2010) Emotional Intelligence Among the B.Ed. teacher Trainees. *Indian Journal of Psychometry and Education*, 41(2), 137-142.

Goyal, A., and Singh, T. (2010) Creativity Among Collegiate Students. *Psycho-Lingua*, 40(1 and 2), 50-52.

Goyal, R.P. (1973) *A Study of Some Personality Correlates of Creativity in Secondary School Teacher Under Training*. Ph.D. Thesis in Education, Punjabi University, Patiala.

Goyal, S., and Duggal, K. (2011) A Study of Teacher Effectiveness in Relation to Locus of Control and Burnout. *Researcher's Tandem.* 2(8), 65-74.

Graves, M.L.M. (2000) *Emotional Intelligence, General Intelligence and Personality: Assessing the Construct Validity of An Emotional Intelligence Test Using Structural Equation Modeling.* Unpublished Doctoral Dissertation, California School of Professional Psychology, California.

Guildford, J.P. (1968) *Intelligence, Creativity and their Educational Implications.* California: Robert R. Knapp Publisher.

Guilford, J.P. (1950) Creativity. *American Psychologist,* 5(9), 444-454.

Guilford, J.P. (1956) Structure of Intellect. *Psychological Bulletin.* 53(4), 267-293.

Guilford, J.P. (1957) *A Revise Structure of Intellect.* Los Angels: University of Southern California, 69-95.

Guilford, J.P. (1961) Creative-Thinking Abilities of Ninth-Grade Students. *Paper Presented at Annual Meeting of American Educational Research Association,* Chicago.

Guilford, J.P. (1963) *An Information Theory in Creative Thinking.* USAF Instructors, 1, 28-33.

Guilford, J.P. (1967) *The Nature of Human Intelligence.* New York: McGraw-Hill.

Guilford, J.P. (1986) *Creative Talents: Their Nature, Use and Development.* Buffalo, New York: Bearly.

Guilford, J.P., and Fruchter, B. (1981) *Fundamental Statistics in Psychology and Education.* Auckland: McGraw-Hill.

Guilford, J.P., and Fruchter, B. (1981) *Fundamental Statistics in Psychology and Education.* Auckland: McGraw-Hill.

Gulati, S. (1979) Creativity as a Function of Intelligence, Artistic Aptitude and Neuroticism. *Educational Trends,* 14(1), 35-44.

Gulati, S. (1995) (Eds.) *Education for Creativity: A Research Book for Teacher Educators.* New Delhi: National Council of Educational Research and Training (NCERT), 16(30-35), 73-74.

Gulati, S. (2000) Teaching of Creative Endeavour. *Journal of Indian Education,* XXVI (3), 1-21.

Gupta, B.D. (1988) *Intelligence, Adjustment and Personality Needs of Effective Teachers in Science and Arts.* Ph.D. Thesis in Education, Agra University, Agra.

Gupta, G.S. (1979) A Comparative Psychological Study of Creativity of Indian Adolescents Students at Various Educational Levels. *Indian Psychological Review.* 18(1 and 4), 42-44.

Gupta, K.K. (1979) Creativity Intelligence and Achievement. *The Educational Review,* 85(11), 208-212.

Gupta, M., and Jain, R. (2007) A Comparative Study of Teaching Effectiveness of the Government and Private School Teachers Trained Through the Formal and Distance Modes. *Indian Journal of Distance Education,* IX, 61-75.

Gupta, M.S. (1984) *Psychology of Engineering Creativity.* New Delhi: Cusmo Publications.

Hallman, R.J. (1971) Techniques of Creative Teaching. Reproduced in G.A. Davis and J.A. Scott. (Eds) *Training Creative Thinking,* New York: Holt, Rinehart and Winston, Inc. 220-224.

Hamann, D.L., Line Burgh, N., and Paul, S. (1998) Teacher Effectiveness and Social Skill Development. *Journal of Research in Music Education,* 46(1), 87-101.

Hameed, A., and Manjusha, M. (2010) Teacher Efficacy of Secondary School Teachers in Relation to Teaching Style and Organizational Culture. *Edusearch,* 1(1), 64-70.

Hargreaves, A. (2001) Emotional Geographies of Teaching. *Teachers College Record,* 103(6), 1056-1080.

Harkeness, S., Blom. M., Oliva, A., Moscardiono, C., Zylicz, P.R., Feng, X., Zylicz, A.C., Ania, G., and Super, C.M. (2007) Teacher's Ethnotheories of the Ideal Student in Five Western Cultures. *Comparative Education,* 43(1), 113-135.

Hassan, N., Jani, S.H.M., Som, R.M., Hamid., N.Z.A and Azizam, A.N. (2015) The Relationship between Emotional Intelligence and Teaching Effectiveness among Lecturers at University Teknologi MARA, Puncak Alam, Malaysia. International Journal of Social Sciences and Humanties, 5(1) 1-5.

Hee, W.J. (1998) *Emotional Intelligence and Cognitive Ability as Predictors of Job Performance in the Banking Section.* Unpublished Master's Thesis, *Ateneo de Manila University, Philippines.*

Hennessey, B.A., and Amabile, J.M. (1988) The Conditions of Creativity. In R.J. Sternberg (Eds.), *The Nature of Creativity.* Cambridge: Cambridge University Press, 11-38.

Hensly, P.A. and Reynolds, C.R. (1989) Creativity and Intelligence. In J.A. Glover, R.R. Ronning and C.R. Reynolds (Eds.) *Handbook of Creativity.* New York: Plenum, 111-132.

Herbert, M. (1986) Social Intelligence: Evidence for Multidimensionality and Construct Independence. *Journal of Educational Psychology,* 70(1), 52-58.

Herr, E.L., Moore, G.D., and Hasen, J. and Castell, C. (1965) Creativity, Intelligence, and Values: A Study of Relationships. *Exceptional Children,* 32(2), 114-115.

Hill, R. (1992) Finding Creativity for Children. *Paper Prepared for Leadership Accessing Symposium.* Lafeyette, in March 4-5.

Hiremath, S.A. (2012) Effectiveness of Secondary School Teachers with their Intelligence. *International Indexed and Referred Research Journal,* 4(39), 51-52.

Hochschild, A. (1983). *The Managed Heart: Commercialization of Human Feeling.* Berkeley: University of California Press.

Horn, J.L. (1965) Fluid and Crystallized Intelligence: A Factor Analytic Study of the Structure Among Primary Mental Abilities. *Journal of Educational Psychology,* 57(5), 253-270.

Horn, J.L. (1968) Organization of Abilities and the Development of Intelligence. *Psychological Review,* 75(3), 242-259.

Horn, J.L. (1994) Theory of Fluid and Crystallized Intelligence. In R.J. Sternberg (Eds.) *The Encyclopedia of Human Intelligence,* New York: Macmillan, 1, 443-451.

Hudson, (1966) *Contrary Imaginations.* London: Methuen.

Hunt, T. (1928) The Measurement of Social Intelligence. *Journal of Applied Psychology,* 12, 317-324.

Hyde, A.P., Sanjyot, P., and Dhar, U. (2002) *Emotional Intelligence Scale.* Lucknow: Vendant Publications.

Indu, H. (2009) Emotional Intelligence of Secondary Teachers Trainees. *Edutracks,* 8(9), 34-36.

Isen, A.M. (1987) Positive Affect, Cognitive Processes and Social Behaviour. In L. Berkowitz (Eds.) *Advances in Experimental Social Psychology,* San Diego; CA: Academic Press, 20, 203-53.

Israeli, N. (1946) Studies in Occupational Analysis: II. Originality. *Journal of Psychology,* 22, 77-87.

Jadhav, V.V., and Patil, A.B. (2010) Emotional Intelligence among Student Teachers in Relation to General Intelligence and Academic Achievement. *Edutracks,* 10(3), 36-37.

Jain, R. (1977) *Proficiency in Teaching as a Function of Creativity, Intelligences and Interest.* Ph.D. Thesis in Psychology, Agra University, Agra.

Jain, R. (2007) Teacher Effectiveness of Teacher Trained through Distance Mode in Relation to Sex, Experience and Type of School. *MERI Journal of Education*, 2(2), 77-83.

Jain, S. (1998) Social Competence Among Tribal and Non Tribal Pupils. *Psycho-Lingua*, July, 28(2), 131-134.

Jarial, G.S. (1981) Instructional Materials for Developing Creativity in Students. *Ph.D. Thesis in Education*, Devi Ahilya Vishwavidyalaya, Indore.

Jarmali, D., Sidani, Y. and Abu-zaki, D. (2008) Emotional Intelligence and Management Development Implications: Insight from Lebanese Context. *Journal of Management Development*, 27(3), 348-360.

Jayanthi and Agarwal, R. (2006) Enhancing, Creativity of the Teachers for Building Positive Socio-Emotional Classroom Climate. *Edutracks*, 6(3), 21-23.

Jayanthi, and Aggarwal, R. (2005) Relationship Between Teachers Creativity (Verbal and Figural) and Socio Emotional Climate of the Classroom. *Indian Psychological Review*, 65(Special Issue), 233-242.

Jelouder, S.Y. (2011) Exploring Relationship between Teachers' Social Intelligence and Classroom Discipline Strategies. *International Journal of Psychological Studies*, 3(2), 149-155.

Jelouder, S.Y. and Lotfi-Goodarzi, F. (2012) The Relationship between Social Intelligence and Job Satisfaction among M.A. and B.A. Teachers. *International Journal of Educational Science*, 4(3) 209-213.

Jennings, P.A., and Greenberg, M.T. (2009) The Pro-social Classroom: Teachers Social and Emotional Competence in Relation to Student and Classroom Outcomes. *Review of Educational Research*, 79(1), 491-525.

Jensen, A.C. (1948) Determining Critical Requirements for Teachers, *Journal of Experimental Educations*, XX (1), 79-85.

John, C.D. (1988) *Familial and School Correlates of Creativity: A Study of Standard IX Students.* M.Phil. Dissertation in Education, Bangalore University, Bangalore.

Johnson, B.L. (1997) An Organizational Analysis of Multiple Perspectives of Effective Teaching: Implications for Teacher Evaluation. *Journal of Personnel Evaluation in Education*, 11(1), 69-87.

Johnson, M. (1980) *Effective Teaching as Perceived by Teachers and Principals in Selected Indiana school Corporations.* Doctoral Thesis, Ball State University, Muncie, USA.

Johnson-Laird, P.N. (1993) *Human and Machine Thinking.* Hillsdale, NJ: Lawrence Erlbaum Associates.

Jones, K., and Day, J.D. (1997) Discrimination of Two Aspects of Cognitive-Social Intelligence from Academic Intelligence. *Journal of Educational Psychology*, 89(3), 486-497.

Jordan, S.P. (1998) Teacher Perception of the Effects of a Social Skills Curriculum on the Social Competence of Primary-Age Students with Learning Disabilities. *DAI*, June, 59(12), 4400-A.

Jubert, M.M. (2001) The Art of Creative Teaching: NACCCE and Beyond in A. Craft, B. Joffery and M. Leibling (Eds.) (2001) *Creativity in Education*: London and New York: Continuum.

Juchniewicz, J. (2010) The Influence of Social Intelligence on Effective Music Teaching. *Journal of Research in Music Education*, 58(3), 276-293.

Jung, C.G. (1928) On the Relation of Analytical Psychology to Poetry, In C.G. Jung (1985.) *The Spirit in Man: Art and Literature*. USA: Routledge Taylor & Francis Group.

Kagathala, A.B. (2002) A Study of the Effectiveness of Teachers of Secondary School in Gujarat. *Journal of Education and Psychology*, 59 and 60(1 and 4), 26-33.

Kala, S. (1988) *Relationship of Selected Psychological Variables with Attitude Toward Teaching of Traditional and Model School Teachers.* Ph.D. Thesis in Education, Panjab University, Chandigarh.

Kalra, R.K. (2010) Effect of Gender and Adjustment on Teaching Effectiveness of Higher Secondary Teachers. *Indian Psychological Review,* 74(3), 141-146.

Kamboj, R.K. (2007) Relationship of Emotional Intelligence with Self-Actualization. *New Frontiers in Education,* 40(3), 224-228.

Kapoor, D.R., and Gupta, A.K. (1983) *Organizational Climate and Innovativeness of School in Relation to Teaching Effectiveness.* Ph.D. Thesis in Education, University of Jammu, Jammu.

Kartz, L.G. (1993) Dispositions Definitions and Implications for Early Childhood Practices. Chamapaigh-Urbana, I.L. ERIC Clearing House on Elementary and Early Childhood Education. http://crc.uluc.edu/eearchieve/books.

Kashyap, R. (2006) Creativity in Design Education. *Indian Educational Review,* 42(1), 51-59.

Kasture, P.B and Bhalerao (2014) Social Intelligence of Pupil Teachers. Scholarly Research Journal for Interdisciplinary Studies, II (XIV) 1912-1923.

Katoch, K.S. (2001) *Cognitive Style, Self Actualization and Temperament as Related to Teacher Effectiveness.* Ph.D. Thesis in Education, Himachal Pradesh University, Shimla.

Katoch, K.S. (2011) Teacher Effectiveness and Temperament. *MIER Journal of Educational Studies, Trends and Practices,* 1(2), 204-212.

Kaukiainen, A., Bjorkquist, K., Osterman, K. Lagerspetz, K.M.J., and Forsbrom (1995) *Peer-Estimated Social Intelligence* (*PESI*) Department of Psychology, University of Turku, Finland.

Kaukiainen, A., Bjorkqvist, K., Kirsti, L., Karn, O., Christina, S., Sari, R., and Arme, A. (1999) The Relationship Between Social Intelligence, Empathy and Three Types of Aggression. *Aggressive Behaviour,* 25(2), 81-89.

Kaur, A. (2007) *A Study of Academic Stress in Relation to Self Concept and Emotional Intelligence of Perspective Teachers.* M.Ed. Dissertation, Panjab University, Chandigarh.

Kaur, Charanjeet (2010) *Relationship of B.Ed. Entrance Test Performance with Scholastic and Attitudinal Variables.* Ph.D. Thesis in Education, Punjabi University, Patiala.

Kaur, D. (2008) *Emotional Intelligence of Teacher Trainees in Relation to their Perceived Stress and Life Satisfaction.* M.Ed. Dissertation, Panjab University, Chandigarh.

Kaur, H. (1989) *A Study of Teacher Effectiveness of Physical Education Teachers In Relation to their Locus of Control, Intelligence, Psychological Adjustment and Self Concept.* Ph.D. Thesis in Education, Punjabi University, Patiala.

Kaur, H. (2011) Impact of B.Ed. Programme on Teacher Effectiveness of Prospective Teachers. *Researcher's Tandem,* 2(5), 56-60.

Kaur, H., (1998) *Attitude Towards Creative Learning and Teaching of Pre-Service Teachers in Relation to Sex, Socio-Economic Status and Academic Discipline.* M.Ed Dissertation, Panjab University, Chandigarh.

Kaur, Harpreet and Kalaramna (2004) Study of Interrelationship Between Home Environment, Social Intelligence and Socio-Economic Status Among Male and Females. *Journal of Human Ecological,* 16(2), 137-140.

Kaur, Manmeet (2001) *Comparative Study of Job Satisfaction Professional and Educational Interests, Creativity, Attitude Towards Teaching of Teacher Educators at Different Levels of Education.* Ph.D. Thesis in Education, Panjab University, Chandigarh.

Kaur, N. (1993) *Comparative Study of Teaching Effectiveness of Navodaya and Traditional School in Relation to Intellective, Non-Intellective and Institutional Variables.* Ph.D. Thesis in Education, Panjab University, Chandigarh.

Kaur, P. (2009) *A Comparative Study of Emotional and Social Intelligence, Educational Aspiration, Mental Health and Personality Characteristics of General and Scheduled Caste Students.* Ph.D. Thesis in Education, Panjab University, Chandigarh.

Kaur, S. (2008) *Correlates of Teacher Effectiveness.* Patiala: 21st Century Publications.

Kaur, S. (2012) *A Study of Social Intelligence of University Students in Relation to Family Environment.* M.Ed. Dissertation, Punjabi University, Patiala.

Kauts.A and Chechi, V. K (2014) Teacher Effectiveness in Relation to Type of Institution, Emotional Intelligence and Teaching Experience, *Anadolu Journal of Educational Sciences International,* 4(2) 63-81.

Kauts, A., and Chechi, V.F. (2011) Emotional Intelligence among Teachers in Relation to Type of Institution and Gender in Schools. *Educational Quest—International Journal of Education and Applied Social Science,* 2(1), 81-87.

Kauts, D.S., and Mittu, G. (2011) Study of Teacher Effectiveness in relation to Locus of Control and Stress of Teacher Educators. *Learning Community,* 2(1), 25-33.

Kavoli, S.N. (1964) Economic Correlate of Artistic Creativity. *American Journal of Sociology,* 70(3), 332-341.

Keating, D.P. (1978) A Search for Social Intelligence. *Journal of Educational Psychology,* 70(2), 218-223.

Kerlinger, F.N. (2012) *Foundation of Behavioural Research.* New Delhi: Surjeet Publications.

Kerlinger, F.N. (1973) *Foundation of Behavioural Research.* USA: Holt, Rinehart and Winston Inc.

Khan, N. (2008) Impact of Creative Talent on the Performance of Teacher Trainees of Distance Mode. *Indian Journal of Open Learning,* 17(1), 95-100.

Khatena, J., and Torrance, E.P. (1973) *Thinking Creatively with Sound and Words.* Norms Technical Manual Princeton, N.J. Personal Press.

Khatoon, S. and Sultana, H. (2012) Effect of Emotional Intelligence of Teacher Trainees. *The CTE National Journal,* X(1), 88-90.

Kosmitzki, C., and John, O.P. (1993) The Implicit Use of Explicit Conceptions of Social Intelligence. *Personality and Individual Difference,* 15(1), 11-25.

Kottler, J.A., Zehm, S.J., and Kottler, E. (2005) *On Being a Teacher: The Human Dimension.* 3/e, California: Conwin Press.

Kris, E. (1952) *Psychoanalytic Explorations in Art.* New York: International Universities Press, Inc.

Krishnan, S.S. and Singh, J.R. (1994) Impact of Teachers Sex, Socio-Economic Status and Locale on Teacher Effectiveness. *Journal of Educational Research and Extension,* 31(2), 104-108.

Kubie, L.S. (1958) *Neurotic Distortion of the Creative Process.* Lawrence: University of Kansas Press.

Kumar, A.G.H., and Awati, R.B. (2012) Teaching Effectiveness of Female Student Teachers in Relation to their Creativity. *International Indexed and Referred Research Journal,* 3(34), 72-73.

Kumar, G., and Sharma, V.K. (2009) A Study of Creative Functioning in Relation to Emotional Intelligence and Accomplishment of Engineering Students. *Journal of Education and Pedagogy,* 1(2), 63-70.

Kumar, K. (1999) *A Study of Teacher Effectiveness Among Scheduled Caste and Non-Scheduled Caste Teachers in Relation to their Teaching Aptitude and Self-Concept.* Ph.D. Thesis in Education, Panjab University Chandigarh.

Kumar, P., and Mutha, D.N. (1999) *Teacher Effectiveness Scale* (*Revised*). Agra: National Psychological Corporation.

Kumar, S., and Rao, S.N. (2009) Social Maturity among Teacher Trainees, *Indian Journal of Psychometry and Education,* 40(1 and 2), 156-158.

Kumar, V.K. (2009) Emotional Intelligence and Learning Styles of School Teachers. *Journal of Psychological Researches,* 53(1), 44-47.

Kurtzman, K.A. (1967) A Study of School Attitudes, Peer Performance Acceptance and Personality of Creative Adolescents. *Exceptional Children*, 34(3), 157-162.

Kwang, A.K., and Lin Hor, N. K., (2005) Teaching attitudes, Emotional Intelligence and Creativity of School Teachers in Singapore. *Educational Research Journal,* 20(2), 207-220.

Lal, G. (1974) *A Study of Relationship Between Creative Thinking and Vocational Anxiety and their Effect on Success in Teaching.* Ph.D. Thesis in Education, Panjab University, Chandigarh.

Langer, J.A. (2000) Excellence in English in Middle and High School: How Teachers' Professional Lives Support Student Achievement. *American Educational Research Journal,* 37(2), 397-439.

Latha, A.R., and Ananthasayanam, E. (2005) A Study of Teacher Effectiveness with Relation to Emotional Intelligence. *Perspectives in Education*, 20(2), 42-46.

Leonard, N.H., and Harvey, M. (2007) The Trait of Curiosity as a Predictor of Emotional Intelligence. *Journal of Applied Social Psychology,* 37(7), 1545-1561.

Locke, E.A. (2005) Why Emotional Intelligence is an Invalid Concept. *Journal of Organizational Behaviour*, 26(4), 425-431.

Lordanoyglou, D. (2007) The Teacher as Leader: The Relationship Between Emotional Intelligence and Leadership, Effectiveness, Commitment and Satisfaction. *Journal of Leadership Studies,* 1(3), 57-66.

Lovejoy, M.S. (2008) Indiana School Superintendents and Relationship Between Gender and Level of Social Intelligence. *DAI,* 69(3), 835-A.

Lowman, R.L., and Leeman, G.E. (1988) The Dimensionality of Social Intelligence, Social Abilities, Interest and Needs. *Journal of Psychology,* 12(2), 279-290.

Lutz, C., and White, G.M. (1986) The Anthropology of Emotions. *Annual Review of Anthropology*. 15, 405-436.

Mackinnon, D.W. (1962) The Nature and Nurture of Creative Talent. *American Psychologist,* 17(7), 484-495.

Mackinnon, D.W. (1963) Personality Correlates of Creativity. *A Paper Presented at the Second Conference on Productive Thinking, National Educational Association.* Washington, D.C., May 2-4.

Mackinnon, D.W. (1967) The Highly Effective Individual in Ross L. Mooney and Taher A. Rozik (Eds.) *Explorations in Creativity.* New York, Evanston, and London: Harper and Raw Publication.

Maddux, C.D., Samples-Lachman, I., and Cummings, R.E. (1985) Preferences of Gifted Students for Selected Teacher Characteristics. *Gifted Child Quarterly,* 29(4), 160-163.

Malekar, S. (2005) Managing Human Capital: An EQ Perspective *Unpublished Paper Presented at the National Conference at Institute of Technology and Management.* Kharagpur, Navi Mumbai, India, December, 7-9.

Malikow, M. (2005) Effective Teacher Study. *National Forum of Teacher Education Journal-Electronic,* 2005-2006, 16(3-E), 1-9.

Mandell, B., and Pherwani, S. (2003) Relationship between Emotional Intelligence and Transformational Leadership Style: A Gender Comparison. *Journal of Business and Psychology,* 17(3), 387-404.

Manhas, K.D. (2004) *Cognitive and Non-Cognitive Cognitive correlates of Emotional Intelligence of Adolescents*. Ph.D Thesis in Education, Panjab University, Chandigarh

Marina, S.P., Maria, G.G., Fec. P., Yolandag, P., Amparoc, T.Y., and Arcadioc, L. (2012) Relationship Between Emotional Intelligence, Job Satisfaction and Teaching Effectiveness Among Faculty Members of ESSU-SALCEDO. *Paper Presented at International Research Conference for Globalization and Sustainability*. August 14-16, 2012, Sarabia Monor Hotel, Iloilo Philippines.

Marlowe, H.A. (1986) Social Intelligence: Evidence for Multidimensionality and Construct Independence. *Journal of Educational Psychology*, 78(1), 52-58.

Martindale, C. (1999) (Eds.) Biological Bases of Creativity in R.J. Sternberg (1999) *Handbook of Creativity*. New York: Cambridge University Press.

Mary, S. (1992) *A Study of Creativity of Classes VI and VII Children in Relation to Some Variables*. M.Phil. Dissertation in Education, Sri Venkateswara University, Tirupati.

Marzano, R.J. Pickering, D., and McTighe, J. (1993). *Assessing Student Outcomes: Performance Assessment using the Dimensions of Learning Model*. Alexandria, VA: Association for Supervision and Curriculum Development.

Marzano, R.J. Pickering, D.J., and Pollock, J.E. (2001) *Classroom Instruction that Works: Research-based Strategies for Increasing Student Achievement*. Alexandria, VA: Association for Supervision and Curriculum Development.

Maslow, A.H. (1957) *Motivation and Personality* (2/e). New York: Harper and Row Publishers, 35-58.

Maslow, A.H. (1971) *The Farther Reaches of Human Nature*. New York: Viking Press.

Mathur, S. (1988) *The Attitude of Teachers Towards Creative Learning and Teaching*. Ph.D. Thesis in Education, Agra University, Agra.

Matieson, D.K. (1974) Personality Traits Associated with Effective Teaching in Rural and Urban Secondary Schools. *Journal of Educational Psychology*, 66(1), 123-128.

Mavroveli, S., Petrides, K.V., Rieffe, C., and Bakker, F. (2007) Trait Emotional Intelligence, Psychological Well-Being and Peer-Rated Social Competence in Adolescence. *British Journal of Developmental Psychology*, 25(2), 263-275.

May, R. (1959) The Nature of Creativity. In H.H. Anderson (Ed.), *Creativity and Its Cultivation*. New York: Harper and Row, 55-68.

May, R. (1975) *The Courage to Create*. New York: Norton.

Mayer, J.D., and Geher, G. (1996) Emotional Intelligence and the Identification. *Intelligence*, 22(2), 89-113.

Mayer, J.D., and Salovey, P. (1993) The Intelligence of Emotional Intelligence. *Intelligence*, 17(4), 433-442.

Mayer, J.D., and Salovey, P. (1997) What is Emotional Intelligence? In P. Salovey and D. Sluyter (Eds). *Emotional Development and Emotional Intelligence*. New York: Cambridge University Press, 396-420.

Mayer, J.D., Caruso, D.R., and Salovey, P. (1999) Emotional Intelligence Meets Traditional Standards for an Intelligence. *Intelligence*, 27(4), 267-298.

Mayer, J.D., Caruso, D.R., Salovery, P., and Sitarenious, G. (2001) Emotional intelligence as a Standard Intelligence. *Emotion*, 1(3), 232-242.

Mayer, J.D., Roberts, R.D., and Barsade, S.G. (2008) Human Abilities: Emotional Intelligence. *The Annual Review of Psychology*, January, 59, 507-536.

Mayer, J.D., Salovery, P., and Caruso, D. (2000) Competing Models of Emotional Intelligence. In R.J. Sternberg (Ed.), *Handbook of Human Intelligence*. 2/e. New York: Cambridge University Press, 396-420.

McCabe, M.P. (1991) Influence of Creativity and Intelligence on Academic Performance. *Journal of Creative Behaviour*, 25(2), 116-122.

McElvain, J.L., Fretwell, L.N., and Lewis, R.B. (1963) Relationship between Creativity and Teacher Variability. *Psychological Reports*, 13(1), 186-188.

McNemar, Q. (1964) Lost: Our Intelligence, Why? *American Psychologist,* 19(12), 871-882.

Medley, D.M. (1982) Teacher effectiveness. In H.E. Mitzel *et al.* (Eds.) *Encyclopedia of Educational Research.* 5/e. New York: Free Press, 1894-1903.

Mednick, M.T., and Andrews, F.M. (1967) Creative Thinking and Level of Intelligence. *Journal of Creative Behaviour*, 1(4), 428-431.

Mednick, M.T., Mednick, S.A., and Jung, C.C. (1964) Continual Association as a Function of Level of Creativity and Type of Verbal Stimulus. *Journal of Abnormal and Social Psychology,* 69(5), 511-515.

Mednick, S.A. (1962) The Associative Basis of the Creative Process. *Psychological Review*, 69(3), 220-232.

Mednick, S.A., and Mednick, M.J. (1964) An Association Interpretation of Creative Process. In C.W. Taylor (Eds.) *Widening Horizons in Creativity*. New York: John Wiley.

Mehdi, B. (1977) Creativity, Intelligence and Achievement—A Correlational Study. *Psychological Studies,* 22(1), 55-62.

Mehta, K. (2005) Holistic Approach to Creativity and Design Education. Design Education, *International Conference Design Education.* Tradition and Modernity, National Institute of Design, Ahmedabad.

Meintjes, H., and Grosser, M. (2010) Creative Thinking in Prospective Teachers: The Status Quo and the Impact of Contextual Factors. *South African Journal of Education,* 30(3), 361-386.

Menon, T.K.N. (1949) Teachers and Educational Reconstruction. *Indian Journal of Psychology,* XXIV, 1-4.

Miller, J.G. (1984) Culture and Development of Everyday Social Explanation. *Journal of Personality and Social Psychology*, 46(5), 961-978.

Mishra, M. (2006) Teaching Work Motivation Among Emotionally Intelligent Student-teachers. *Journal of Educational Studies*, 4(1 and 2), 40-41.

Mishra, P.S., and Mohapatra, A.K.D. (2010) Relevance of Emotional Intelligence for Effective Job Performance: An Empirical Study. *VIKALPA—The Journal of Decision Makers*, 35(1), 53-61.

Misra, G. (2001) Cultural and Self-Implications of Psychological Inquiry. *Journal of Indian Psychology,* 19, 1-20.

Mitchell, R.D. (1998) World Class Teachers: When Top Teachers Earn National Board Certification, Schools—and Students—Reap the benefits. *The American School Board Journal,* 185(9), 27-29.

Mitzel, H.E. (1960) Teacher Effectiveness. In C.W. Harris (Eds.) *Encyclopedia of Educational Research*. 3/e. New York: Macmillan.

Moffitt, J.E., Casri, A., Harkness, A.R., and Silva, P.A. (1993) The Natural History of Change in Intellectual Performance: Who Changes? How Much? Is it Meaningful? *Journal of Child Psychology and Psychiatry,* 34(4), 455-506.

Mohan, J. (2003) Emotional Intelligence Questionnaire *Training Instrument.* Chandigarh: Panjab University.

Molnar, A., Smith, P., Zahorik, J., Palmer, A., Halbach, A., and Ehrle, K. (1999) Evaluating the SAGE Program: A Pilot Programme in Targeted Pupil-Teacher Reduction in Wisconsin. *Educational Evaluation and Policy Analysis,* 21(2), 165-178.

Mooney, R.L. (1963) A Conceptual Model for Integrating For Approaches to The Identification of Creative Talent. In C.W. Taylor and F. Barron (Eds.) *Scientific*

Creativity: Its Recognition and Development. New York: Willey, 331-340.

More, R.T. (1988) A Study of Relationship Between Personality, Aptitude for Teaching and Effectiveness of Secondary Teachers. *Ph.D. Thesis in Education,* Nagpur University, Nagpur.

Morris, A.J (1997) Perceptions of Serial Structure, Others and Self: The Role of Social Intelligence in Managerial Effectiveness. *DAI,* May, 57(11), 4823-A.

Morrison, D.F. (1976) *Multivariate Statistical Methods*. New York: McGraw Hills.

Mortiboys, A. (2005) *Teaching with Emotional Intelligence*, London: Routledge.

Moss, F.A., and Hunt, T. (1927) Are You Socially Intelligent? *Scientific American*, 137, 108-110.

Muddu, V. (1982) Relationship Between Creative Abilities (Dimensions) Creativity and Intelligence. *Experiments in Education,* 9(2), 189-191.

Muijs, O., and Reynolds D. (2001) *Effectiveness Teaching: Evidence and Practice.* London: Paul Chapman Publishing.

Mulia, R.D. (1991) A Comparative Study of Social Maturity of Higher Secondary School Students in the Context of their Streams, Sex and DIQs. *Journal of Education and Psychology,* 48(3-4), 145-155.

Murthy, H.N. (1966) Relation of Intelligence and Emotional Stability. *Journal of Education and Psychology,* 23, 243-247.

Nair, S.R. (1974) Intelligence and Teacher Effectiveness. *Journal of Educational Research and Extension,* 10(4), 225-229.

National Association of Secondary School Principles (NASSP) (1997) Students say: What Makes a Good Teacher? School in the Middle, 6(5), 15-17.

Neelkandan, R. (2007) Emotional Competence of Primary School Teachers. *Edutracks,* 6(9), 31-33.

Neil, John O' (1996) On Emotional Intelligence: A Conversation with Daniel Goleman. *Educational Leadership,* 54(1), 6-11.

Neisser U. (1979) The Concept of Intelligence. *Intelligence*. 3(3), 217-227.

Nelson, D., and Low, G. (1999) *Exploring and Developing Emotional Intelligence Skills.* Kings Ville, TX: EI Learning systems.

Nelson, D.B., Low, G., and Nelson K., (1999) The Emotionally Intelligent Teacher: A Transformative Learning Model. *www.tmuk.edu/edu/kwei000/research articles_files.*

Newa, D.R. (2007) *Teacher Effectiveness in Relation to Work Satisfaction, Media Utilization and Attitude Towards the Use of Information and Communication Technology Among Secondary School Teachers of Nepal.* Ph.D. Thesis in Education, Panjab University Chandigarh.

Nickerson, R.S., Perkins, D.N., and Smith, E.E. (1985) *The Teaching of Thinking.* Hillsdal, N.J. Erbaum.

Nikose, R.L. (2010) Social Intelligence of Prospective Teachers. *Psycho-Lingua,* 40(1 and 2), 30-33.

Noor, A. (2001) *A Study of Creativity of B.Ed Teacher Trainees in Banglore City in Relation to their Values, Personality Adjustment and Achievement Motivation.* Ph.D. Thesis in Education, University of Mysore, Mysore.

O'Boyle Jr. E.H., Humphery, R.H., Pollack, J.M., Howver, T.H. and Story, P.A. (2011) The Relation Between Emotional Intelligence and Job Performance: A Meta-Analysis. *Journal of Organizational Behaviour,* 32(5), 788-818.

Olatoye, R.A., and Oyundoyin, J.O. (2007) Intelligence quotient as a Predictor of Creativity Among Nigerian Secondary School Students. *Educational Research and Review,* 2(4), 92-95.

Onderi, H., and Croll, P. (2009) Teacher Self-Perceptions of Effectiveness: A Study in

District of Kenya. *Educational Research,* 51(1), 97-107.

Ornstein. A.C. (1991) Teacher Effective Research: Theoretical Considerations. In H.C. Waxman and H.J. Walberg (Eds.) *Effective Teaching: Current Research.* Berkeley. CA: Mccuttan, 63-80.

Osborn (1948) *Your Creative: Power How to Use Imagination.* New York: Charles Scribner's Sons.

Pachauri, D. (2010) Emotional Intelligence of three Faculties Members. *Indian Journal of Psychometry and Education*, 41(1), 67-69.

Pachaury, A.C. (2000) Initiating Creative Thinking in Five-Six-Year-Old Children. *Journal of Indian Education,* XXVI(3), 23-38.

Pal, M. (2001) *A Comparative Study of Attitude of School and College Teacher Towards Creative Learning and Teaching.* Ph.D. Thesis in Education, Panjab University, Chandigarh.

Palsane, M.N., and Law, D.J. (1996) Stress and Coping from Traditional Indian and Chinese Perspectives. *Psychology and Developing Societies,* 8, 128-153.

Panda, M. (2004) Prediction of Teaching Competency from Creativity, Intelligence and Teacher Attitude: A Study. *Indian Educational Review,* 40(2), 80-88.

Panda, M., and Yadva, R. (2005) Implicit Creativity Theories in India an Exploration. *Psychological Studies,* 50(1), 32-39.

Pandey, M., and R. Maikhuri (1999) A Study of the Attitude of Effective and Ineffective Teachers Towards Teaching Profession. *Indian Journal of Psychometry and Education,* 30(1), 43-46.

Panton, J.H. (1948) *Modern Teaching Practice and Technique.* London: Longmans Green and Co.

Parnes, S.J. (1966) *Work Book for Creative Problem Solving Institutes and Courses.* Buffalo Creative Education Foundation.

Patel, A.S., and Joshi, R.J. (1978) An Enquiry into the Relation of Creativity to Intellectual Giftedness. *Indian Journal of Psychology,* 53(3), 140-144.

Patil, B., and Kumar, A. (2006) Emotional Intelligence among Students Teachers in Relation to Sex, Faculty and Academic Achievement. *Edutracks,* 6(7), 38-39.

Peart, N.A., and Campbell, F.A. (1999) At-Risk Students' Perceptions of Teacher Effectiveness. *Journal for a Just and Caring Education,* 5(3), 269-284.

Penrose, A., Perey, C., and Ball, I. (2007) Emotional Intelligence and Teacher Self Efficacy: The Contribution of Teacher Status and Length of Experience. *Issues in Educational Research,* 17(1), 1-17.

Perkins, D.N. (1988) The Possibility of Invention. In R.J. Sternberg (Eds.). *The Nature of Creativity.* Cambridge: Cambridge University Press, 362-385.

Petrides, K.V., and Furnham, A. (2000) Gender Differences in Measured and Self-Estimated Trait Emotional Intelligence. *Sex Roles*, 42(5 and 6), 449-461.

Phaewsakul, N. (1989) *Effect of Clinical Supervision on Teacher Effectiveness in Relation to Intelligence and Self Concept of Secondary School Teachers in Thailand. Ph.D. Thesis In Education, Panjab University, Chandigarh.*

Pllazza, R., and Bar-On, R. (1995) A Study of the Emotional Intelligence of Convicted Criminals, *Unpublished Manuscript.* Quoted from Dean, E. Frost, The Psychological Assessment of Emotional Intelligence, 203-213.

Prithima, H.P.and. Kulsum, U. (2013) Relationship between Social Intelligence and Mental Health of Secondary School Teachers.*PARIPEX-Indian Journal of Research*, 2(11), 60-62.

Promin, R., and Petrill, S.A. (1997) Genetics and Intelligence. *Intelligence,* 24(1), 53-77.

Punia, B.K. (2005) Impact of Development Variables on Emotional Intelligence and

Leadership Behaviour of Corporate Executives. *Journal of Organizational Behaviour,* April, 4(2), 7-22.

Puri, S. (2008) *Study of Teacher Effectiveness of Teacher Educators in Relation to Cognitive and Non-Cognitive Variables.* Ph.D. Thesis in Education, Panjab University, Chandigarh.

Qureshi, A.N. (1980) *A Study of Creativity in Relation to Intelligence Manifest Anxiety and Level of Aspiration of High School Girls.* Ph.D. Thesis in Psychology, Agra University, Agra.

Raghuvansh, H.S. (2008) Emotional Intelligence: A Key Ingredient of Leadership. *Business Perspective,* 10(1), 85-95.

Rai, R.P., and Rai, V.K. (2006) *Teaching Effectiveness and Student Evaluation of Teaching: A Study.* Allahabad: Sharda Pustak Bhawan.

Rai, V.K. (2005) Teaching Effectiveness and Student Evaluation of Teaching: A Study. *Indian Educational Abstracts*, January and July 2007, 7(1 and 2), 12-13.

Rai, V.K. (2005) Teaching Effectiveness and Students Evaluation of Teaching-A Study. *Indian Educational Abstract*, January and July, 7(1 and 2), 12-13.

Raina, N.K. (1970) A Study of Creativity in Teachers. *Psychological Studies*, 15(1 and 2), 28-33.

Raina, T.N. (1982) Sex Differences in Creativity in India: A Second Look. *Indian Educational Review,* 17(3), 122-128.

Raina, V.K. (1990) Personality Characteristics of Graduated Student Teachers: Does Specialisation Make Differences? *Indian Educational Review*, 25(1), 106-113.

Raj, T. (2000) An Empirical Study of Correlates Teacher Effectiveness. *The Educational Review,* 107(1), 6-7.

Raja Gopalan, S. (1976) Measurement of Teaching Success. *Experiments in Education*, 3(4), 78-83.

Raja, B. William Dharma and Thiagarajan, (1998) School Organizational Climate and Teacher effectiveness of Boys Higher Secondary Schools in Tripura. *Journal of Educational Research and Extension,* 35(1), 20-27.

Ramalingam, P., and Mani, P. (2009) Social Maturity of Elementary Pupil Teachers. *Psycho-Lingua,* 39(2), 168-170.

Rao (1978) *A Study of Socio-Psychological Correlates of Social Development of High School Children in Grades VIII, X in Some High Schools of Bangalore City.* Unpublished Doctoral Thesis, Bangalore University, Bangalore.

Rao, G.K. (1995) Evaluation of Teacher Effectiveness of Primary and Secondary Level Teachers with Creativity and Inter-personal Relationships. *Sixth Survey of Educational Research,* New Delhi: NCERT, II, 509.

Rao, O., and Bandkumar, D.N. (2004) *School Teacher Effectiveness.* New Delhi. Discovery Publishing House.

Rao, V.K., and Reddy, V.S. (1982) *Instructional Objectives and Teacher Education.* New Delhi: Common Wealth Publishers.

Raven, J.C. (1958) *Standard Progressive Matrices.* London: H.K. Lewis & Co. Ltd.

Reddy, T.R, Reddy, V.D., and Geetanath, P.S. (1999) A Study of Creativity of Teacher Trainees of DIETS. *Sixth Survey of Educational Research,* NCERT, New Delhi, II, 522.

Renzulli, J.S. (1986) The Three-Ring Conception of Giftedness: A Developmental Model for Creative Productivity. In R.J. Sternberg and J.E. Davidson (Eds.) *Conceptions of Giftedness.* Cambridge University Press. 53-92

Repucci, L.C. (1960) Definitions of Creativity. In Sternberg R.S. (Ed.). *The Nature of Creativity.* Cambridge: Cambridge University Press, 118-119.

Rhodes, M. (1961) An Analysis of Creativity. *The Phi Delta Kappan*, 42(7), 305-310.

Riggio, R.E., Messamer, J., and Throckmorton, B. (1991) Social and Academic Intelligence Conceptually Distinct but Overlapping Constructs. *Personality and Individual Difference,* 12(7), 695-701.

Riti (2010) *A Study of Teacher Effectiveness in Relation to School Organizational Climate and Administrative Behaviour of School Heads of Himachal Pradesh.* Ph.D. Thesis in Education, Punjabi University, Patiala.

Rogers, C.R. (1954) Towards a Theory of Creativity, in P.E. Vernon (Eds.) (1970). *Creativity.* Penguin, Harmondsworth, 139, 147-149.

Rogers, C.R. (1959) Toward a Theory of Creativity. In H.H. Anderson (Eds.). *Creativity and its Cultivation.* New York: Harper and Bros, 69-82.

Rosenshine, B., and Furst, N. (1971) Research on Teacher Performance Criteria in Teacher Characteristics In H.E. Mitzel *et al.* (Eds.) *Encyclopedia of Educational Research,* 5/e, New York: Free Press, 1894-1903.

Rosenthal, R. (1977) *The PONS Test: Measuring Sensitivity to Non-Verbal Cues.* In P. McReynolds (Ed.) *Advances in Psychological Assessment.* San Francisco, CA: Jossey-Bass.

Rossman (1937) *The Psychology of Inventor*. Washington: Investors Publishing Company.

Roul, S. (2007) Teacher Effectiveness of Autonomous and Non-Autonomous College Teachers. *Journal of Community Guidance and Research*, 24(3), 326-339.

Roy, M. (2005) *To Study the Effect of Creativity Appreciation Training Programme (CATP) on the Teachers' Attitudes Towards Creative Teaching and Learning.* Ph.D. Thesis in Education, Nagaland University, Nagaland.

Rushton, J.P., Murray, H.G. and Paunonen, S.V. (2005) Personality, Research Creativity and Teaching Effectiveness in University Professors. *Scientometrics,* 5(2), 93-116.

Rushton, J.P., Murray, H.G., and Paunonen, S.V. (1983) Personality, Research Creativity and Teaching Effectiveness in University Professors. *Sociometrics,* 5(2) 93-116.

Russell (1974) *Creativity and the Individual.* New York: Hudson Valley Free Press.

Ryans D.G. (1969) *Characteristics of Teachers.* Delhi: Sterling Publishers.

Saini, S. (1998) *Self-Esteem of Student Teachers as Related to their Personality, Creativity and Attitude Towards Teaching Profession.* Ph.D. Thesis in Education, Panjab University, Chandigarh.

Salovey, P., and Mayor, J.D. (1990) Emotional Intelligence. *Imagination, Cognition and Personality,* 9, 185-211.

Salovey, P., Hsee, C.K., and Mayer, J.D. (1993) Emotional Intelligence and the Self Regulation of Affect. In D.M. Wegner and J.W. Penn (Eds.) *Handbook of Mental Control*. Eagenwood Cliffs, NJ: Prentice Hall, 258-77.

Sameer, B.M. (2008) Family Related Psychological Problems as Moderating Factor of Emotional Intelligence. *Psycho-Lingua.* 38(1), 48-51.

Sansanwal, D.N., and Jarial, G.S. (1974) Personality Differences Among High and Low Creative Teacher Trainees. *Journal of the Institute of Educational Research,* 3(3), 24-26.

Sansanwal, D.N., and Jarial, G.S. (1983) Creativity and Its Components in Relation to Different Levels of Intelligence and Academic Subjects Among High School Students. *Asian Journal of Psychology and Education,* 11(2), 9-13.

Santhana, K.S. (1990) *A Study of Creativity in Relation to Some Selected Variables.* Ph.D. Thesis in Education, Annamalai University, Chidambaram, Tamil Nadu.

Sanwal, V. (2004) *Emotional Intelligence: The Indian Scenario*, New Delhi: Indian Publisher Distributors.

Saxena, S. and Panigrahi, (2010) Social Intelligence of High and Low Achiever

Undergraduate Students. *Journal of Educational Studies,* 1(7), 31-34.

Scheider, R.J., Ackerman, R.J., and Kanger, R., (1996) To Act Wisely in Human Relations: Exploring the Dimensions of Social Competencies. *Personality and Individual Differences,* 21(34), 469-482.

Schulte, D.P., Slate, J.R. and Onwuegbuize, A.J. (2008) Effective High School Teachers: A Mixed Investigation. *International Journal of Educational Research,* 47(6), 351-361.

Schutte, N.S., Malouff, J.M., Hall, L.E., Haggerty, D.J., Cooper, J.T., Golden, C.H., and Dornheim, L. (1998) Development and Validation of a Measure of Emotional Intelligence. *Personality and Individual Differences*, 25(2), 167-177.

Selsor, K., (2003) Rural and Suburban Community College Students Perceptions of Teaching Effectiveness. *DAI,* August, 64(2), 380-A.

Seng, Q.K., Keung, H.K., and Cheng, S.K., (2008) Implicit Theories of Creativity: A Comparison of Student Teacher in Hong Kong and Singapore. *A Journal of Comparative and International Education,* 38(1), 71-86.

Service, R.W. (2005) S.Q. Versus Intelligent Quotient: Successful Intelligence Measuring and Teaching What Matters. *The International Journal of Business Disciplines,* 16(1), 81-96

Sharma, A.K. (1979) *A Study of Creativity in Relation to Intelligence, Personality, Socio-Economic Status and Sex of the High School Students of Indore City.* Unpublished M.Ed. Dissertation, Indore University, Indore.

Sharma, K.N. (1971) *Creativity as Function of Intelligence, Interest and Culture.* Ph.D. Thesis in Psychology, Agra University, Agra.

Sharma, K.N. (1972) Creativity as a Function of Intelligence, *Psychological Studies,* 17(1 and 2), 64-67.

Sharma, K.N. (2006) *Divergent Production Abilities* (*DPA*). Agra: National Psychological Corporation.

Sharma, M.L. (1977) *Success in Teaching in Relation to Self-Concept, Intelligence, Experience and Academic Achievement of Teachers.* Ph.D. Thesis in Education, Panjab University, Chandigarh.

Sharma, R. (2007) A Study of Art Competencies of B.Ed Pupil Teachers as Correlates of Emotional Intelligence, Creativity and Achievement Motivation. *KMR-Journal of Teacher Education*, 3(1), 37-41.

Sherry, G.P. (1964) *A Battery of Psychological Tests for Prediction of Success in Teaching.* Ph.D. Thesis in Education, Agra University, Agra.

Sibia, A., and Misra, G. (2004) Towards Understanding Emotional Intelligence in Indian Context. Perspectives of Parents, Teachers and Children. *Psychological Studies,* 49(2-3), 114-123.

Silvera, D.H., and Martinussen, M. and Dahi, T.I. (2001) The Tromso Social Intelligence Scale: A Self Report Measure of Social Intelligence. *Scandinavian Journal of Psychology*, 42(4), 313-19.

Sinclair, R.C and Mark, M.M. (1992) The Influence of Mood State on Judgement and Action: Effects on Persuasion, Categorization, Social justice, Person Perception and Judgemental Accuracy. In L.L. Martin and A. Tesser (Eds.) *The Construction of Social Judgements.* Hillsdale, N.J: Erlbaum, 165-93.

Singarvalu, S., (2007) Emotional Intelligence of Student Teacher (Pre Service) at Primary Level in Puducherry. *Journal of all India Association of Educational Research,* 19(3), 3-4.

Singh, I and Jha, A. (2012) Teacher Effectiveness in Relation to Emotional Intelligence among Medical and Engineering Faculty Members, Europe's Journal of Psychology, 8(4) 667-685.

Singh and Koteswari, V.B. (2006) Emotional Intelligence and Coping Resources of Stress among Project Managers. *Edutracks.* August 2006, 5(11), 33-36.

Singh, D. (1991) *Creativity and Intelligence as Correlates of Teacher Effectiveness of Secondary School Teachers.* Ph.D. Thesis in Education, Punjabi University, Patiala.

Singh, D. (2003) *Emotional Intelligence At Work: A Professional Guide.* 3/e New Delhi, India: Sage Publication.

Singh, D. (2003) *Emotional Intelligence at Work: A Professional Guide*. 2/e New Delhi, Sage Publications.

Singh, D. (2006) *Emotional Intelligence at Work.* 3/e New Delhi: Response Books.

Singh, G. (2002) *A Comparative Study of Job Satisfaction of Teacher Educators in Relation to their Values, Attitude Towards Teaching and Teacher Effectiveness.* Ph.D. Thesis in Education, Panjab University Chandigarh.

Singh, G., and Kumar, G. (2009) Emotional Intelligence Among Convent and Saraswati School Teachers. *Psycho-Lingua,* 39(2), 139-141.

Singh, G., and Kumar, G. (2009) Emotional Intelligence and Medium of Instruction. A Study Among Secondary School Teachers. *Experiments in Education,* XXXVII(3), 43-46.

Singh, H.I. (1996) Identification of Creative Teaching Skills for Secondary School Teachers. *The Progress of Education,* LXX(II), 255-257.

Singh, R. (1985) Attitude of High School Teachers Towards Creative Learning and Teaching. *Prachi Journal of Psycho-cultural Dimensions,* 1(1), 7-12.

Singh, R.B. Mathur, S.R., and Sexena, S. (1977) Creativity as Related to Intelligence, Achievement and Security-Insecurity. *Indian Psychological Review,* 14(3), 84-88.

Singh, R.P., and Dass, M. (1989) Attitudes of Teachers Towards Creative Learning Teaching in *Fifth Survey of Educational Research.* New Delhi: NCERT, II, 1488.

Singh, R.S. (1987) Teaching Effectiveness and Its Correlates at Higher Secondary Stage in Eastern U.P. *Ph.D. Thesis in Education*, Gorkhpur University, Gorkhpur, Uttar Pradesh.

Singh, S. (2007) *Emotional Inelligence, Social Intelligence, Adjustment and Personality Differentials of Adolescents with High and Low Creativity.* Ph.D. Thesis in Education, Panjab University, Chandigarh.

Singh, S. (2010) *Classroom Interaction of High School Teachers as a Function of their Teaching Style, Creativity and Some Selected Variables.* Ph.D. Thesis in Education, Punjabi University, Patiala.

Singhal S. (1990) Effective and Ineffective Teachers Do Students Differentiate? *Perspectives in Education,* 6(3), 237-242.

Sitaram, Lakshmi (2005) *Relationship between Emotional Quotient and IQ among Adolescents.* Ph.D. Thesis in Education, University of Bangalore, Bangalore.

Smith, I.L. (1970) IQ, Creativity, and the Taxonomy of Educational Objectives: Cognitive Domain. *Journal of Experimental Education*, 38(4), 58-60.

Snarey, J.R., and Vaillant, G.E. (1985) How Lower and Working Class Youth Become Middle-Class Adults: The Association Between Ego, Defence Mechanisms and Upward Social Mobility. *Child Development*, 56(4), 899-910.

Sodhi, B. (2010) *Teacher Effectiveness of Secondary School Teachers of Punjab in Relation to School Organizational Climate.* Ph.D. Thesis in Education, Punjabi University, Patiala.

Sofaya (1981) Academic Achievement of B.Ed. Trainees as Related to Intelligence, Creativity and adjustment. *Trends in Education,* 8(1 and 2), 18-25.

Soloman, D., Rosenberg, L., and Bazdek, W.E. (1965) Teacher Behaviour and Student Learning. *Journal of Educational Psychology,* 55(1), 23-30.

Southeast Center for Teaching Quality (SECTQ) (2003) How do Teachers Learn to Teach Effectively? Quality Indicators From Quality Schools, *Teaching Quality in the Southeast: Best Practices and Policies*, 7(2) 1-2

Spearman, C. (1927) *The Nature of Intelligence and Principles of Cognition*. London: Macmillan.

Spencer, L., and Spencer, S. (1993) *Competence at Work*. New York: John Wiley.

Sridhar, Y.N., and Badici, H.R.C. (2007) Teacher Efficacy and Emotional Intelligence of Primary School Teachers. *Edutracks*, 7(3), 25-31.

Srinivasan, P.T. (2005) Relationship of Emotional Intelligence and Conflict Management Style Among Management Teachers. *UAC Funded Field Study*, Department of Management Studies, University of Madras, Chennai, Tamil Nadu.

Srivastava, A.K., and Misra, G. (2007) *Rethinking Intelligence Conceptualizing Human Competence in Cultural Context*. New Delhi: Concept Publishing Company.

Srivastava, G.N.P., and Bhargava, A. (1984) Personality Factors and Teaching Effectiveness of Science Pupil-Teachers. *Journal of Educational Research and Extension*, 21(2), 103-111.

Srivastava, N., and Mallick, S. (2010) A Study of Social Competence Among Emotionally Intelligent Students. *Journal of Educational Studies*, 1(7), 23-27.

Srivastava, S., and Thomas, A. (1991) Creativity of Pre-School Children—Effect of Sex, Age, Birth Order and Intelligence. *Journal of Psychological Researchers*, 36(2), 92-98.

Stein, M.I. (1963) A Transactional Approach to Creativity. In C.W. Taylor and F. Barron (Eds.) *Scientific Creativity its Recognition and Development*. New York: Johnwiley, 217-227.

Stein, M.I., and Shirley Heinze (1960) (Eds.) *Creativity and Individual*. Chicago: Free Press.

Stein, S.J., and Book, H.E. (2001) *The EQ Edge*. New Delhi: Macmillan India.

Stern, W. (1912) *Die Psychologischen Methods de Intelligenzpsufeing*. Leipzig: Baith.

Sternberg, R., Conway, B.E., Ketron, J.L., and Bernstein, M. (1981) People's Conception of Intelligence. *Journal of Personality and Social Psychology*, 41(3), 37-55.

Sternberg, R.J and O-Hara, L. (2000) Intelligence and Creativity, in R.L. Sternberg (Eds.) *Handbook of Intelligence*. U.K. Cambridge University Press.

Sternberg, R.J. (1985) *Beyond IQ, A Triarchic Theory of Human Intelligence*. New York: Cambridge University Press.

Sternberg, R.J. (1985) Implicit Theories of Intelligence, Creativity, and Wisdom. *Journal of Personality and Social Psychology*, 49(3), 607-627.

Sternberg, R.J. (1986) Intelligence, Wisdom and Creativity: Three is Better than One. *Educational Psychologist*, 21(3), 175-190.

Sternberg, R.J. (1988) (Eds.) *The Nature of Creativity: Contemporary Psychological Perspective*. USA: Cambridge University, Press.

Sternberg, R.J. (1990) *Metaphors of Mind: A New Theory of Human Intelligence*. New York: Cambridge University Press.

Sternberg, R.J. (1996) *Successful Intelligence*. New York: Viking.

Sternberg, R.J. (2000) Creativity is a Decision. In A.L. Costa (Eds.) Teaching for Intelligence II. Arlington Heights, IL: Sky Light Training and Publishing.

Sternberg, R.J. (2003) *Wisdom, Intelligence and Creativity Synthesized*. New York: Cambridge University Press.

Sternberg, R.J., and Determan, D.R. (1986) *What is Intelligence*? Norwood, NJ: Ablex.

Sternberg, R.J., and Lubart, T.I. (1995) *Defying the Crowd: Cultivating Creativity in a Culture of Conformity*. New York: Free Press.

Sternberg, R.J., and Lubart, T.I. (1995) Investing in Creativity. *American Psychologist*, 51(7), 677-688.

Sternberg, R.J., and Wagner, R.K. (1986) *Practical Intelligence: Everyday World*. New York: Cambridge University Press.

Strang, R. (1930) Measures of Social Intelligence. *The American Journal of Sociology*, 36(2), 263-269.

Stranger, R., and Karwoski, T.F. (1973) quoted by L.D. Crow and A. Crow, *Educational Psychology*. New Delhi: Eurasia Publishing House, 164-180.

Strenberg, R.J., and Lubart, T.I. (1991) An Investment Theory of Creativity and its Development. *Human Development*, 34(1), 1-31.

Stronge, J.H. (2007) *Qualities of Effective Teachers*. 2/e. U.S.A: Association for Supervision and Curricular Development.

Suresh, K. and Rao, D.B. (2009) *Social Intelligence of Student Teachers*. New Delhi: Discovery Publishing House.

Sutton, R.E. and Wheatery, K.F. (2003) Teachers' Emotions and Teaching: A Review of the Literature and Directions for Future Research. *Educational Psychology Review*, 15(4), 327-358.

Tafuri, D.M. (1995) The Effects of Creativity on Teacher Students Interactions. *DAI*, 55(10), 3087-A.

Tajudin, A., Omar, C.M.Z.C., Yunus. N.KY., Tajuddin, A.F.A., Aziz, R.A and Hadi, N.F.A (2014) The Effect of Emotional Intelligence and Job Stress on the Teaching Effectiveness among Malaysia Polytechnic Lectureres. *International Journal of Sciences: Basic and Applied Research*, 17(1), 226-235.

Tan, Ai-Girl (2000) Teachers Conceptions of Creativity, in Ai-Girl. Tan (Eds.) *Psychology of Cultivating Creativity: Conceptions and Competence* (Singapore, National Institute of Education, Nanyang Technological University)

Tardif, T.Z., and Sternberg, R.J. (1988) What Do We Know About Creativity? In R.J. Sternberg. *The Nature of Creativity*. Cambridge: Cambridge University Press, 429-440.

Tatsuoka, M. (1970) *Discriminant Analysis: The Study of Group Differences*. Champaign III: Institute for Personality and Ability Testing.

Tatsuoka, M. (1970) *Discriminant Analysis: The Study of Group Differences*. Champaign III: Institute for Personality and Ability Testing.

Taylor, B., and Wash (2003) 3000 Educators Respond to Preferred Dispositions. *Paper Presented at the Second Annual Symposium on Educator Dispositions*, November 20-21, in Richmond, Kentucky.

Taylor, B., Pressley, M., and Pearson, D. (2000) *Effective Teachers and Schools: Trends Across Recent Studies*. Stronge, J.H. (2007) *Qualities of Effective Teachers*. 2/e, U.S.A: Association for Supervision and Curricular Development.

Taylor, C.W. (1988) Various Approaches to and Definitions of Creativity. In Sternberg (Eds.). *The Nature of Creativity*. Cambridge: Cambridge University Press, 99-121.

Taylor, C.W., and Bawon, F. (1963) (Eds.) *Scientific Creativity: Its Recognition and Development*. New York: John Wiley and Sons.

Teddlie, C., and Liu, S. (2008) Examining Teacher Effectiveness with Differently Effective Primary Schools in the People's Republic of China. *School Effectiveness and School Improvement: An International Journal of Research, Policy and Practice,* 19(4), 387-407.

Teddlie, C., and Reynolds, D. (2000) *International Handbook of School Effectiveness Research*. London: Falmer.

Thomson, G.H. (1939) *The Factorial Analysis of Human Ability*. London: University of London Press.

Thorndike, E.L. (1920) Intelligence and Its Users. *Harper's Magazine*, 140, 227-235.

Thurstone, L.L. (1938) *Primary Mental Abilities*. Chicago: University of Chicago Press.

Topping, K., Bremmer, W., and Holmer, E.A. (2000) Social Competence: The Social Construction of the Concept. In R. Bar-on and J.D.A. Parker (Eds.) *The Handbook of Emotional Intelligence*. San Francisso: Jossy, 28-29.

Torrance, E.P. (1962) *Guiding Creative Talent.* N.J. Prentice-Hall, Inc. 2-7, 30-31, 84-103, 193-195, 206.

Torrance, E.P. (1965) *Rewarding Creative Behaviour*. New Jersey: Prentice Hall Englewood Cliffs.

Torrance, E.P. (1966) *Torrance Tests of Creative Thinking: Norms Technical Manual.* Princeton NJ: Personnel Press.

Torrance, E.P. (1975) Creativity Research in Education: Still Alive. In I.A. Taylor and J.W. Getzels (Eds.), *Perspective in Creativity.* Chicago: Aldine. 278-296

Torrance, E.P. (1975) *Prodiminary Manual: Ideal Child Checklist.* Athens, Georgia: Georgia Studies of Creative Behaviour.

Torrance, E.P. (1988) The Nature of Creativity as Manifest in its Testing. In R.J. Sternberg (Eds.) *The Nature of Creativity: Contemporary Psychological Perspectives.* Cambridge: Cambridge University Press, 43-75.

Torrance, E.P. and Myers, R.E. (1974) *Creative Learning and Teaching.* (6/e). New York: Dodd, Mead and Company, 13, 22, 37, 83, 156, 189, 195, 219-238, 252-55, 289.

Triandis, H.C., Bontempo, R., and Villareal, M.J. (1988) Cited in A. Sibia, G. Misra and A.K. Srivastava (2004) Towards Understanding Emotional Intelligence in the Indian Context. *Psychological Studies*, 49(2 and 3), 114-123.

Tripathi, S.N. (1996) *Talent and Creativity*. Agra: National Psychological Cooperation.

Tuckman, Bruce, W. (1978) *Conducting Educational Research*. New York: Harcourt Brace College Publishers.

Turner, J.C., Meyer, D.K., Midgley, C., and Patrick, H. (2003) Teacher Discourse and Sixth Graders Reported Affect and Achievement Behaviours in Two Mastery, High Performance Mathematics Classrooms. *Elementary School Journal*, 103(4), 357-382.

Tyagi, S.K. (2004) Emotional Intelligence of Secondary Teachers in Relation to Gender and Age. *Journal of Educational Research and Extension,* 41(3), 39-45.

Upadhaya, P. (2006) Personality of Emotionally Intelligent Student-Teachers. *Journal of Educational Studies,* 4(1 and 2), 37-41.

Upadhyaya, P. (2008) *Emotional Intelligence in Teacher Education.* Allahabad: Anubhav Publishing House.

Valeski, T.N., (2000) Young Children's Social Competence and Relationship with Teacher: Pathway to Early Academic Success. *DAI*, December, 61(6), 2189-A.

Van Rooy, A.A., and Viswas V.C. (2005) Group Difference in Emotional Intelligence Scores: Theoretical and Practical Implications. *Personality and Individual Differences,* 38(3), 689-700.

Varshney, S.P. (2007) Effect of Parental Encouragement on Emotional Intelligence of Adolescents. *Psycho-Lingua,* 37(2), 152-155.

Vasilova, K., and Baumgartner, P. (2004) Why is Social Intelligence Difficult to Measure. *Research Supported by Grant Agency VEGA and Centre of Excellence of the Slovak Academy of Science-CEVIT.*

Venkatarami, Reddy, A. and Bala Krishna, Reddy, P. (1983) Creativity and Intelligence. *Psychological Studies,* 28(1), 20-24.

Vernon, P.E. (1933) Some Characteristics of the Good Judge of Personality. *Journal of Social Psychology*, 4(1), 42-57.

Vernon, P.E. (1971) *The Structure of Human Abilities.* London: Methuen.

Vesanthi, R., and Anandi, E. (1997) A Study of Some Factors Effecting Teacher Effectiveness. *The Progress of Education,* 71(6), 137-140.

Vijyalakshmi, G., and Mythill, B. (2004) Impact of Some Personal and Professional Variables on the Teacher Effectiveness and Work Orientation. *Recent Researches in Education and Psychology,* 9(1), 15-21.

Vora, J.J. (1980) *An Investigation into Social Maturity of Students of Colleges of Education in the Context of Some-Socio Correlates.* Ph.D. Thesis in Education, Shilong University, Shillong.

Walberg, H.J. (1983) Scientific Literacy and Economic Productivity in International Perspective. *Daedalus,* 112, (2), 1-28.

Walberg, H.J. (1986) Synthesis of Research on Teaching. In M.C. Whittrock (Ed.). *Handbook of Research on Teaching.* 3/e. New York: Macmillan, 214-229.

Walker, R.E., and Foley, J.M. (1973) Social Intelligence: Its History and Measurement.*Psychological Reports*, 33(3), 839-869.

Walker, W.J. (1964) Creativity and High School Climate in John Curtis Gowan, GEORGED Demos and E. Paul Torrancc (Eds.) (1967) *Creativity: Its Educational Implications.* New York: John Wiley and Sons Inc., 296.

Walker-Dalhouse, D. (2005) Discipline: Responding to Socio-economic and Racial Differences. *Childhood Education,* 82(1), 24-30.

Wallach, M.A. and Kogan, N. (1966) *Models of Thinking in Young Children.* New York: Holt, Rinechart and Winston in C.

Wallach, M.A., and Kogan N. (1965) *Modes of Thinking in Young Children: A Study of the Creativity—Intelligence, Distinction.* New York: Holt Rinehart and Winston, Inc., 14-15.

Wallas, G. (1926) *The Art of Thought.* New York: Harcourt, Brace, Jovanovich.

Walls, R.T., Nardi, A.H., Vonminden, A.M., and Hoffman, N. (2002) The Characteristics of Effective and Ineffective Teachers. *Teacher Education Quarterly, Winter,* 29(1), 39-48.

Walter, O. and Marcel, A. (2013) Emotional intelligence and Teaching efficacy as Predictors of Teaching Ability.*Journal of Studies in Education*, 3(3), 57-74.

Wang, M., Haertel, G.D. and Walberg, H. (1993) Toward A Knowledge Base for School Learning. *Review of Educational Research,* 63(3), 249-294.

Wannamaker, C.M. (2005) *A Study of the Need for Emotional Intelligence in University Judicial Officers.* Ph.D Thesis in Educational Leadership and Learning Technology, Drexel University, Philadelphia.

Wechsler, N. (1958) *The Measurement and Appraisal of Adult Intelligence.* 4/e. Baltimar: Williams and Wilkins.

Wedeck, J. (1947) The Relationship Between Personality and Psychological Ability. *British Journal of Psychology*, 37(3), 133-151.

Weinstein, E.A. (1969) The Development of Interpersonal Competence. In D.A. Gosein (Eds.) *Handbook of Socialization Theory and Research.* Chicago: Rand MacNally.

Weisberg (1986) *Creativity: Genius and Other Myths.* New York: W.H. Freeman.

Welsch, P.K. (1980) Cited in Isaksen and Murdock, *et al.* 1993, p. 18). *The Nurturance of Creative Behaviour in Educational Environments: A Comprehensive Curriculum Approach.* Unpublished Doctoral Thesis, University of Michigan. U.K.

Wenglinsky, H. (2002) How Schools Matter: The Link Between Teacher Classroom Practices and Student Academic Performance. *Educational Policy Analysis Archives,* 10(2). Retrieved from http://epaa.asu.edu/epaa/v10n12/.

Wentzel, K.R. (1997) Student Motivation in Middle School: The Role of Perceived Pedagogical Caring. *Journal of Education Psychology,* 89(3), 411-419.

Wharton-McDonald, R., Pressley, M., and Hampston, J.M. (1998) Literacy Instruction in Nine First-Grade Classrooms: Teacher Characteristics and Student Achievement. *The Elementary School Journal,* 99(2), 101-128.

Whitney, F.L. and Frasier, C.M. (1930) The Relations of Intelligence to Students Teaching Success. *Peabody Journal of Education,* 8(1), 3-6.

Williamson, J.N. (2006) The Relationship Between Teacher's Level of Social Interest and Teacher Efficacy and their Degree of Job Satisfaction. *Psychological Abstract, July,* 93(7), 26-35.

Willis, S.L., and Schair, K.W. (1986) Practical Intelligence in Later Adulthood. In R.J. Sternberg and R.K. Wagner (Eds.) *Practical Intelligence: Nature and Origins of Competence in the Everyday World.* New York: Cambridge Press, 236-268.

Wimberly, R.C. Faulker, G.L. and Moxly, R.D. (1978) Dimensions of Teacher Effectiveness. *Teaching Sociology*, 6(1), 7-20.

Witte, R. (2004) Emotional Intelligence and Career Success among the Highly Intelligent. *www.hamiltoninstitute.com/docs/witey/ thesis.*

Wong, C.M.T., Day, J.D. Maxwell, S.E., and Meera, N.M. (1995) A Multi Trait Multi Method Study of Academic and Social Intelligence in College Students. *Journal of Educational Psychology*, 87(1), 117-133.

Woolfolk, A. (2004) *Educational Psychology*. 9/e. New Delhi: Pearson Education.

Wu, S. (2004) Development and Application of Brief Major of Emotional Intelligence for High School Teachers. *Psychology Reports*, 95(2 and 3), 1207-1218.

Yamamato, K. (1964) Creative Thinking Thoughts on Research, *Exceptional Children,* 30(9), 403-410.

Yamamoto, K. (1964) Creativity and Sociometric Choice among Adolescents. *Journal of Social Psychology*, 64(2), 249-261.

Yang, Y., and Sternberg, R.J. (1997) Taiwanese Chinese People's Conceptions of Intelligence. *Intelligence*, 25(1), 21-36.

Zahorik, J., Halbach, A., Ehrle, K., and Molnar, A. (2003) Teaching Practices for Smaller Classes. *Educational Leadership,* 61(1), 75-77.

Zembylas, M. (2004) The Emotional Characteristics of Teaching: An Ethnographic Study of One Teacher. *Teaching and Teacher Education,* 20(2), 185-201.

Zinkel, S. (2000) Social Intelligence: The Development and Maintenance of Purposive Behaviour. In R. Bar-on and J.D.A. Parker (Eds.) *The Handbook of Emotional Intelligence*, Sanfrancisco: Jossey-Bass.

Index

Abstract reasoning, 18
Achievement level, 12
Achievement motivation, 50–51
Adaptability, 4, 18, 22, 24–26, 30, 38, 136, 138
Adaptive flexibility, 63–64, 69, 78
Adjustment, 3, 50–51, 53
Administrative behaviour, 50
Affective Regulation Model of Emotional Intelligence, 24
Analytic procedures, 40
Approaches, 15, 17, 19–20, 34, 38, 41, 44–45, 47, 69, 138–39
  analytic, 100
  assessment, 33
  explicit, 15
  goal-oriented, 21
  holistic, 39
  imaginative, 48
  multivariate analysis, 74
  psychoanalytic, 39
  psychometric, 20
  theoretical, 20
  traditional, 6, 29
  triangulation, 70
Associational fluency, 68, 77
Associationistic Approach to Creativity, 38
Attitude information technology, 50
Auditory perceptions, 17
Awareness, 28–30, 39
  emotional, 26, 138

Basic skills, development of, 5, 141
Behavioural
  correlates, 17
  domains, 20
  expectations, 11
  flexibility, 44
  management, 7, 141
  manager, 51
  research, 81, 139
  scientist, 81, 140
Behaviour management, 5
Benevolence, 28
Best predictors, 112, 115, 117
Binet-Simon Intelligence Test, 13

Canonical correlation, 81, 103, 136, 139
Canonical Discriminant Function, 103, 136
Capacity
  cognitive, 29, 113
  global, 29
  intellectual, 61
  pedagogic, 130
  sensory, 14
Cause-and-effect relationships, 137
Chinese conceptualization of intelligence, 15
Classification Table, 136
Classroom
  activities, organization of, 8, 140
  competence, 75
  conductive, 55
  environment, 135
  experiences, 47

situations, 4
strategies, 52
management, 4–5, 8, 11, 140
climate, 6–7, 12, 45, 137
practices, 3–4

Cognitive
abilities, 17, 31, 34, 52, 113
characteristics, 34
model, 23

Communication skills, 51
Comparison of Creativity, 91
Competent behavior, 50
Complex interrelations, 98
Componential Intelligence, 17
Concept learning, 16
Conceptual
definitions of intelligence, 14
dimensions, 15
framework, 9
proximity, 19

Confidence dimension, 68
Content knowledge, 8, 118, 138
Contextual Intelligence, 17
Context validity, 61
Convergent-Divergent Thinking, 40
Convergent production, 41
Cooper's Model of emotional intelligence, 26
Cordial relationship, 107
Correlational analysis, 94, 112, 120, 137
Correlation
analysis, 70, 98, 137
coefficient, 94–98, 137

Covariance matrices, 136
Creative
act, 36–39
activity, 36, 38
behaviour, 38, 53, 115
people, 39, 42–43
teacher, qualities of, 53
thinking, 36–37, 40, 48, 64, 73, 110, 112, 133

Creativity
ability, 17
definitions of, 36–37
developing, 134
fluency, dimensions of, 112, 120
high-level, 38, 108, 119
holistic approach to, 39
language, 109
measuring, 63
nurture, 56
scores, 43, 69, 78, 80–81, 83, 109
tests, 35
verbal, 54

Criterion variable, 117
Cultural-historical contexts, 37
Curvilinear relationship, 43
Cyclical concept, 19

Defence mechanisms, 38
Demographic variables, 50
Dependent variables, 98, 100, 102, 136, 138–39
Desirability, 132
Differences
fundamental, 31
individual, 5, 16
significant, 102, 105–6, 108–9, 114

Differential pupil characteristics, 9, 137
Differentiated teacher effectiveness, 9, 137
Discriminant
analysis, 70, 81, 101–2, 105, 136, 138–39
function, 103–5, 136

Divergent Production Abilities (DPA), 63–64, 68, 72, 77

Education administrators, 5
Educational research, 49
Effectiveness, 1, 3–4, 6, 9–10, 49, 54–55, 75, 87, 103, 110, 112, 132, 135
defined, 4
dictionary meaning of, 3

differentiated, 137
interactive effect of type of school and teacher, 89–90, 93
personal, 135
Effectiveness of teachers, dimensions of, 141
Elaboration Test, 64, 69
Elicit information, 59
Emotional
behaviour, 12, 76
capabilities, 118
challenges, 47, 107
climate, 107
competence, 15, 29
competencies, 46, 111
content, 30
expression, 26, 28, 46, 138
imbalances, 39
information, 23, 30–31, 138
Emotional intelligence, 22–32, 45–47, 49–59, 62, 70, 74–76, 78–81, 89–90, 94–95, 97–103, 105–7, 110–21, 127–28, 131–35, 138
coefficients of correlation of, 98
comparison of, 89
conceptualized, 22
creativity and, 97, 127
dimensions of, 26
measuring, 61
scale, 61, 67, 71, 76
scope of, 32
skills, 106, 111
Emotionality, 55
Emotional learning, 28
Emotional maturity, 29, 112
Emotional Self-management, 24, 138
Emotional skills, developing, 132
Emotional stability, 3, 10, 48, 54, 110, 112–13, 115, 117
Emotional strengths, 46
Emotional variability, 44
Emotions, 15, 22–24, 26–31, 35, 46, 50, 54, 106–7, 110, 113, 115–18, 131, 133, 138
complex, 24
expressing, 118
identifying, 24
individuals approach, 28
internal, 31
managing, 24, 29
negative, 47, 107
personal, 118
positive, 107
strong, 26, 141
Emotions transit, 24
Encyclopedia of Educational Rresearch, 5
Environment
changing, 17
conductive, 11
creatiity, 37
cultural, 37, 61
democratic school, 131
emotional, 8
experiences, 131
home, 35, 52
physical, 137
positive, 41
socio-psychological, 134
Evaluation procedures, 4
Experimental Intelligence, 17
Expressional fluency, 77

Factor analysis, 20, 81, 103, 138–39
Factorial
approach factor, 16
design, 82, 123, 138
experiment design, 138
purification, 138
Factor loading, 103
Fair grading procedures, 6
Fluency factor, 109
Formal education, 1
Function, 1, 18, 22–23, 34, 103–5, 121, 136–37
canonical, 103, 136
reliable, 137
social, 38

F-value, 84–87, 89–91, 93

Gender differences, 56
General intelligence, 13, 18, 29–31, 49–51, 54, 57–60, 74–76, 78–81, 84–85, 94, 97–103, 112–15, 117, 119–21, 126–28
  comparison of, 84
  contribution of, 128
  determining, 87
  inter-correlation of, 57, 97
  path model showing effects of, 101
  test, 30
  value, 76, 79
George Washington Social Intelligence Test, 20
Goleman's model, 24
Group covariance matrices, 136
Group differences, 102, 138
Group membership, 102
Group variability, 105, 121

Harmonious relationship, 23
H-creativity, 40
Hierarchical model, 17, 21
Homogenous trait, 28
Human dimensions, 130
Humanistic concept, 39
Humour and Recognition of Social Environment, 68

Ideational fluency, 63, 77
Implicit concept, 50, 52
Independent variables, 81–83, 94, 98, 100, 102, 104, 136, 138–40
Individualistic cultures, 28
Individual student characteristics, 6
Influence creativity, 41
Initial teacher education, 130
Intellect model, 16
Intellectual behaviour, 17
Intelligence
  abstract, 19–20
  analytic, 42–43
  cognitive, 23, 31, 113, 138
  concrete, 19
  creative, 42
  crystallized, 17, 41
  defined, 29
  distinct, 41
  fluid, 32, 41
  inter-personal, 15, 23, 30–31, 118, 139
  intra-personal, 15, 23, 30–31, 139
  measuring, 15
  non-cognitive, 113
  skills, 48
  spatial, 18
  tests, 43
  verbal, 18, 42
Intelligent behaviour, 14, 17, 48, 133
Interpersonal
  behaviour, 115
  goals, 19
  skills, 10, 45, 113, 117
Interrelated concept, 29
Intrapersonal understanding, 117
IQ, 32, 42–43, 45, 80, 111, 113, 116

Jack-knife classifications, 136
Job satisfaction, 50–53

Knowledge
  declarative, 45, 113
  discipline, 8, 137–38
  emotional, 23, 50
  pedagogical, 8, 140
  procedural, 45, 113
  scanty, 109
  social, 21, 52
Kothari Education Commission, 2

Leadership
  behaviour, 50–51
  skills, 20, 52
Learning
  climate, 8
  creative, 53, 109

environment, 11
rote, 109
stimulation, 6, 141
Life satisfaction, 50–51
Linear association, 137
Literacy rate, 65
Locality of residence, 50–51
Longitudinal research, 135

MANOVA, 81, 138–39
Mcber's model, 7
Memorization, 12
Mental ability, 18, 28, 34, 50, 60, 137, 139
identified primary, 16
tasks, 84
Mental capabilities, 113
Mental health, 3, 39, 45, 48, 52
Mental processes, 31, 34, 137
Mill Hills Scales, 71
Mill Hill Vocabulary (MHV), 61
Moral code of behaviour, 9, 140
Moral-developmental level, 21
Motivational characteristics, 35
Multi-dimensional concept, 33
Multiple
domains, 9
intelligences, 41
regression, 81, 102–3, 136
regression analysis, 81, 98, 102, 139–40
Multivariate analysis, 81, 139

National Advisory Committee on Creative and Cultural Education, 36
National Curriculum Framework for Teacher Education, 133
Neurosis, 39, 44
Non-cognitive capabilities, 25
Non-significant gender difference, 106

Organizational productivity, 140
Originality dimension, 96
Originality score, 69

Parent teacher association, 132
Path analysis, 70, 81, 100, 140
P-creativity, 40
Pearson Product Moment Correlation, 63
Pedagogical content knowledge, 8
Peer-Estimated Social intelligence (PESI), 20
Personal
characteristics, 4, 6, 45, 141
disposition, 4
exploration, 28
knowledge, 8–9, 140
optimism, 29
performance, 27
projects, 21
qualities, 3
relationships, 131
soundness, 48
strengths, 18, 139
Personality traits, 55
Predictors, 45, 99, 101, 103, 105, 113–14, 116–17, 121, 136
determining, 99
important, 116
psychological, 121
significant, 99–100, 105, 121
strongest, 103
variables, 104–5
Problem
-finder, 49
-poser, 49
-solver, 49
solving, 5, 9, 16–18, 21, 29, 40, 49, 110, 133, 137
Product-oriented psychologists, 35
Professional dimensions, 112
Progressive matrices, 61
Pro-social values, 51, 111, 116
Psychic life, 36
Psychoanalytic Approach to Creativity, 38

Psychological
  dimensionality, 1, 74, 81
  dimensions, 29, 138
  process, 109
Punjab School Education Board, 58
Pupils perceptions, 137

Qualities
  academic, 55
  emotional, 116
  leadership, 77
  moral, 45
  motivational, 34
  professional, 3, 75
Quality education, 55
Quality of life, 26, 138

Raven Progressive Matrices, 32
Real-life creative performance, 41
Reasoning, 14–16, 18, 22–23, 31, 50, 60, 139
  analogical, 44
  logical, 113
  non-verbal, 15
  verbal, 15
Recognition of Social Environment, 62–63, 68
Regulation of emotion, 27
Relationship
  management, 25, 140
  quotient, 26, 138
Reliability, 60–64, 134
  index of, 60, 62
  split-half, 60, 63
  test-retest, 60–61, 63
Remedial inputs, 132
Research
  methodology, 59
  tools, 59, 67
Rule learning, 16

School
  effectiveness, 135
  improvement, 9, 137
  management factors, 135
  principles, 5
Scoring, 67–68, 75–78, 82
  procedures, 64
Self actualization, 39, 50–51
Self-assessment, 24, 138
Self-awareness, 22, 31, 106, 117
Self belief, 9, 140
Self confidence, 24, 35, 50–51, 138
Self-control, 24, 110, 138
Self-criticism, 35, 45
Self efficacy, 20, 50, 135
Self-esteem, 50, 53, 134
Self-expression, 33, 37
Self-knowledge, 45, 113
Self-management, 45, 48, 113
Self-perception, 28, 75
Self-ratings, 21, 135
Self-regulation, 22, 53, 77
Sentence Construction Test (SCT), 64, 68, 77
Similarities Test (ST), 64, 68, 77
Skewness, 75, 79
Skill of teaching, 5
Skills
  cognitive, 45, 113
  communication technology, 5
  conceptual thinking, 7, 140
  emotional, 48, 107
  intellectual, 6, 141
  inter-personal, 25
  intra-personal, 25, 45
  logical thinking, 34
  multitude of, 3, 141
  numerical, 15
  organizational, 10, 112
  pedagogical, 47
  professional, 116
  pro-social, 20, 52
  psychoticism, 45, 113
  social-intelligence, 21
  social interactional, 8, 140
  verbal, 15

Social
adaptability, 18, 141
cognition, 21, 140
desirability, 62
experimental approach uses measures, 21
flexibility, 20
Social intelligence, 18–23, 29–31, 49–50, 52–55, 57–59, 62, 74–75, 77–84, 90–91, 94–95, 97–103, 108, 110–15, 117, 119–21
defining, 19, 21
Definitional approach of, 19
high, 30, 108
behaviour, 111
of secondary school teachers, 77, 90
of teachers, 49, 52, 62
scale, 62–63, 67, 71–72, 77
Social perceptions, 21
Social skills, developing, 5
Split-half reliability coefficient, 62, 72
Standardized regression coefficients, 100, 103, 137
Sternberg's triarchic theory, 41
Stratified random sample technique, 65
Stratum Theory of Cognitive Abilities, 17
Structural model, 140
Structure matrix correlation, 103, 129
Structure of the Intellect (SI), 40–41
Student learning experience, 6

Tactfulness dimensions, 62, 68
Teacher education, 8, 133
Teacher effectiveness, 3, 5–7, 9, 49–59, 66–67, 70, 74–75, 81–102, 105, 108, 110–12, 115, 117–29, 134–35, 140–41
coefficient of correlation of, 95
correlational analysis of, 110, 119
effect of, 84, 89–91
incidence of, 57, 74–75
predictor of, 117, 121
values on, 128
factorial design, 83
Teacher Effectiveness Scale (TES), 59–63, 66–67, 75, 78, 82
Teacher efficiency, 45, 132
Teacher fairness, 7, 137
Teacher performance, 5–6, 9, 141
Teacher quality, 56, 135
Teacher-student interactions, 45
Test-Retest Reliability, 71

Uses of Things Test (UTT), 64, 68, 77

Wechsler Adult Intelligence Scale (WAIS), 14, 32
Word Production Test (WPT), 63, 68

Zero correlation, 32
Zero order correlation, 70